Esther Unmasked

Solving Eleven Mysteries of the Jewish Holidays and Liturgy

MITCHELL FIRST
with an Introduction by
Rabbi Hayyim Angel

KODESH PRESS

978-0692375426

Cover image is cropped from Rembrandt van Rijn's *Ahasuerus and Haman at the Feast of Esther* (1660).
Additional formatting and layout by Kodesh Press.

Published & Distributed by

Kodesh Press L.L.C.
New York, NY
www.KodeshPress.com
kodeshpress@gmail.com

This book is dedicated to my wife Sharon, my children Shaya, Daniel and Rachel, and my parents Harry First, Esq. and Judge Lee First.

I have learned much, in different ways, from all of them.

מכל מלמדי השכלתי

— תהלים קיט: צט

TABLE
OF
CONTENTS

Introduction
by Rabbi Hayyim Angel

One of the thirty-nine categories of prohibited labor on Shabbat is *soter*, pulling down a building. The Talmud explains that destructive knocking down is not considered creative labor that is biblically prohibited on Shabbat. Only *soter al menat livnot*, pulling down for the sake of rebuilding, constitutes creative, thoughtful labor.

On the intellectual plane, the questions of scholars can be *soter*, as they tend to challenge commonly held assumptions. Within such questioning, however, there are two approaches. Some scholars use their questions to weaken or dismiss commonly held views without providing constructive alternatives. Good scholarship, on the other hand, follows the premise of *soter al menat livnot*. Responsible scholars first challenge our most basic assumptions, and make us realize how unfounded many of our suppositions really are. These scholars then dig to the foundations of each issue using sound research, and construct a stronger basis of understanding. Their work constitutes creative, thoughtful labor and it builds a stronger structure for those who delve into their ideas.

Mitchell First is from the scholarly school of being *soter al menat livnot*. He forthrightly questions several basic traditional Jewish assumptions and demonstrates why they often lack a sound foundation. He then combines extensive research into primary sources, the contributions of other contemporary scholars, and his own original ideas to build stronger structures in the pursuit of truth. By doing so, readers with a historical sense will grow intellectually, and religious Jewish readers also stand to gain a deeper understanding of their observances, prayers, and other elements within tradition. By doing so, they may grow religiously through sound Torah learning.

For example, First argues that the inspiring expression from the second paragraph of the daily *Aleinu* prayer, לתקן עולם במלכות ש-די (to improve the world under God's sovereignty), might not be the original text. Based on a survey of early versions of the prayerbook and analysis of the competing versions of לתכן and לתקן, First submits that the likely original version is לתכן עולם במלכות ש-די, to *establish* the world under God's sovereignty. Don't worry, *tikkun olam* is still an ancient idea deriving from the Mishnah and Gemara and of course a valuable and inspiring concept to apply in our times. However, First maintains that this ubiquitous phrase should not be associated with the original text of *Aleinu*.

In a similar vein, First provides extensive evidence from rabbinic sources and the Cairo Geniza that the traditional "Four Questions" of the *mah nishtannah* recited at the Passover Seder originally consisted of, well, three questions. He carefully traces the evolution of that liturgy so that we can see how we eventually arrived at what has become our "traditional" text with four questions.

In several essays, First explores the interrelationship between Jewish historical traditions and external histories. For example, he identifies Achashverosh of the Book of Esther with the king known as Xerxes by the Greek historian Herodotus, and then explains that Esther is likely Amestris, Xerxes' only wife in the writings of Herodotus. Despite the similarities of the names Esther and Amestris, some have dismissed this link because the main story that Herodotus tells about Amestris depicts her as unusually cruel. In contrast, Esther in the Megillah is a delightful character. First counters this argument by noting that Herodotus admitted that he did not subject the stories he heard to critical scrutiny, and Herodotus also had a strong political and ideological agenda. Therefore, Herodotus should not be considered an "objective" historian against which the Book of Esther should be held. Rather, Herodotus' story about Amestris' cruelty must be taken with many grains of salt. Indeed, First points out that a widespread view of scholars today is that the stories regarding the Persian queens told by the Greek historians should be treated as "literature" (i.e., fiction designed to entertain the reader) rather than as "history."

Particularly intriguing is First's final article in this collection, which explores the *pe-ayin* order in the original Hebrew alphabet. Although chapters 1-4 in Lamentations follow an *aleph-bet* acrostic, the *pe* verses precede the *ayin* verses in chapters 2, 3 and 4. First argues that the reason for this deviation is that the original Hebrew *aleph-bet* had *pe* before the *ayin*, and this order changed to the current order of *ayin* before *pe* only at the beginning of the Second Temple period. This transition likely occurred because other Semitic alphabets, including the Aramaic version used in Babylonia at that time, placed the *ayin* before the *pe*.

Archaeologists have identified several Hebrew abecedaries (lists of the *aleph-bet*) from various parts of Israel dated from the period of the Judges through the period of the First Temple. All of them have the *pe* before the *ayin*. Additionally, the one surviving Dead Sea text of Lamentations chapter 1 presents the *pe* verse before the *ayin* verse, whereas the Masoretic Text has the *ayin* verse before the *pe* verse. The two earliest manuscripts of the Septuagint similarly place the *pe* verse before the *ayin* verse in the "*eshet ḥayil*" (woman of valor) acrostic poem in Proverbs chapter 31. This evidence suggests that the *pe* used to precede the *ayin* in the early Biblical period.

First attempts to demonstrate that Proverbs chapter 31, and Psalms 25 and 34 read more smoothly if the *pe* verses are moved before the *ayin* verses. If he is correct, it would demonstrate that the original version of these chapters followed the earliest known Hebrew *aleph-bet* order, and later editors transposed those verses to reflect the updated order of the *aleph-bet*. The most compelling example is Psalm 34:16-19, where commentators recognized the obvious difficulty with the current Masoretic order:

> (*ayin*) The eyes of the Lord are on the righteous, His ears attentive to their cry.
> (*pe*) The face of the Lord is set against evildoers, to erase their names from the earth.
> (*tzaddi*) They cry out, and the Lord hears, and saves them from all their troubles.
> (*kuf*) The Lord is close to the brokenhearted; those crushed in spirit He delivers.

Who are "they" in verse 18 (beginning with *tzaddi*)? Based on the flow, it appears that God listens to the *wicked*, who are the subject of the previous verse (beginning with *pe*)! However, it appears far more likely that God would listen to the cries of the righteous, mentioned two verses earlier (beginning with *ayin*).

Rashi and Radak therefore maintain that one must skip over the *pe* verse when interpreting the *tzaddi* verse. Indeed, God hears the cries of the righteous. Alternatively, Ibn Ezra proposes that God listens to the wicked *who repent* and cry out to God. Ibn Ezra turns to the following verse (beginning with a *kuf*), and argues that "the brokenhearted" refers to previously wicked people who repented and turned to God.

With First's presentation of the ancient evidence, however, another possibility arises: the original psalm may have placed the *pe* verse before the *ayin* verse, since the *aleph-bet* was still written in that order! If this is true, then the psalm originally read:

(*pe*) The face of the Lord is set against evildoers, to erase their names from the earth.
(*ayin*) The eyes of the Lord are on the righteous, His ears attentive to their cry.
(*tzaddi*) They cry out, and the Lord hears, and saves them from all their troubles.
(*kuf*) The Lord is close to the brokenhearted; those crushed in spirit He delivers.

This flow makes eminent sense, and reflects the understanding of Rashi and Radak. In this instance, the scholarship pertaining to the ancient abecedaries and other versions (Septuagint and Dead Sea Scrolls) shed valuable light on this interpretive conundrum.

Deciding whether this compelling example is sufficient to draw the sweeping conclusions First does regarding the Book of Psalms can be left to each reader. Regardless, his historical survey and analysis provide an illuminating perspective on the *aleph-bet* acrostics in *Tanakh*.

All eleven essays in this collection are clear and accessible to interested laypeople, and will be stimulating for rabbis and scholars as well. Readers who enjoy having their assumptions challenged stand to gain a broader and deeper grasp of each topic after reading these essays. Through this process, one can build a deeper learning foundation, through which one may enhance one's religious experience.

Rabbi Hayyim Angel
National Scholar, Institute for Jewish Ideas and Ideals
Bible Faculty, Yeshiva University

Preface

This book consists of eleven articles that address interesting questions that arise in connection with the liturgy and origin of the Jewish holidays. Too often, Orthodox Jews take the liturgy and the origin of the holidays for granted, without adequate investigation.

For example, regarding the liturgy:

- The Jewish obligation of תקון עולם, "improving the world," is widely referred to and it is traditionally assumed that the *Aleinu* prayer is one of the texts upon which this obligation is based. The first article shows that a very strong case can be made that the original version of *Aleinu* read לתכן עולם, "to *establish* the world under God's sovereignty," and not לתקן עולם, "to *perfect/improve* the world under God's sovereignty." If so, the concept of תקון עולם has no connection to the *Aleinu* prayer.
- A phrase that is part of the traditional Sukkot *hoshanot* liturgy is אני והו הושיעה נא, based on the text of a Mishnah at *Sukkah* 4:5. The meaning of the phrase אני והו has been a puzzle throughout the centuries. The third article shows that almost certainly the original text of the Mishnah read אני והוא. With this reading, the statement can be explained.
- It is usually assumed that the Passover recital of "Four Questions" is one of the fundamental rituals of rabbinic Judaism. The ninth article explains that the original *mah nishtannah* only included three questions. The variation in the number of questions in the *mah nishtannah* over the centuries is then described, and the evolution of the number of questions into the present four is then explained.

Regarding the origin of the Jewish holidays:

- The sixth article discusses what motivated Antiochus to undertake his persecution of the Jews. The three main theories will be discussed and evaluated.
- In the seventh article, the origin of the fast of the 13th of Adar (*Taanit Esther*) will be addressed. No fast in Adar is mentioned in the book of Esther or the Talmud, and the origin of this fast has always been difficult to understand. The 13th of Adar was even a holiday (*Yom Nikanor*) in the late Second Temple period, a day on which fasting was prohibited. Based on a careful examination of Geonic sources, the seventh article will explain how this fast first came into existence in Geonic Babylonia.
- The identification of Achashverosh in secular sources had always been a puzzle. The eighth article will explain how, in the middle of the nineteenth century, Achashverosh was finally able to be identified. He is the king that the Greek historians referred to as "Xerxes." The article will detail the basis for this identification, and will show that Esther can be identified in secular sources as well.

Regarding the balance of the articles:

- The second article suggests explanations for the origin of the mysterious Tannaitic root מחל, a root not found in the Bible. The article further attempts to distinguish this root from its synonym סלח.
- The fourth article explains the correct spelling of the term Maccabee (מקבי) and points to its likely original meaning.
- The fifth article discusses the identity and meaning of חשמונאי.
- The tenth article conducts an analysis of Mishnah *Pesaḥim* 10:4. It shows that it is likely that this Tannaitic source understood *arami oved avi* to mean "my father was a homeless/wandering/lost Aramean." Typically, it is assumed that this interpretation of *arami oved avi* did not arise until the time of the Rishonim.
- The final article explains the reason why the *pe* verses preceded the *ayin* verses in the acrostics in chapters 2-4 of the book of *Eikhah* (and in the acrostic in chapter 1 in the Dead Sea text of *Eikhah*). It turns out that *pe* preceded *ayin* in the order of the alphabet in ancient Israel! The implications of this explanation for dating the book of *Tehillim* (interspersed with many acrostics) are then addressed.

◆ ◆ ◆

Many of the articles included in this book have been published in earlier forms in *Ḥakirah, Biblical Archaeology Review*, *AJS Review*, *Journal for the Study of the Old Testament* and seforim.blogspot.com. (For the references to the earlier articles, see the first footnote in each article.)

Several of the articles: the first (establishing the reading לתכן עולם), seventh (origin of *Taanit Esther*), eighth (the identification of Esther in secular sources), and eleventh (the implications of the ancient *pe/ayin* order) have been viewed by many as groundbreaking.

Acknowledgements

It is said that "it takes a village" to raise a child. The production of a work of Jewish scholarship is not very different. In this spirit, I would like to thank Sam Borodach and Rabbi Moshe (Jordan) Yasgur for the extensive discussions I had with them over many years. I could never have written the articles I did without these discussions. I would also like to thank Rabbi Avrohom Lieberman for reviewing the articles. He has a tremendous breadth of knowledge. It is hard to imagine a better reviewer. I would also like to acknowledge Dr. Ezra Chwat of the Jewish National and Hebrew University Library who was always there to offer his expertise. Finally, I would like to acknowledge Rabbi Ezra Frazer, Allen Friedman, and Meylekh Viswanath, with whom I have also had the privilege of sharing ideas and sources for many years.

I would also like to acknowledge some of the many others who contributed over the years towards my efforts, either by sharing particular ideas and sources, or by encouraging me in my research. First and foremost is my *ḥavruta* Josh Teplow. In addition: Ze'ev Atlas, David Barach, Lazer Borgen, Menachem Butler, Myron Chaitovsky, Ben Cooper, Yisrael Dubitsky, Yakov Ellenbogen, David Fisher, Howard Friedman, Rabbi Mordy Friedman, Rachel Friedman, David Gertler, Jeff Glazer, Binyamin Goldstein, Azriel Haimowitz, Dick Harris (of blessed memory), Ziggy Hirsch, Rabbi Aryeh Kaplan, Daniel Klein, Heshie Klein, Rabbi Stephen Knapp, Steve and Abby Leichman, Ari Leifer, Arvin Levine, Josh Levy, Yehiel Levy, Moshe Markovitz, Rabbi

Michael Pariser, Lenny Presby, Rabbi Baruch Price, Michael Rapoport, Chanani Sandler, Eli Schaap, David Schachter, Steve Schaffer, Richie Schiffmiller, Fred Schulman, Mark Siletski, Kal Staiman, Zalman Suldan, Zvi Weissler, Rabbi Richard Wolpoe, Rabbi Benjamin Yablok, Neal Yaros, Joshua Zakheim, Rabbi Alan Zelenetz, and Ariel Zell.

I have also gained much over the years from the *shiurim* of Rabbi Ephraim Kanarfogel and Rabbi Laurence Rothwachs. I would like to thank them for the many opportunities I was given to deliver *shiurim* in Congregation Beth Aaron. These *shiurim* helped lay the groundwork for these articles.

I have benefited much from exchanging ideas with my children: Shaya, Daniel, and Rachel. In addition to her linguistic insights, Rachel provided much-needed computer assistance.

Special thanks to Alec Goldstein of Kodesh Press for his hard work in bringing this book to publication.

Finally, I would like to thank my wife Sharon for allowing me to live this additional life as a scholar, outside my legal career, and pursue these research interests.

All the views expressed are my own. Please feel free to contact me with insights or additional material on any of the topics I have addressed.

Mitchell First
Teaneck, NJ
January 2015
MFirstAtty@aol.com

1

לתכן עולם: Establishing the Correct Text in *Aleinu*[1]

The Jewish obligation of תקון עולם, "improving the world," is widely referred to and it is traditionally assumed that the *Aleinu* prayer is one of the texts upon which this obligation is based. This article will show that a very strong case can be made that the original version of *Aleinu* read לתכן עולם, "to *establish* the world under God's sovereignty," and not לתקן עולם, "to *perfect/improve* the world under God's sovereignty."[2] If so, the concept of תקון עולם has no connection to the *Aleinu* prayer.[3]

---

1. I would like to thank Yehiel Levy for showing me his Yemenite *siddur* which read לתכן and inspired this research. I would like to dedicate this article to my beloved wife Sharon. Though the *gematria* of her name is תקון, she needs no improvement.

Earlier versions of this article were published in *Ḥakirah*, vol. 11 (2011): "*Aleinu*: Obligation to Fix the World or the Text?" and seforim.blogspot.com (Sept. 3, 2013): "*Le-Tacen Olam* (לתכן עולם) Establishing the Correct Text in *Aleinu*."

2. The above is how this phrase is usually translated. However, *The Complete ArtScroll Siddur* (Brooklyn: 1990, 3rd ed.) p. 161, translates: "to perfect the universe through the Almighty's sovereignty." Others adopt this translation as well. See, e.g., J. David Bleich, "*Tikkun Olam:* Jewish Obligations to Non-Jewish Society," in *Tikkun Olam: Social Responsibility in Jewish Thought and Law*, eds. David Shatz, Chaim I. Waxman, and Nathan J. Diament (Northvale, N.J.: 1997), p. 61.

3. Meir Bar-Ilan already intuited that the original reading may have been לתכן. See his "*Mekorah shel Tefillat 'Aleinu le-Shabbeaḥ*,'" *Daat* 43 (1999), pp. 5-24 (20, n. 72).

The articles by Gerald Blidstein and J. David Bleich in *Tikkun Olam: Social Responsibility in Jewish Thought and Law* assume that the reading is לתקן (see pp. 26, 61 and 98). But the article in this volume by Marc Stern mentions the alternate reading of לתכן, citing R. Saadiah (see p. 165, n. 24).

It is reasonable to assume that *Aleinu* was already included in the *Amidah* of Rosh Hashanah (herein, "RH") by the time of Rav (early third century C.E.).[4] But no text of *Aleinu* is included in the Talmud,

---

In 2005, Gilbert S. Rosenthal wrote a detailed article about the concept of *tikkun olam* throughout the ages and merely assumed that the reading in *Aleinu* is לתקן. See his "*Tikkun ha-Olam:* The Metamorphosis of a Concept," *Journal of Religion* 85:2 (2005), pp. 214-40.

4. The Jerusalem Talmud (JT), at *Avodah Zarah* 1:2 (39c), includes the following passage:

א"ר יוסי בי רבי בון מאן סבר בראש השנה נברא העולם? רב,
דתני בתקיעתא דבי רב זה היום תחילת מעשיך זכרון ליום ראשון וכו'.

A very similar passage is found at JT *Rosh Hashanah* 1:3 (57a), where the reading is בתקיעתא דרב. The sentence from the liturgy referred to (זה היום...) is from the introductory section to the ten verses of *zikhronot*. A reasonable inference from these Talmudic passages is that Rav composed (at least) the introductory sections to *zikhronot*, *malkhuyyot* and *shofarot*. *Aleinu* is part of the introductory section to *malkhuyyot*. Since the sentence from the introduction to *zikhronot* quoted corresponds to the present introduction to *zikhronot*, it is reasonable to assume that their introduction to *malkhuyyot* corresponded to the present introduction to *malkhuyyot*, i.e., that it included *Aleinu*. Admittedly, Rav could have made use of older material in the introductory sections he composed. The fact that *Aleinu* has been found (in a modified version) in *heikhalot* literature is some evidence for *Aleinu*'s existence in this early period, even though the prayer is not specifically mentioned in any Mishnaic or Talmudic source. (Regarding the dating of *heikhalot* literature, see below.) On the version of *Aleinu* in *heikhalot* literature, see Michael D. Swartz, "*'Alay Le-Shabbeaḥ*: A Liturgical Prayer in *Ma'aseh Merkabah*," *JQR* 77 (1986-1987), pp. 179-190, and Bar-Ilan, above (note 3). We will discuss the version of *Aleinu* in *heikhalot* literature further below. For parallels in later sources to the two passages from the Jerusalem Talmud, see Swartz, p. 186, n. 20. See also *Rosh Hashanah* 27a.

A statement that *Aleinu* was composed by Joshua appears in a collection of Geonic responsa known as *Shaarei Teshuvah* (responsum #44). But the statement was probably a later addition by the thirteenth-century kabbalist Moses de Leon. See Elliot R. Wolfson, "Hai Gaon's Letter and Commentary on '*Aleynu*: Further Evidence of Moses De León's Pseudepigraphic Activity," *JQR* 81 (1990-91), pp. 365-410 (379-380). The idea that *Aleinu* was composed by Joshua is first reliably found in statements recorded in the name of R. Judah he-Ḥasid (d. 1217). This attribution to Joshua is

nor is a text of *Aleinu* included in any of the classical *midrashim*.[5] Therefore, we must look to later sources for texts of *Aleinu*.

---

then repeated by various Ashkenazic Rishonim. (For the references, see Wolfson, pp. 380-381.) Over time, what was probably only a suggestion by R. Judah he-Ḥasid came to be viewed as a reliable ancient tradition.

There is much evidence that *Aleinu* could not have been composed by Joshua. For example: (1) *Aleinu* cites verses from the prophet Isaiah (this will be discussed below); (2) The epithet *ha-kadosh barukh hu* was not an appellation for God in Biblical times; and (3) terms are found in *Aleinu* that are characteristic of *heikhalot* literature. Also, for almost the entire Biblical period, the word *olam* is only a time-related word. It is not until Dan. 12:7 and perhaps Eccles. 3:11 that *olam* means "world" in the Bible. (*Olam* definitely means "world" at Ben Sira 3:18.) See Kirsten A. Fudeman and Mayer I. Gruber, "'Eternal King/King of the World' From the Bronze Age to Modern Times: A Study in Lexical Semantics," *REJ* 166 (2007), pp. 209-242. See also *Daat Mikra*, comm. to Ps. 89:3 and Eccles. 3:11, and R. Abraham Ibn Ezra, comm. to Ex. 21:6 and Eccles. 3:11. Based on the language, it is very clear that Ecclesiastes is a late Biblical book. See *Encyclopaedia Judaica* (Jerusalem: 1972) 2:349.

Regarding the roots תק"ן and תכ"ן, the root תק"ן does not appear in *Tanakh* until the book of Ecclesiastes, and the root תכ"ן probably did not mean "establish" in the period of the *Tanakh* (see below).

5. As noted, *Aleinu* has been found (in a modified form) in *heikhalot* literature. There are five manuscripts that include this *Aleinu* text. But four of these only include *Aleinu* in an abbreviated form and are not long enough to include the phrase לתכן/לתקן עולם. See Peter Schäfer, *Synopse zur Hekhalot-Literatur* (Tübingen: 1981), sec. 551, pp. 206-207. The only manuscript that includes the phrase reads לתקן. But this manuscript, N8128, dates from around 1500. See Ra'anan S. Boustan, "The Study of *Heikhalot* Literature: Between Mystical Experience and Textual Artifact," *Currents in Biblical Research* 6.1 (2007), pp. 130-60 (137).

Regarding the dating of *heikhalot* literature, Bar-Ilan (*Mekorah*, p. 22, n. 85) estimates this literature as dating from the 3rd through 5th centuries. See also more recently his "*Shalshelet ha-Kabbalah be-Sifrut ha-Heikhalot*," *Daat* 56 (2005), pp. 5-37. Moshe Idel, *Encyclopaedia Judaica* (Detroit and Jerusalem: 2006) 11:592, summarizes the subject as follows:

> Even though it is quite possible that some of the texts were not edited until this period [the Geonic era], there is no doubt that large sections originated in talmudic times, and that the central ideas, as well as many details, go back as far as the first and second centuries.

Among the later sources, the reading לתכן is found in the text of the RH *Amidah* in the *Siddur Rav Saadiah Gaon* (d. 942),[6] and in the text of the RH *Amidah* in the *Mishneh Torah* of the Rambam (d. 1204).[7] Moreover, numerous prayer texts from the Cairo Genizah include this line of *Aleinu*.[8] For example, it is found in: (1) a fragment of the RH *Amidah* first published by Jacob Mann in 1925;[9] (2) a fragment of the RH *Amidah* first published by Richard Gottheil and William H. Worrell in 1927;[10] (3) a fragment of the RH *Amidah* first published by Mordecai Margaliot in 1973;[11] and (4) a fragment of *Aleinu* first published by Mann in 1925.[12] It is found in many other *Aleinu* prayer texts from the

---

6. *Siddur Rav Saadiah Gaon*, eds. Israel Davidson, Simḥah Assaf, and Yissakhar Joel (Jerusalem: 1941), p. 221. Admittedly, the manuscript which forms the basis for this edition was not composed by R. Saadiah himself. It is estimated to date to the 12th or 13th century.

Neither R. Saadiah nor Rambam recited *Aleinu* in the daily service.

7. See the *Seder Tefillot Kol ha-Shanah* section at the end of *Sefer Ahavah*. I have looked at the *Or ve-Yeshuah* edition, the Frankel edition, the Mechon Mamre edition (www.mechon-mamre.org), and the editions published by R. Yitzḥak Sheilat and by R. Yosef Kafaḥ. All print לתכן. (In the authoritative manuscript Huntington 80, this reading is found at p. 178b.)

In the standard printed *Mishneh Torah*, in the *al kein nekavveh* section of the RH *Amidah* (*Sefer Ahavah*, p. 154), only the first ten words were included (up to עוזך), followed by a וכו'.

8. Most of the texts from the Cairo Genizah date from the 10th through the 13th centuries. See Robert Brody, *The Geonim of Babylonia and the Shaping of Medieval Jewish Culture* (New Haven: 1998), p. 32. All of the texts from the Cairo Genizah that I refer to can be seen at genizah.org.

9. See his "Genizah Fragments of the Palestinian Order of Service," *HUCA* 2 (1925), pp. 269-338 (329). The fragment is known as Cambridge Add. 3160, no. 10. When Mann published the fragment, he erroneously printed לתקן.

10. See their *Fragments from the Cairo Genizah in the Freer Collection* (New York: 1927), plate XLIII (opposite p. 194). The fragment is labeled F42 at genizah.org.

11. See his *Hilkhot Eretz Yisrael min ha-Genizah* (Jerusalem: 1973), p. 148. The fragment is known as Cambridge T-S 8H23.1.

12. See above, pp. 324-325. See also, more recently, Ezra Fleischer, *Tefillah u-Minhagei Tefillah Eretz-Yisre'eliyyim bi-Tekufat ha-Genizah* (Jerusalem: 1988), p. 238. The fragment is known as Cambridge Add. 3160, no. 5. Neither Mann nor Fleischer printed the full text of *Aleinu* in this fragment.

Cairo Genizah as well.[13] (In the fragment of *Aleinu* first published by Mann in 1925, *Aleinu* is included in the *Pesukei de-Zimra* section of the Palestinian *Shaḥarit* ritual.[14])

Furthermore, the reading לתכן survives in Yemenite *siddurim* to this day. It was also the reading in the original tradition of the Jews of Persia.[15]

Admittedly, the reading in Europe since the time of the Rishonim has been לתקן. See, for example, the following texts of *Aleinu*:

---

13. See the following fragments: Cambridge Or. 1080 2.46; Cambridge T-S Misc. 10.27, 34.5, and 34.23; Cambridge T-S NS 150.235, 154.19, 155.23, 157.6, 157.37, 157.176, 158.69, 195.55, and 273.38; Cambridge T-S AS 101.64; and New York ENA 1878.8. I was able to find only one fragment that read לתקן: Cambridge T-S NS 122.33. (An interesting fragment is T-S NS 153.64, 8R. Here, only the top line of the letter remains and it is hard to determine if it is the top of a כ or the top of a ק.)

I have been able to examine most of the *Aleinu* prayer text fragments from the Cairo Genizah. I would like to thank Prof. Uri Ehrlich of Ben Gurion University of the Negev for referring me to them. (Not all of these *Aleinu* prayer text fragments were long enough to include the relevant passage.)

14. Since the second word of the *Aleinu* prayer is לשבח, it was probably seen as fitting to include this prayer in the *Pesukei de-Zimra* section. A main theme of both *Barukh she-Amar* and *Yishtabbaḥ*, as well as of the entire *Pesukei de-Zimra*, is שבח. See also *Berakhot* 32a: *le-olam yesadder adam shivḥo shel HKBH ve-aḥar kakh yitpallel.*

A Palestinian practice of reciting *Aleinu* in *Pesukei de-Zimra* may also explain a statement found in several Rishonim (e.g., *Sefer ha-Maḥkim, Kol Bo,* and *Orḥot Ḥayyim*) in the name of *Pirkei de-Rabbi Eliezer* (a work composed in 8th-century Palestine): שבח גדול יש בעלינו לשבח לכך צריך לאומרו מעומד. The statement is obviously not giving an instruction regarding the RH *Amidah* recited by individuals. Nor does the language of the statement (לאומרו) fit as an instruction to individuals listening to the repetition of the RH *Amidah*. Rather it seems to be referring to reciting *Aleinu* in a context outside of the RH *Amidah*. (The statement is not found in the surviving texts of *Pirkei de-Rabbi Eliezer*.)

15. See Shelomoh Tal, *Nusaḥ ha-Tefillah shel Yehudei Paras* (Jerusalem: 1981), p. 154 (RH). The Persian-Jewish prayer ritual followed that of R. Saadiah in many respects. At the end of the 18th century, the Persian Jews were influenced to adopt a Sefardic prayer ritual and their own ritual was forgotten.

- *Maḥzor Vitry* of R. Simḥah of Vitry (daily *Shaḥarit* and RH);[16]
- *Siddur Ḥasidei Ashkenaz* (daily *Shaḥarit* and RH);[17]
- *Peirush ha-Tefillot ve-ha-Berakhot* of R. Judah b. Yakar (RH);[18]
- *Peirushei Siddur ha-Tefillah* of R. Eleazar b. Judah of Worms (RH);[19] and
- *Sefer Arugat ha-Bosem* of R. Abraham b. Azriel (RH).[20]

The three main manuscripts of *Seder Rav Amram Gaon* also read לתקן.[21]

16. Ed. Aryeh Goldschmidt (Jerusalem: 2004), pp. 131 (daily *Shaḥarit*) and 717 (RH). The earliest surviving manuscript of *Maḥzor Vitry* dates to the first half of the 12th century.
17. Ed. Moshe Hirschler (Jerusalem:1972), p. 125 (daily *Shaḥarit*), and p. 214 (RH). (This work was published by Hirschler together with another work, *Siddur Rabbenu Shelomoh*; both are integrated into the same volume.) *Siddur Ḥasidei Ashkenaz* was compiled by the students of R. Judah he-Ḥasid (d. 1217) and presumably reflects his text of *Aleinu*. Hirschler's edition of this *siddur* is based on several manuscripts.
18. Ed. Samuel Yerushalmi (Jerusalem: 1979), sec. 2, pp. 91-92. R. Judah flourished in Spain and died in the early 13th century. Aside from the text of *Aleinu* in the manuscript published by Yerushalmi including the reading לתקן, it is also clear from the various explanatory comments by R. Judah that he was working with a text that read לתקן.
19. Ed. Moshe Hirschler (Jerusalem: 1992), p. 659. R. Eleazar died circa 1230. The text of *Aleinu* is found in his commentary to the *Aleinu* of RH. In his commentary on the daily *Shaḥarit*, only the first two words of *Aleinu* and the last two (*timlokh be-kavod*) are recorded. In his *Sefer ha-Rokeaḥ*, his references to *Aleinu* in both the RH *Amidah* and the daily *Shaḥarit* are similarly very brief.
20. Ed. Ephraim E. Urbach (Jerusalem: 1963), vol. 3, pp. 469-470. *Sefer Arugat ha-Bosem* was composed in 1234, in Bohemia. Aside from the text of *Aleinu* published here including the word לתקן, it is clear from R. Abraham's explanatory comment (p. 469, lines 8-9) that he was working with a text that read לתקן.

Other early European texts of *Aleinu* include the three texts of *Aleinu* in manuscript Oxford, Corpus Christi College 133 (late 12th century; daily *Shaḥarit*, RH and one other) and the text of *Aleinu* in manuscript Cambridge Add. 667.1 (early 13th century; daily *Shaḥarit*). The former has לתקן in the first two; the third *Aleinu* does not include the second paragraph. In Cambridge Add. 667.1, the text of *Aleinu* does not include the second paragraph.
21. See *Seder Rav Amram Gaon*, ed. Daniel Goldschmidt (Jerusalem: 1971), p. 142.

But these manuscripts are not from the time of R. Amram (d. 875); they are European manuscripts from the time of the later Rishonim.[22]

Earlier than *Maḥzor Vitry*, we have circumstantial evidence for the reading לתקן in comments on *Aleinu* that were probably composed by R. Eliezer b. Nathan of Mainz (c. 1090-1170). Here, in Hamburg MS 153,[23] the following explanatory comment about *Aleinu* is expressed (without a text of the line itself):

ויהיו כל העולם מתקנים מלכותך וכולם יקראו בשמך...[24]

Another manuscript also largely composed of the comments of R. Eliezer b. Nathan has essentially this same reading, in two places.[25] Another manuscript, which is probably the *siddur* of R. Eliezer b. Nathan, has a similar reading:

ויהיו כל העולם מתקנים במלכותך. וכולם יקראו בשמך...[26]

Admittedly, it cannot be proven that לתכן was the original reading.

22. Ibid., introduction, pp. 11-13. A few fragments of the *Seder Rav Amram Gaon* have been found in the Genizah, but these are very short and do not include our passage.

23. This manuscript is generally considered to be largely composed of the comments of R. Eliezer b. Nathan. See, e.g., Urbach, *Sefer Arugat ha-Bosem*, vol. 4, p. 24 and the facsimile edition of this manuscript published by Abraham Naftali Tzvi Rot (Jerusalem: 1980), pp. 21-30. The manuscript itself is estimated to have been copied in the 14th century (Rot, p. 21).

24. See Rot, p. 20a (comm. to RH *Aleinu*).

25. See Alter Yehudah Hirschler, "*Peirush Siddur ha-Tefillah ve-ha-Maḥzor Meyuḥas le-Rabbi Eliezer ben Natan mi-Magenza (ha-Ravan)*," in *Genuzot* vol. 3 (Jerusalem: 1991), pp. 1-128. In this *siddur* commentary (pp. 78 and 114), ויהיו כל העולם מתקני' מלכותך וכלם יקראו בשמך is found in the commentary to daily *Aleinu* in *Shaḥarit*, and ויהיו כל העולם מתקנין מלכותך וכלם יקראו בשמך is found in the commentary to RH *Aleinu*. (One should not deduce from this manuscript that R. Eliezer b. Nathan recited *Aleinu* daily in *Shaḥarit*.)

26. See *Siddur Rabbenu Shelomoh*, p. 212 (commentary on RH *Aleinu*). Hirschler published this work as the siddur of Shelomoh b. R. Shimson of Worms (1030-1096), but it is probably that of R. Eliezer b. Nathan. See, e.g., Avraham Grossman, *Ḥakhmei Ashkenaz ha-Rishonim* (Jerusalem: 2001), pp. 346-348.

But this seems very likely, as לתכן is by far the better reading in the context. This can be seen by looking at all the other scenarios that are longed for in this section:

לראות מהרה בתפארת עזך להעביר גילולים מן הארץ
והאלילים כרות יכרתון לתכן/ לתקן עולם במלכות שד-י
וכל בני בשר יקראו בשמך להפנות אליך כל רשעי ארץ
יכירו וידעו כל יושבי תבל כי לך תכרע כל ברך תשבע כל לשון
לפניך ה׳ אלקינו יכרעו ויפולו ולכבוד שמך יקר יתנו
ויקבלו כולם את עול מלכותך ותמלוך עליהם מהרה לעולם ועד
כי המלכות שלך היא ולעולמי עד תמלוך בכבוד....

Beginning with להעביר, every clause expresses a hope for either the removal of other gods or the universal acceptance of our God. With regard to the first line, properly understood and its mystical and elevated language decoded,[27] it is almost certainly a request for the

---

27. Gershom Scholem recognized long ago that *Aleinu* includes several terms that are not only post-Biblical, but are characteristic of *heikhalot* literature. See his *Jewish Gnosticism, Merkabah Mysticism and Talmudic Tradition*, (New York: 1965, 2d. ed.), pp. 27-28. He points to the terms *yotzer bereshit*, *moshav yekaro*, and *shekhinat uzzo*. Bar-Ilan (Mekorah, p. 8) also points to the term *adon ha-kol*. (The phrase *aleinu le-shabbeaḥ u-lefaerkha u-legadlekha u-leyaḥedkha* is also found in *heikhalot* literature. See Moshe Ḥallamish, *Ḥikrey Kabbalah u-Tefillah* [Beer Sheva: 2012], p. 60.)

Most importantly, *heikhalot* literature includes the *Aleinu* prayer in the singular form (*alay le-shabbeaḥ...*) as a prayer of gratitude purportedly recited by R. Akiva on return from a safe journey to heaven. See the article by Swartz referred to above and see Schäfer, sec. 551, pp. 206-207. (R. Akiva and R. Ishmael serve as central pillars and chief mouthpieces in this pseudepigraphic literature. See *Encyclopaedia Judaica* 11:591 [2006].)

Based on all of this, many have argued that our RH *Aleinu* originated in *heikhalot* literature. Perhaps it originated in the singular in the above pseudepigraphic prayer of R. Akiva, and was then changed to the plural and borrowed into the RH *Amidah*. Or perhaps it originated elsewhere in *heikhalot* literature in the singular or plural and was then borrowed into the RH *Amidah* (and into the pseudepigraphic prayer of R. Akiva). Meir Bar-Ilan strongly argues that *Aleinu* originated in *heikhalot* literature. See his *Mekorah*, pp. 12-24.

But there are too many themes in *Aleinu* that are out of context and extraneous under the assumption that *Aleinu* originated in the above

speedy rebuilding of the Temple.[28] Taken together, this whole section is a prayer for the rebuilding of the Temple and the establishment of God's

---

pseudephigraphic prayer of R. Akiva, and to date we have not found the *Aleinu* prayer anywhere else in *heikhalot* literature, in either the singular or the plural. The second paragraph of *Aleinu* fits well as an introduction to the verses of *malkhuyyot*, and I argue below that both paragraphs of *Aleinu* were composed at the same time. Therefore, it is more likely that *Aleinu* originated as a prayer composed for the RH *Amidah*. The presence of terms characteristic of *heikhalot* literature merely reflects that *Aleinu* was composed for the RH *Amidah* by someone connected to or familiar with *heikhalot* literature, or composed at a time after terms originating in *heikhalot* literature came to be in normative rabbinic use. (Later, as Scholem points out, due to the common terms, the authors of *heikhalot* literature may have seen *Aleinu* as a text related to their own hymnology and hence incorporated it into their own literature. See Scholem, p. 28.)

28. The idiom is based on verses such as Ps. 78:60-61 (ויתן לשבי עזו ותפארתו ביד צר) and 96:6 (עז ותפארת במקדשו), and Is. 60:7 (ובית תפארתי אפאר) and 64:10 (בית קדשנו ותפארתנו). Also, Ps. 63:3 (כן בקדש חזיתיך לראות עזך וכבודך). This interpretation is probably implicit in the commentary of R. Judah b. Yakar. On לראות מהרה בתפארת עזך, he writes:

> ע"ש (= על שם) כי תפארת עוזמו אתה, ונזכה לראות פני שכינה ולראות בתפארת בית המקדש דכתי' ובית תפארתך אפאר.

See the *Peirush ha-Tefillot ve-ha-Berakhot* of R. Judah b. Yakar, part II, p. 91. R. Judah's statements are adopted by R. David Abudarham in his commentary to the *Aleinu* of RH. See also R. Shemtob Gaugine, *Keter Shem Tov* (Kėdainiai, Lithuania: 1934), vol. 1, p. 104. Unfortunately, this interpretation of the phrase תפארת עזך has generally been overlooked. Numerous are scholars who have written that the prayer includes no request for the Temple's rebuilding.

Scholem (p. 28, n. 18) notes the following passage found in other *heikhalot* texts:

> ברוך שמו במושב הדרו ומבורך בתפארת עזו.

The parallel to מושב הדרו strongly suggests that תפארת עזו represents the physical Temple in this passage. For *heikhalot* texts with this passage, see Mordecai Margaliot, *Sefer ha-Razim* (Jerusalem: 1966), pp. 107-109, and Martin Samuel Cohen, *The Shi'ur Qomah: Texts and Recensions* (Tübingen: 1985), pp. 173 and 175.

kingdom on earth. This fits the reading לתכן perfectly.[29] It is appropriate that this section of *Aleinu* is fundmentally a prayer for the establishment of God's kingdom on earth. Most likely, this section was composed as an introduction to the *malkhuyyot* section of the RH *Amidah*.[30]

---

29. The use of the root תכ"ן to mean "establish" does require some explanation. In *Tanakh*, the root תכ"ן means to "weigh," "examine," "measure," or "place in order." (At Ps. 75:4, תכנתי עמודיה, the root is commonly translated as "establish," but even here it probably means something like "properly apportion" or "place in order." See, e.g., the commentary of S. R. Hirsch.) תכ"ן with the meaning "establish" is not found in the Mishnah or Tosefta, but it may mean "establish" in the Dead Sea text 4Q511: תכן למועדי שנה (*DJD* VII [Oxford: 1982], p. 221), and perhaps in other Dead Sea texts as well.

In *paytanic* literature, an early use of תכ"ן to mean "establish" is found in the *piyyut Emet Emunatkha* (כי בששת ימים עולמך תכנת). This *piyyut* is preserved in the *Siddur Rav Saadiah Gaon* (p. 110) and in several Genizah fragments. It has a tetrastichic structure (as does *Aleinu*), and is generally viewed as a pre-classical *piyyut*, i.e., a *piyyut* from the late Tannaitic/early Amoraic period. See, e.g., Ezra Fleischer, *Ha-Yotzrot be-Hithavutam ve-Hitpaḥutam* (Jerusalem: 1984), p. 55, n. 47. The Academy of the Hebrew Language, in its Historical Dictionary Project database (*Ma'agarim*), estimates the date of composition of this *piyyut* as the late 2nd century C.E.

In the *Musaf Amidah* for *Shabbat*, תקנת, not תכנת, may be the original reading. See, e.g., *Siddur Rav Saadiah Gaon*, p. 112 and the Genizah fragment quoted by Fleischer, *Tefillah u-Minhagei Tefillah*, p. 52. (For more sources on this spelling issue, see *Maḥzor Vitry*, ed. Goldschmidt, p. 199, n. 1.)

Probably, the use of the root תכ"ן to mean "establish" arose based on the usage of the root at Psalms 75:4, or perhaps from the words תכן and תכון (both from the root כון) found numerous times in the *Tanakh*. (See Jer. 30:20; Ps. 89:22, 93:1, 96:10, and 141:2; Prov. 12:19 and 20:18; 1 Kings 2:12; 1 Chron. 16:30; and 2 Chron. 8:16, 29:35, 35:10 and 35:16).

30. Aside from the fact that the theme of the section fits as an introduction to verses of *malkhuyyot*, the section ends with four words from the root מל"ך:

> ויקבלו כולם את עול מלכותך ותמלוך עליהם מהרה לעולם ועד כי המלכות שלך
> היא ולעולמי עד תמלוך בכבוד

I have little doubt that the first section of *Aleinu* (which includes the words *melekh malkhei ha-melakhim* and *malkeinu*) was also composed at the same time. This is contrary to the view of many scholars who point to the two separate themes in the two sections as evidence of different authors.

Moreover, we can easily understand how an original reading of לתכן עולם might have evolved into לתקן עולם, a term related to the familiar term תקון העולם. The term תקון העולם (always with the definite article) is widespread in early rabbinic literature.[31] It is found thirteen

---

Aleinu is a short prayer, and in the earliest texts of *Aleinu* there is no division into sections. Therefore, our presumption should be one of unitary authorship. Close analysis of the verses cited shows that both sections quote or paraphrase from the same chapter of Isaiah (45:20: *u-mitpallelim el el lo yoshia* and 45:23: *ki li tikhra kol berekh tishava kol lashon*; there are quotes and paraphrases of other verses from chapter 45, and from 44:24 and 46:9 as well.) This strongly suggests that both sections were composed at the same time. (I have not seen anyone else make this point.) Terms characteristic of *heikhalot* literature are found in both sections as well.

While it cannot be proven that Rav was the author of *Aleinu*, it has been observed that "in some of Rav's homilies a tendency to a certain mystical thinking is discernible." See *Encyclopaedia Judaica* 13:1578 (1972) and the citations there, as well as the following statement of Rav at *Berakhot* 55a:

יודע היה בצלאל לצרף אותיות שנבראו בהן שמים וארץ.

Also, several Talmudic passages record Rav's authorship or contribution to the texts of other prayers. Most of these passages are collected at Ismar Elbogen, *Jewish Liturgy: A Comprehensive History*, translated by Raymond P. Scheindlin (New York: 1993), pp. 207-208. Most relevant is *Berakhot* 12b where the המלך הקדוש and המלך המשפט changes for the Ten Days of Repentance are recorded in the name of Rav.

The literary style and meter of *Aleinu* (unrhymed, with parallel paired stichs of approximately four beats each) also point to its authorship in or around the century of Rav. (According to the Letter of R. Sherira Gaon, Rav died in 247.) As one scholar has written recently (and many have observed prior to this): "In literary style, [*Aleinu*] is consistent with the earliest forms of rabbinic-era liturgical poetry from the land of Israel...." See Ruth Langer, "The Censorship of *Aleinu* in Ashkenaz and Its Aftermath," in Debra Reed Blank, ed., *The Experience of Jewish Liturgy: Studies Dedicated to Menahem Schmelzer* (Leiden and Boston: 2011), p. 148. Although Rav gained prominence in Babylonia, he had been a student of R. Judah ha-Nasi in Israel.

31. תקון העולם was the correct classical term, even though it has now been replaced in popular parlance by תקון עולם. Rosenthal, p. 214, n. 1.

times in the Mishnah, and seventeen times in the Babylonian Talmud.[32] The alternative scenario, that the original reading was לתקן עולם and that this evolved in some texts into the unusual reading לתכן עולם, is much less likely.[33]

Finally, the ב of במלכות שד-י seems to fit better in לתכן עולם במלכות שד-י (to establish the world under God's sovereignty) than in either of the two ways of understanding לתקן עולם במלכות שד-י.[34] Also, the use of the word עולם instead of העולם and the lack of an את before the object עולם perhaps fit the reading לתכן better. I leave a detailed analysis of these aspects to grammarians.

---

32. Rosenthal, p. 214, n. 1. It is also found eight times in the Jerusalem Talmud and four times in the Tosefta. Most of the time, the term is used in the context of the laws of divorce, but it is found in other contexts as well (e.g., Hillel's enactment of *prozbol* at M. *Gittin* 4:3). Rosenthal suggests that the concept originated in the context of the laws of divorce, and was later expanded into the other contexts. See Rosenthal, pp. 217-219. The latest discussion of the term is by Levi Cooper. See his "The Assimilation of *Tikkun Olam*," *Jewish Political Studies Review* 25, no. 3-4 (Fall 2014) (forthcoming).

33. Admittedly, the root תק"ן can often be translated as "established." But in many of these cases the context is that of establishing a legal ordinance or procedure, and a better translation would be "instituted." On the other hand, the *Musaf Amidah* for festivals includes the phrase ושמחנו בתקונו (the subject being the *beit ha-mikdash*) and this seems to be an example of the root תק"ן meaning "establish" in a non-legal context. Another such example is the phrase...והתקין לו ממנו of *sheva berakhot* (*Ketubbot* 8a).

Nevertheless, I strongly believe that לתכן was the original reading in *Aleinu*. It is easily understandable how an original reading of לתכן עולם might have evolved into לתקן עולם; the reverse scenario is much less likely. Moreover, R. Saadiah's text in the *Musaf Amidah* for *Shabbat* read תכנת שבת. Yet he recorded לתכן in *Aleinu*.

34. As mentioned earlier, in the reading לתקן עולם, there are two ways to translate במלכות: "under the sovereignty" or "through the sovereignty." If the translation is "under," establishing a world under the sovereignty of God is a simpler reading than perfecting a world under the sovereignty of God. If one wants to advocate for the translation "through," it requires investigation whether the prefix ב could have been used to mean "through" in the Tannaitic and Amoraic periods.

Conclusion

There is no question that social justice is an important value in Judaism.[35] Moreover, classical rabbinical literature includes many references to the concept of תקון העולם, both in the context of divorce legislation and in other contexts. The purpose of this article was only to show that is almost certainly a mistake to read such a concept into the *Aleinu* prayer, a prayer most likely composed as an introduction to the *malkhuyyot* section of the *Amidah*, and focused primarily on the goal of establishing God's kingdom on earth. Even if we do not change the text of our *siddurim*, we should certainly have this alternate and almost certainly original reading in mind as we recite this prayer.[36]

35. See, e.g., Shatz, Waxman, and Diament, eds., *Tikkun Olam: Social Responsibility in Jewish Thought and Law*, and Jacob J. Schacter, "*Tikkun Olam*: Defining the Jewish Obligation," in *Rav Chesed: Essays in Honor of Rabbi Dr. Haskel Lookstein*, ed. Rafael Medoff (Jersey City: 2009), vol. 2, pp. 183-204. For some citations to Biblical verses on justice, see Rosenthal, p. 215, n. 2.

36. R. Chaim Brovender suggested to me that after *Aleinu* shifted to becoming primarily a daily prayer, reciting a statement about perfecting/improving the world would have been seen as appropriate. By the 12th century, *Aleinu* was being recited as a daily prayer in *Shaḥarit* in parts of France (see above, n. 16) and probably in parts of Germany and England as well. (For Germany, see above, n. 17, and for England, see Ms. Oxford, Corpus Christi College 133.)

The recital of *Aleinu* in the evening prayer in Europe is a slightly later development. For some early references to this practice, see *Sefer ha-Minhagot* of R. Moshe b. R. Shmuel of Marseilles (early 13th century), published in *Kobetz Al Yad* 14 (1998), pp. 81-176 (103), and *Kol Bo*, sec. 11, citing R. Meir of Rothenberg (13th century). The recital of *Aleinu* in the afternoon prayer is a later development.

Regarding the recital of *Aleinu* as a *daily* prayer in Palestine, see above, n. 14.

2

What is the Origin of the Word מחילה?

Introduction[1]

The concept of מחילה is commonly assumed to be integral to our *Yamim Noraim*. Yet surprisingly, neither the word מחילה nor the verb מחל appears in *Tanakh*.[2]

When do the terms מחילה and מחל first appear and in what contexts? What is their precise meaning? Can we differentiate between the meaning of the verb מחל and the meaning of the verb סלח? (The latter appears 50 times in *Tanakh*.) This article will attempt to deal with these issues.

1. A very similar version of this article is forthcoming shortly in vol. 18 of *Ḥakirah*. I would like to acknowledge the article by Jed H. Abraham, "A Literary Solution to the Name Variations of Esau's Wives," *The Torah U-Madda Journal* 7 (1997), pp. 1-14, which provided many useful references.

2. There are people in *Tanakh* with names built around the letters מחל. These are: מחול (1 Kings 5:11, but see Rashi), מחלה (daughter of Zelophehad, mentioned several times, and a male referred to at 1 Chron. 7:18), מחלון (son of Elimelech), מחלי (two different individuals), and מחלת (a wife of Esau; later, a wife of Rehoboam). The *Tanakh* also refers to a place called אבל מחולה (Judg. 7:22, and 1 Kings 4:12 and 19:16; see also 1 Sam. 18:19 and 2 Sam. 21:8). Based on all of this, it can be argued that the verb מחל and a concept of מחילה did exist in Biblical times. This will be discussed further in Part III. The *Tanakh* also includes words like מחלת (musical instrument) and מחול (musical instrument, dancing). But almost certainly the initial *mem* in these is not a root letter and these derive from חלל or חול.

That the verb מחל is not found in *Tanakh* explains many instances in our *tefillot* where a citation to a verse about מחילה might be expected and yet none is provided. See, for example, the *zekhor lanu* section of our *seliḥot*. See *Siddur Kol Yaakov: The Complete ArtScroll Siddur* (Brooklyn: 1990, 3rd ed.), p. 830. See also *Machzor Zichron Yosef: The Complete ArtScroll Machzor: Yom Kippur: Nusach Ashkenaz* (Brooklyn: 1986), p. 682: *timḥol ve-tislaḥ la-avoneinu ka-katuv...vesalaḥta....*

I. The First Appearances

Although the noun מחילה and the verb מחל do not appear in *Tanakh*, the noun מחילה (in the form מחילת) and various forms of the verb מחל do appear in the *mishnayyot* of *Bava Kamma*, *Terumot*, *Sotah*, *Yoma*, and *Avot*.[3] Similarly, the noun מחילה (in the form מחילת) and various forms of the verb מחל also appear in the Tosefta.[4]

The fact that the root מחל does not appear in *Tanakh* and then appears in Mishnaic Hebrew is surprising, but not unusual. This is the case with many other roots as well.[5]

The word מחול with the meaning "waive" or "forgive" also appears once in a very fragmentary passage in a text from the Dead Sea.[6]

II. What is the Origin and Meaning of the Root מחל?

I will now present three suggestions for the origin and meaning of the root.

(1) The root derives from the noun חלל, and its meaning of "open space" or "emptiness."

There is a noun in Mishnaic Hebrew חלל, which seems to have "open space" or "emptiness" as its fundamental meaning.[7] It is fairly clear that this word lies behind Biblical words such as חליל (flute), מחלות[8] (caves,

3. *Bava Kamma* 8:7 and 9:6, *Avot* 6:1, *Terumot* 6:1, 7:1, 7:3 and 7:4, *Sotah* 7:7 and 7:8, and *Yoma* 7:1.

4. *Bava Metzia* 8:9, *Bava Batra* 5:4, *Yoma* 3:13, 4:9 and 4:12, *Sukkah* 4:2, *Gittin* 5:11, *Sanhedrin* 9:3, and *Shevuot* 3:2-3.

5. See Menaḥem Moreshet, *Leksikon ha-Poal she-Nitḥaddesh bi-Leshon ha-Tannaim* (Ramat Gan: 1980). (His discussion of מחל is at pp. 86 and 209.) Admittedly, many of the new Tannaitic roots can be easily connected to earlier Hebrew or Aramaic roots, or to earlier roots in other Semitic languages. But in the case of מחל, this is not the case.

6. See 4Q267 4:4 (*DJD* XVIII, Oxford, 1996, p. 99): מחול לוא יביאנו. The surrounding words have not survived, so the context is unknown. The handwriting is an "early Herodian formal hand" (ibid., p. 96).

7. See, e.g., *Bava Batra* 3:8, *Uktzin* 2:8, and *Maaser Sheni* 3:7. This word is also known to us from the blessing *asher yotzar* (חלולים) .

8. 1 Sam. 10:5 and elsewhere.

hollows),[9] and חלון (opening, window).[10] Probably, the Hebrew word for bread, חלה, derives from חלל as well.[11] Ancient Middle Eastern bread probably looked like pita, i.e., had a hollow center.[12]

Perhaps the verb מחל originated in the form מחלל, the *hif'il* (causative) of חלל, meaning "to turn something into a void."[13] Subsequently, the second *lamed* dropped.[14]

(2) The root derives from the verb חל"ל, and its meaning "release, make loose, untie."

A root חל"ל with the meaning of "release, make loose, untie" is found in Arabic.[15] There is no such root in Hebrew,[16] and our sources for חל"ל in Arabic with this meaning are many centuries after the period of Mishnaic Hebrew. But the root in Arabic raises the possibility that Hebrew may

9. Is. 2:19.

10. Gen. 8:6 and many other places. See, e.g., Samuel David Luzzatto, comm. to Gen. 8:6.

11. See, e.g., Solomon Mandelkern, *Heikhal ha-Kodesh* (Lipsiae: 1896), p. 396 and Ernest Klein, *A Comprehensive Etymological Dictionary of the Hebrew Language for Readers of English* (New York: 1987), p. 217.

12. In a different context, R. Shlomo Riskin writes: "The word *ḥol*, as in *ḥol ha-moed*, means 'empty'; it does not mean "profane." There exist the holy and the still-empty-of holiness, the holy, and the not-yet-holy, which is waiting for us to express its inherent sanctity." See his *The Passover Haggadah* (New York: 1983), p. 25. Although his idea is a profound one, almost certainly *ḥol* does not mean "empty" in the expression *ḥol ha-moed*; it means "common, profane." See similarly the meaning of the term *ḥol* at Lev. 10:10 (*bein ha-kodesh u-vein ha-ḥol, u-vein ha-tame u-vein ha-tahor*).

13. See, e.g., Yehoshua Steinberg, *Mail-Jewish*, vol. 50, number 31 (2005).

14. The dropping of the second of two *lameds* is not an infrequent occurrence.

15. See Avraham Even-Shoshan, *Millon Even-Shoshan* (Israel: 2003), vol. 2, p. 565, entry חלל. (Klein, p. 219, lists the Arabic word as having the meaning "united [sic], undid." But "united [sic]" is surely a typographical error for "untied.")

16. It is possible to argue that חלל means "release" in the *Tanakh*, Mishnah, and Tosefta any time the term is used to describe an object going from a holy state to a profane state. But much more likely, the meaning of חלל in this context is "profane/make common," and not "release."

once have had such a root and that this underlies the word מח"ל.[17] If the verb חלל was one that was conjugated in the *pi'el* construct, the present tense would have had an initial *mem* (מחלל, *meḥallel*). Over time, this *mem* could have become part of the root, and the second *lamed* could have dropped.[18]

The derivation of מח"ל from חל"ל is supported by the fact that there is a root חל"ל in Aramaic with the meaning of "forgive" or "relinquish."[19]

---

17. See, e.g., Ḥanokh Yehudah (Alexander) Kohut, *Sefer Arukh ha-Shalem* (1970), vol. 5, p. 110, entry מחל, and Yeḥezkel Kutscher, *Erkhei ha-Millon he-Ḥadash le-Sifrut Ḥazal*, vol. 1 (Ramat Gan: 1972), pp. 5 and 66.

18. Alternatively, perhaps the verb מחל originated in the form מחלל as the *hif'il* of חלל, meaning "to cause something to be released, made loose, or untied." Subsequently, the second *lamed* dropped. Or the verb חלל generated a noun מחלל, an object that was released, and this noun later generated the verb מחל. Such a development occurred in the case of the verb תר"ם. The original verb רו"ם (raise) led to the creation of the noun, תרומה. This noun later generated the verb תר"ם.

19. See Michael Sokoloff, *A Dictionary of Jewish Babylonian Aramaic of the Talmudic and Geonic Periods* (Ramat Gan and Baltimore: 2002), entry חל"ל. Sokoloff categorizes the Babylonian Aramaic root as חל"ל, even though none of his references have a double *lamed* following the *ḥet*. Marcus Jastrow had listed the relevant Aramaic root for these references as חו"ל. See his *A Dictionary of the Targumim, the Talmud Babli and Yerushalmi, and the Midrashic Literature* (London and New York: 1903), p. 432.

It is unclear whether there was an Aramaic root מח"ל with a meaning of "forgive" or "relinquish" in the Amoraic period. Words such as מחל, מחיל, מחלי, and מחילנא, with a meaning of "forgive" or "relinquish" are found in the Babylonian and Palestinian Talmuds. (For the references, see Sokoloff's above dictionary, entry חל"ל, and his *A Dictionary of Jewish Palestinian Aramaic of the Byzantine Period*, entry מח"ל.) But some scholars believe that the initial *mems* here are not root letters. See, e.g., Kutscher, vol. 1, pp. 5 and 66, and Moreshet, p. 209, n. 8** . If the initial *mem* is a root letter, the Aramaic root מח"ל may derive from the Hebrew root.

Sokoloff seems to believe that there was a root מח"ל in the Palestinian Aramaic of the Amoraic period, but not in the Babylonian Aramaic of this period. His *Dictionary of Jewish Babylonian Aramaic*, entry מח"ל, lists only Geonic usages of the root. The words in the Babylonian Talmud with the initial *mem* are categorized in the entry חל"ל. But in his *Dictionary of Jewish Palestinian Aramaic*, he categorizes the words in the Jerusalem

(3) The root מח"ל is related to the root מח"ה:

The root מחה is attested to many times in *Tanakh*.[20] It has the meaning "to erase, blot out, remove, wipe away." It has been suggested that מחל is related to this root.[21] Supporting this is the possibility that, in the earliest stages, Hebrew roots had only two letters.[22] There may have been an original two-letter root מח, which had some meaning related to "erase, blot out, remove," from which מח"ה and מח"ל ultimately derive.

Interestingly, an anonymous passage in *Midrash Tanḥuma* seems to assume a close relationship, and perhaps an identity of meaning, between מח"ל and מח"ה. The passage makes a statement about God being מוחל, but then cites a verse referring to מחה:[23]

> אמר הקדוש ברוך הוא: בעולם הזה נתכפר להם על ידי קרבן ולעולם הבא אני מוחל פשעיך בלא קרבן שנאמר אנכי אנכי הוא מחה פשעיך למעני....

◆ ◆ ◆

Talmud with the initial *mem* in an entry מח"ל. Similarly, Ludwig Koehler and Walter Baumgartner, in *The Hebrew and Aramaic Lexicon of the Old Testament* (Leiden-New York-Köln: 1994), entry מחלי, take the position that Palestinian Aramaic had a root מח"ל with the meaning "forgive."

20. For example, it is the verb used in connection with the commandment to remember Amalek. See Ex. 17:14, and Deut. 25:19.

21. See, e.g., R. Jacob Emden, *Siddur Beit Yaakov* (Lemberg: 1904), p. 68: והוא ענין המחייה והמחיקה לגמרי יותר מהסליחה. Jastrow, p. 761, seems to believe there is a relation between them as well.

Pinchas H. Peli, in setting forth the view of Rabbi Joseph B. Soloveitchik, uses the phrase *meḥikat ha-avon* in discussing the meaning of the root מח"ל. See *Al ha-Teshuvah* (Jerusalem: 1975), p. 265. Regarding the root מח"ק, see below.

22. See, e.g., Kutscher, *A History of the Hebrew Language* (Jerusalem: 1984), p. 6. The one example that Kutscher provides are the several verbs whose first two root letters are פר: פרר, פרק, פרס, פרם, פרך, פרט, פרד and פרץ. They all seem to have an underlying notion of "divide." Another example may be נג: נגש, נגע, נגד. These all relate to "coming close to something." (Perhaps נגח and נגף are related as well.) In the two-letter root model, the third letter acts as a semantic modifier, distinguishing between the different types of the verb.

23. *Midrash Tanḥuma, Shemini* 10. The verse cited is Is. 43:25.

Admittedly, our first and second suggestions are difficult because they have to postulate that an initial *mem* eventually became part of the root. Although we have suggested scenarios in which this could have occurred, these scenarios are farfetched.

Therefore, of our three suggestions, the third seems most likely: a connection between מח"ה and מח"ל based on an original two-letter root מח. But it may just be coincidence that מח"ל and מח"ה begin with the same two letters; there may be no relationship between the two at all. After all, the Biblical verbs מח"א and מח"ץ (both meaning "strike") are probably not related to the verb מחה.[24]

III. Light Shed by Archaeology

It has long been observed that there are people and places in *Tanakh* with the names מחלת ,מחלי ,מחלון ,מחלה ,מחול, and אבל מחולה.[25] These can support an argument that the root מחל and the concept of מחילה existed in Biblical times.[26] But one can easily respond that these names were

24. The verb מח"ק appears only once in *Tanakh*: *mahakah rosho* (Judg. 5:26). From the context, its meaning seems to be "hit," "crushed," "split," or "destroyed." In Mishnaic Hebrew, the root מח"ק means "rub out," "blot out," "scrape," or "smooth." It is possible to interpret Judg. 5:26 using the Mishnaic meaning, but such an interpretation seems farfetched in the context. Most likely, the מח"ק of Judg. 5:26 is related to the Biblical מח"א. See, e.g., Moreshet, p. 209, n. 13*.

It is noteworthy that the *Avinu Malkeinu* prayer includes the lines for מח"ה, מח"ל, and מח"ק in direct succession. (The first of these begins סלח ומחל.)

25. See above, n. 2.

26. For example, JT *Bikkurim* 3:3 (65d) and *Genesis Rabbah* 67:13 read into the name מחלת (Gen. 28:9) an allusion that God forgave Esau's sins. See also Rashi to Gen. 36:3.

The Sages have found other ways to read the concept of *mehilah* into *Tanakh*. For example:

- *Shabbat* 118b reads the term homiletically into מחללו (Is. 56:2).
- *Midrash Tehillim* 88:1 interprets the musical instrument מחלת (Ps. 88:1) as an allusion that God forgave David's sins.
- *Sifrei, Haazinu* 319 records a view that ותשכח א-ל מחללך (Deut. 32:18) refers to God as a forgiver of sins. But the parallel ילדך in the same verse indicates clearly that מחוללך here means "the

much more likely founded upon the "musical instrument," "dancing," or "joy" meanings of the letters מח"ל.[27]

But archaeology has now provided us with a name from the late Biblical period that is likely related to a "forgiveness" or "relinquish" meaning of מח"ל. An incense altar from Lachish has been discovered that names מחליה בן יאש as its owner.[28] The altar dates from the fifth century B.C.E. and most likely, this owner was a Jew.[29] The name מחליה is undoubtedly meant to provide a description of God, and God is much more likely to be described as a "forgiver" or "relinquisher (of punishment)" than as a "musician" or "dancer," or described with some meaning related to "sickness."[30] Thus, the meaning of the name מחליה is almost certainly: "God has forgiven/relinquished." We now have a reasonable basis to infer that the root מח"ל with a meaning relating to "forgive" or "relinquish" existed at least in late Biblical times.[31]

---

one who gave birth to you." ילד and חלל are parallel many times in *Tanakh* (Ps. 90:2 and Is. 23:4, 54:1, and 66:8). (Some suggest that the root of חל"ל in its "birth" meaning is חי"ל, due to the trembling of the birth mother. Others suggest that the root is חו"ל and point to the whirling and writhing of the birth mother. Others suggest that the root is חל"ל, alluding to the womb.) Peli, in setting forth the view of R. Soloveitchik, writes that the term *meḥilah* is not found anywhere in *Tanakh* except "perhaps" at Deut. 32:18, and cites to this *Sifrei*. See *Al ha-Teshuvah*, p. 265.

27. The "musical instrument" and "dancing" meanings derive from חל"ל or חו"ל. Very likely, מחול eventually took on the meaning "joy." See Ps. 30:12 and Lam. 5:15. If so, the birth name can be seen as a commemoration of the joy that the parents felt at the time of the birth. See *Encyclopedia Mikrait*, vol. 4 (Jerusalem: 1962), entry מחול (by Yaakov Shalom Licht), p. 788.

It seems very unlikely that someone would give a child a birth name related to "sickness," or that someone's name would later be changed to reflect such a meaning.

28. See Yohanan Aharoni, *Investigations at Lachish* (Tel Aviv: 1975), pp. 6-7.

29. Aharoni considers the inscription to be Hebrew and its owner to be a Jew. He points out that Neh. 11:30 refers to a Jewish community at Lachish. There are scholars who argue that the owner of the altar was an Arab, or an Edomite, or a Canaanite. But the last two letters of the name מחליה point strongly to its Jewishness; non-Jews probably did not utilize such name endings in this period.

30. "Joy" seems unlikely here as well. Also, it would require a spelling of מחוליה.

31. I had initially thought it possible that מח"ל originated as a contraction

IV. Can We Differentiate Between סליחה and מחילה?

Over the centuries, many rabbinic authorities have attempted to differentiate between סליחה and מחילה.[32] For example, R. David Abudarham writes that סליחה is more efficacious, since with סליחה, there will not remain a *hakpadah muetet* (lingering minor ill-feeling).[33] R.

of מח"ה and the prefix ל. In the Mishnah and the Tosefta, מח"ל is often followed by the prefix ל. But the Biblical verb מח"ה, used in connection with an object, is typically followed by את. See, e.g., the commandment to remember Amalek at Ex. 17:14 and Deut. 25:19. Sometimes the Biblical verb מח"ה is not followed by את and one time it is followed by אל, but it is never followed by the prefix ל. If מח"ל with a meaning related to "forgive" or "relinquish" already existed as a verb in Biblical times, it would seem extremely unlikely that its origin was as a contraction of מח"ה ל.

32. The difference between them is not just relevant to the *Yamim Noraim*. For example, in the prevalent version of the daily *Amidah*, the sixth berakhah uses both סל"ח and מח"ל. (From the Cairo Genizah, we learn that the Palestinian versions of the *Amidah* did not include מח"ל here. After the initial phrase beginning with סל"ח, the next phrase began with מח"ה in the Palestinian versions. See Uri Ehrlich, *Tefillat ha-Amidah Shel Yemot ha-Ḥol* [Jerusalem: 2013], pp. 99-104.)

There are passages in classical rabbinic literature where the roots סל"ח and מח"ל are found together. For example, at *Taanit* 30b and *Bava Batra* 121a, an anonymous passage describes Yom Kippur as a day of both סליחה and מחילה. At *Berakhot* 32a, the Palestinian amora R. Abbahu describes Moses as declaring that he is not going to let go of God *ad she-timḥol ve-tislaḥ lahem*. See also JT *Yoma* 8:7 (8:9, 45c). (Here, a possible distinction is implied: מחילה is requested from עון, while סליחה is requested from חטא. But compare *Leviticus Rabbah* 3:3. See further Isaac Baer, *Avodat Yisrael* [Rödelheim: 1868], p. 416, notes.)

There are many passages in the Yom Kippur and yearly liturgies in which both סל"ח and מח"ל are included and a possible distinction between the roots could be implied (as in the above passages from the Jerusalem Talmud and *Leviticus Rabbah*). But it is doubtful that these passages are Tannaitic, and the original distinction between סל"ח and מח"ל was most likely lost by the time these passages were composed. Moreover, the original distinction between סל"ח and מח"ל may have been lost even in the Tannaitic period.

33. *Sefer Abudarham ha-Shalem* (Jerusalem: 1995), pp. 110-111 (*Shaḥarit shel ḥol*). Interestingly, the earliest edition of *Siddur Kol Yaakov: The Complete ArtScroll Siddur* cites Abudarham as saying the exact opposite! This error was corrected in subsequent editions. See the comm. to *Amidah*

Jonathan Eybeschuetz writes that סליחה is לגמרי, while one still receives יסורים in the case of מחילה.[34] On the other hand, R. Jacob Emden writes that מחילה is a מחייה and מחיקה, and that these are לגמרי, unlike סליחה.[35] Similarly, R. Ḥanoch Zundel writes that מחילה has the implication of לגמרי, while סליחה just delays the time of the punishment.[36]

A most interesting differentiation is made by R. Samson Raphael Hirsch:[37]

> סליחה is *personal forgiveness* granted so that the transgression that was committed may not permanently blight the *relationship* of the transgressor to the one against whom he has sinned. מחילה is objective pardon, the *waiver of the punishment* which the transgressor would have deserved (emphasis added).

---

of daily *Shaḥarit*, p. 103. (But the language in the corrected passage remains awkward.)

Also, Rabbi Joseph B. Soloveitchik has expressed the view that סליחה is more efficacious. See Peli, p. 265. R. Soloveitchik takes the position that even after מחילה (which is described as *meḥikat ha-avon*), one still needs סליחה to purify the soul and return it to its former status. R. Soloveitchik takes the position that מחילה is the equivalent of כפרה, and סליחה is the equivalent of טהרה. See also Isaac Wohlgemuth, *A Guide to Jewish Prayer* (Brookline, MA: 1999), p. 165:

> *Slach* involves divine grace. If we sin, we have done something wrong.... But God in His divine grace can elevate us above our sins and treat us as though they never occurred. It is a complete forgiveness by divine grace. *Mchal*, however, means canceling the debt. It means that you really did sin, but God will not collect the "payment" for the sin by punishing you.

34. See his *Yearot Devash*, cited in *Siddur Otzar ha-Tefillot: Nusaḥ Ashkenaz* (Vilna: 1914), vol. 1, p. 326 (comm. of *Etz Yosef*). On the other hand, an argument can be made from Num. 14:20-23 that סליחה does not preclude punishment.

35. *Siddur Beit Yaakov*, p. 68. He is obviously taking the third approach.

36. See his *Siddur Otzar ha-Tefillot*, vol. 1, p. 385, *Etz Yosef* comm.

According to R. Judah he-Ḥasid (d. 1217), commenting on Num. 14:20-23, סליחה means additional time is given for repentance that will lead to complete forgiveness. מחילה means the forgiveness is total. See *Perushei ha-Torah le-R. Yehudah he-Hasid*, ed. Yitzḥak Shimshon Lange (Jerusalem: 1975), pp. 174-75.

37. Samson Raphael Hirsch, *Siddur Tefillot Yisrael: The Hirsch Siddur* (Jerusalem and New York: 1972), pp. 136-37.

This suggestion is attractive because it clearly delineates two different concepts, each deserving of its own root. One is the psychological forgiveness granted so that the relationship between the transgressor and the other party can be maintained. The other is the waiver or relinquishment of the objective punishment or financial penalty.

The problem with this suggestion is that by the time the root מח"ל appears in the Mishnah and Tosefta, it appears in the contexts of both waiver[38] of objective punishment or financial penalty and psychological forgiveness.[39] Most probably, the name in the altar from Lachish from the fifth century B.C.E. also alludes to the psychological forgiveness aspect of מח"ל.[40] But it is at least possible that originally מח"ל had only the meaning of waiver of an objective punishment and/or financial penalty, and that סל"ח had only the meaning of psychological forgiveness, and over time the root מח"ל expanded to include psychological forgiveness.

An alternative suggestion can be made, based on the fact that the root סל"ח only appears in *Tanakh* in the context of the Divine.[41]

---

38. From now on, for the sake of simplicity, I will use the term "waiver," instead of "waiver/relinquishment."

39. For מח"ל as psychological forgiveness in the Mishnah, see *Bava Kamma* 8:7 (*af-al-pi she-hu noten lo, eino nimḥal lo ad she-yevakesh mimenu*) and *Avot* 6:1 (*u-moḥel al elbono*). In the case of *meḥilat ha-avon* (*Yoma* 7:1, *Sotah* 7:7 and 7:8), it is unclear if the reference is to Divine waiver of punishment or to Divine psychological forgiveness.

For מח"ל as Divine psychological forgiveness in the Tosefta, see *Shevuot* 3:2-3, *Yoma* 3:13, 4:9 and 4:12, *Sukkah* 4:2, and *Sanhedrin* 9:3. But admittedly one could interpret all of these as referring to Divine waiver of punishment.

The context of מחול in the Dead Sea text 4Q267 is unknown. The passage is too fragmentary.

40. Since God both forgives us and imposes punishments or financial penalties, the allusion in the name מחליה could be to either aspect. But probably the psychological forgiveness aspect is primary and is what would be emphasized in the name.

41. The root never appears in *Tanakh* as something given by, or requested from, a human being. See Stefan C. Reif, "The Amidah Benediction on Forgiveness: Links Between Its Theology and Its Textual Evolution," in Mark J. Boda, Daniel K. Falk, and Rodney A. Werline, eds., *Seeking the Favor of God* (Leiden and Boston: 2006), p. 87 and J. Hausmann, entry סל"ח, *The Theological Dictionary of the Old Testament*, vol. 10 (Grand Rapids and Cambridge: 1999), pp. 258-265. (Interestingly, in Akkadian, סלח occurs in non-Divine contexts as well. Hausmann, ibid.) In Akkadian,

סל"ח was the root used for Divine forgiveness or waiver of an objective punishment or financial penalty, while מח"ל arose as the root for human beings, whether they were giving out psychological forgiveness or waiving an objective punishment or financial penalty. Over time, מח"ל also began to be used in the context of the Divine, as evidenced by the altar from Lachish from the 5th century B.C.E.[42]

Summary and Conclusion

We provided three suggestions to connect מח"ל to the roots חל"ל and מח"ה. Of these, the third is most likely: a connection between מח"ה and מח"ל based on an original two-letter מח root. But it is possible that there was an original Hebrew root מח"ל that has no connection to the root מח"ה.

We suggested that מח"ל originally meant waiver of an objective punishment or financial penalty, while סל"ח had the meaning of psychological forgiveness. We suggested alternatively that מח"ל originally arose as the root applicable to human beings, whether they were giving out psychological forgiveness or a waiver of an objective punishment or financial penalty.

---

the root has the meaning "sprinkle." Some believe that this was the original meaning of the root. (Words normally have concrete meanings before they develop abstract meanings.) See, e.g., Hausmann, p. 259 and *Encyclopaedia Judaica* (Jerusalem: 1972) 6:1433. The Aramaic root זל"ח, "sprinkle" (see, e.g., Jastrow, p. 401), is also perhaps related to סל"ח. A relationship between סל"ח and סל"ק (go up, go away) has also been suggested. See, e.g., Mandelkern, p. 799.

Malbim had pointed out that the root סל"ח only appears in *Tanakh* in the context of the Divine. See his comm. to Ps.130:4. He suggests that סליחה treats the sin as if it had never occurred, and only God is capable of doing this. He suggests that this may be the meaning of *ki imkha ha-seliḥah* at Ps. 130:4.

42. Also, over time, the root סל"ח began to recede from common use, since it was a word used only in Divine contexts. The root סל"ח is never found in the Mishnah and is found only twice in the Tosefta (both in *Nazir* 3:6). In both Talmuds, its use is limited to discussions of forgiveness by God, and quotations from Biblical verses and *nusaḥ ha-tefillah*. It is never used in either Talmud to describe forgiveness by an individual. It is very ironic that the expression in modern Hebrew for "excuse me" is סליחה.

But admittedly, all of this is mere speculation. מח"ל in the context of the Divine, and probably in the context of psychological forgiveness, is already found in the altar from Lachish from the fifth century B.C.E.

If מח"ל was not originally synonymous with סל"ח, this makes it more of a possibility that מח"ל existed as a root in the early Biblical period, even though our earliest clear evidence for it is only from the fifth century B.C.E. altar from Lachish. The *Tanakh* may simply have not had the occasion to use the root.[43] The possibility that the root existed in the early Biblical period encourages us to look again at all the people and places in *Tanakh* with names based on the letters מח"ל. That a concept of מחילה may be reflected in some of these names becomes more of a possibility.

◆ ◆ ◆

I will close on a homiletical note.[44] The *Yamim Noraim* are a time when God has a special relationship with the Jewish people.[45] Since the concept of מחילה is not found explicitly in *Tanakh*, it can be considered a special Divine gift, appropriate to this unique period!

---

43. If we follow the suggestion of R. Hirsch, there is little reason for מח"ל to have appeared in the *Tanakh*. When the *Tanakh* sets forth legal provisions affecting the rights of individuals, it is concerned with setting forth fundamental principles. The concept of someone waiving his entitlement is just a side matter, not a subject that we should expect to be mentioned. If we follow our alternative suggestion, there is also perhaps little reason for מח"ל to have appeared in *Tanakh*. *Tanakh* is a work much more concerned with Divine forgiveness and waiver than forgiveness and waiver by human beings.

In his entry נח"ל (p. 734), Mandelkern was willing to suggest that Ex. 34:9, *ve-salaḥta la-avoneinu u-le-ḥattateinu u-neḥaltanu* originally read *ve-salaḥta la-avoneinu u-le-ḥatateinu u-meḥaltanu*. Then the root מח"ל would be found in *Tanakh*! Even though *mem* and *nun* do look somewhat similar in Old Hebrew, there is no reason to take Mandelkern's speculation seriously. On the other hand, it has been suggested that the root נח"ל once had a meaning of "forgive" and that this was its meaning here. See Zev Ben-Ḥayyim, *Ivrit ve-Aramit Nusaḥ Shomron*, vol. 3, part II (Jerusalem: 1967), pp. 358-359. (If this is correct, perhaps מח"ל derives from נח"ל!)

Ben-Ḥayyim suggested that מח"ל is related to the Arabic root מה"ל, which means, "acting kindly or patiently."

44. For some humerous material in connection with the terms מח"ל and מחילה, see Michael Wex, *Just Say Nu* (New York: 2007), pp. 24-25.

45. See Is. 55:6 and *Rosh Hashanah* 18a.

3

אני והו:

What is the Meaning of this Cryptic Mishnaic Statement?

The Mishnah at *Sukkah* 4:5 preserves a description of the *aravah* ceremony in the Temple during the *Sukkot* holiday. In the standard printed text of the Babylonian Talmud (*Sukkah* 45a), the Mishnah reads as follows:

> בכל יום מקיפין את המזבח פעם אחת ואומרים אנא ה' הושיעה נא אנא ה' הצליחה נא ר' יהודה אומר **אני והו** הושיעה נא

The first statement about the required recitation during the ceremony is straightforward. It records the recitation of a verse, or part of a verse, from Psalms.[1] But the meaning of R. Judah's statement is much less clear.

Rashi presents us with a fascinating interpretation.[2] The verses at Exodus 14:19-21 (ויסע ... ויבוא ... ויט) have 72 letters each. Rashi records a tradition that 72 three-letter Divine names can be derived from these verses.[3] According to this tradition, the first letter of the first verse (ו), the last letter of the second verse (ה), and the first letter of the

1. Ps. 118:25. Above I recorded the text of the Mishnah in the standard printed text of the Babylonian Talmud. But it seems from the manuscripts that אנא ה' הצליחה נא was not in the statement of the anonymous Tanna in the original Mishnah. Rather, the statement of the anonymous Tanna was אנא ה' הושיעה נא twice (but many manuscripts omit the 'ה).
2. Before he presents this explanation, Rashi remarks that אני והו is the equivalent of אנא ה' in *gematria*.
3. This tradition clearly preceded Rashi. See my discussion in the appendix to this article.

third verse (ו) yield the first Divine name; by continuing in this manner with the adjacent letters, 72 three-letter Divine names are derived.[4] According to this method, והו and אני are the first and thirty-seventh Divine names.[5]

Why should Divine names be found in these particular verses? Rashi does not say but that is surely because it was obvious to him.

---

4. For a chart presenting all seventy-two names, see *Jewish Encyclopedia* (New York: 1901-06) 9:164.

Interestingly, name 22 is ייי. In the post-Talmudic period, scribes began to use three *yods* to represent the Divine name. See Jacob Z. Lauterbach, "Substitutes for the Tetragrammaton," *Proceedings of the American Academy for Jewish Research* 2 (1930-31), pp. 39-67. Lauterbach finds evidence for this practice as early as the 8th century. (This is prior to the later practice of representing the Divine name with two *yods*, which is probably an offshoot of the three *yods* practice.) One source from the period of the early Rishonim states that the practice of representing the Divine name with three *yods* arose because it was one of the 72 Divine names derived from our three verses. See *Sefer ha-Maasim*, quoted in Benjamin Menashe Lewin, *Iggeret R. Sherira Gaon* (Haifa: 1921), pp. xxxi-xxxii. (The work is found in the collection *Neveh Shalom*, ed. Shelomoh Zalman Toisik, Munich, 1872). I believe that this explanation for the practice is the correct one. (Lauterbach proposes a different explanation. But neither Lauterbach's explanation nor any of the others he mentions are convincing.)

R. Eleazar of Worms points to the absence of a *gimmel* in Ex. 14:19-21 and suggests that this alludes to the fact that one needs to join three letters together to form each name. See Elliot R. Wolfson, *Through a Speculum That Shines* (Princeton: 1994), p. 235. (Obviously, it is very strange that the counting in the second verse proceeds in a reverse direction. One source that suggests an explanation is *Zohar, Beshallaḥ*.)

5. Probably, these two names symbolize all the names, since if the names would be divided into two columns, names 1 and 37 would be at the head of each column. Rashi probably understood that this was the significance of the choice of names 1 and 37, even though he does not state this explicitly. Later commentators state this explicitly. See, e.g., R. Yom Tov Lipmann Heller, *Tosefot Yom Tov*. In *Sefer ha-Bahir*, sec. 110 (ed. Reuven Margaliot, Jerusalem, 1951), the names are divided into three groups of twenty-four. Interestingly, והו appears as the forty-ninth name as well.

הו is stated to be a Divine name at *Shabbat* 104a. (Rashi there writes כמו אני והו שמות הם. This statement is surprising because, based on Rashi's understanding of והו at Mishnah *Sukkah* 4:5, there should be no connection between the names הו and והו).

The Divine names are found here because these are the verses of the splitting of the sea.[6] The three verses read:

19. (ויסע) The angel of God, who went before the camp of Israel, moved and went behind them; and the pillar of the cloud went from before them, and stood behind them.
20. (ויבא) It came between the camp of the Egyptians and the camp of Israel; and there were cloud and darkness, while it illuminated the night; and one came not near the other all the night (הלילה).
21. (ויט) Moses stretched out his hand over the sea, and the Lord caused the sea to go back by a strong east wind all that night, and made the sea dry land, and the waters were split.

The implication of there being Divine names in these verses is that Moses was able to split the sea using these Divine names. The later commentator Ḥizzekuni adds that these Divine names are being recited on *Sukkot* because *Sukkot* is when the world is judged on water![7]

Of course, there are difficulties with Rashi's interpretation.[8] Nevertheless, it is still a fascinating and profound one. Could it be the correct understanding of R. Judah's statement? Some scholars have suggested that R. Judah was not disagreeing when he said אני והו; he was

6. Why rabbinic literature refers to this event as קריעת ים סוף and not בקיעת ים סוף is itself an interesting issue, beyond the scope of this study.

7. Mishnah, *Rosh Hashanah* 1:2.

8. The main difficulty with reading the 72 three-letter Divine names explanation into our Mishnah (assuming והו is the correct text, which it almost certainly is not, see below) is that והו is name #1 and אני is name #37. If R. Judah was alluding to the 72 three-letter Divine names in two columns, his statement should have been והו אני הושיעה נא.

In interpreting our Mishnah the way he did, Rashi was probably following an earlier tradition that this was the interpretation of our Mishnah. (But at present there is no clear evidence for the reading והו prior to Rashi. I will discuss this below.)

Eliezer Ben-Yehuda's comment on our Rashi is noteworthy. He remarks that this is the only time in all of Rashi's commentaries that דעתו הצלולה did not prevent him from following an explanation that was כל כך לא טבעי. See his *Millon ha-Lashon ha-Ivrit ha-Yeshanah ve-ha-Ḥadashah* (New York and London: 1960), entry והו.

merely describing how אנא ה' was actually pronounced in the ritual.[9] Other scholars have suggested that he was disagreeing and making a statement about how the Divine name should be altered and disguised in the ritual.[10]

However, R. Judah's statement reads differently in the standard printed text of the Mishnah in the Jerusalem Talmud: רבי יהודה אומר אני והוא הושיעה נא. In fact, this is the reading in the earliest manuscripts of the Mishnah.[11]

Moreover, all of the other sources for the text of the Mishnah prior to Rashi read והוא. Specifically:

- והוא is the reading in the *She'iltot* of R. Aḥai.[12]
- והוא is the reading of R. Hai.[13]

---

9. Ben Yehuda, ibid.

10. See, e.g., Moses Gaster, *The Sword of Moses* (London: 1896), p. 12, and Abraham Geiger, *Ha-Mikra ve-Targumav* (Jerusalem: 1949), p. 332. See also R. Barukh Epstein, *Barukh She-Amar* to *Avot* 1:14 (אם אין אני לי מי לי). In his view, אני and הו are just abbreviations for the Divine names ADNI and YHVH. While the first Tanna focused on the name YHVH, R. Judah felt that both Divine names were required. However, because he believed that it was forbidden to recite these names outside of the time of *tefillah*, he abbreviated them to אני and הו. R. Epstein points out that R. Judah is known for abbreviations in other contexts. See, for example, his well-known statement in the Haggadah: דצ"ך עד"ש באח"ב and his statement at M. *Menaḥot* 11:4.

11. E.g., Kaufmann, Parma 3173 (=De Rossi 138), and Lowe. (The Ritva writes that בכל המשניות, old and new, and בכל הספרים, it is written with an *aleph*. See Ritva to *Sukkah* 45a.) Menaḥem Tzvi Fox, in his *Mahadurah Bi-Koratit Shel Mishnayyot Massekhet Sukkah Im Mavo ve-He'arot* (Hebrew Univ. dissertation, 1979), vol. 2, p. 131, lists only one Genizah fragment on our Mishnah. It too has the reading אני והוא. (Fox gives it the symbol ג11. It is T-S E1.64 at genizah.org and was previously published by L. Ginzberg as TS 10/64.) There are other Genizah fragments to Mishnah *Sukkah* 4:5, such as T-S K7.46 and T-S NS 57.54. Unfortunately, they are fragmentary and do not include the words relevant to us.

12. See the edition of Samuel Kalman Mirsky (Jerusalem: 1960-77), vol. 5, sec. 191, p. 102. This particular *she'ilta* came to light from the Genizah.

13. See *Toratan Shel Rishonim*, ed. Chaim M. Horowitz (Frankfurt: 1881), vol. 1, p. 51, quoting a responsum of R. Hai. This responsum was reprinted in Benjamin Menashe Lewin, *Otzar ha-Geonim* (Haifa and Jerusalem:

- והוא is the reading of the מפרשי התלמוד and גאונים cited by Rambam.[14]
- והוא is the reading of R. Ḥananel.[15]
- והוא is the reading of R. Isaac b. Judah Ibn Ghayyat.[16]
- והוא is the reading of R. Nathan b. Yeḥiel.[17]

Furthermore, as we will see shortly, the explanation of our Mishnah provided by the Jerusalem Talmud is based on the reading והוא. Finally, R. Judah's statement is quoted at *Leviticus Rabbah* 30:5 and here too the reading seems to be והוא.[18]

Based on all the above evidence, almost certainly והוא was the

---

1928-43), *Sukkah*, p. 66. There, והו is printed when R. Hai quotes the question, and והוא is printed in R. Hai's response. But the only source that Lewin cites for this responsum is *Toratan Shel Rishonim*, which has והוא throughout. Thus, the והו in Lewin's printing of the question seems merely to be a typographical error.

Some claim that R. Sherira (father of R. Hai) also had the reading והוא. The claim is based on a reference to a responsum of R. Sherira in R. Judah Ibn Balam (quoted at Lewin, *Otzar ha-Geonim, Sukkah*, p. 66). But Ibn Balam seems to be referring to this same responsum of R. Hai, which for some reason he attributed to R. Sherira. (Perhaps the responsum is from R. Sherira, and the attribution to R. Hai in *Toratan Shel Rishonim* is erroneous.)

14. See his comm. to M. *Sukkah* 4:5. It is also the reading in the manuscript of the Mishnah used by Rambam. See the edition of R. Yosef Kafaḥ (Jerusalem: 1963), p. 185.

15. See the critical edition of his *Sukkah* commentary by Eliahu Soloveitchik and David Metzger (Jerusalem: 1994), p. 93, based on manuscripts. They do not list any variants on this passage, implying that there are none. The explanation that R. Ḥananel provides also strongly suggests that he had the reading והוא. In the standard printed edition of his commentary, at *Sukkah* 45b, the word והו is found, but the standard printed edition is not reliable. See Soloveitchik and Metzger, p. 10.

16. *Shaarei Simḥah, Hilkhot Lulav*, vol. 1, p. 113, ed. Isaac Dov Bamberger (1964).

17. *Arukh*, entry אן.

18. Although the standard printed edition has והו here, a look at Mordecai Margaliot's critical edition (Jerusalem: 1953-58), vol. 4, p. 700, reveals that he cites only one manuscript with the reading והו. It would appear that all his other manuscripts had והוא.

original reading in the Mishnah.[19] Probably, the alternative reading והו

---

19. See, e.g., Fox, vol. 2, pp. 137-38 and Jeffrey L. Rubinstein, *The History of Sukkot in the Second Temple and Rabbinic Periods* (Atlanta: 1995), p. 112. והוא is also the reading of R. Judah Ibn Balam (Lewin, *Otzar ha-Geonim, Sukkah*, p. 66) and R. Abraham Ibn Ezra (*Sefer ha-Atzamim*, ed. Menashe Grossberg, London, 1901, p. 6).

Note also the following passage at *Rosh Hashanah* 17b:

אני הוא קודם שיחטא האדם... ואני הוא לאחר שיחטא האדם

The following statement appears in the Jerusalem Talmud on our Mishnah:

ר' אבהו בשם ר' יוחנן כיני מתניתא אני והוא הושיעה נא. אני והוא הושיעה נא.

Some have argued that the import of this statement is an awareness of a reading והו and a rejection of it. See, e.g., *Korban ha-Eidah*, Jacob Naḥum Epstein, *Mavo le-Nusaḥ ha-Mishnah* (Jerusalem: 1963), pp. 276-77 (mentioning it as one of several possibilities), and the ArtScroll Jerusalem Talmud (Brooklyn: 2008). But given the lack of other early evidence for the reading והו, there is insufficient reason to adopt this approach. For a different approach to the passage, see the *Melekhet Shelomoh* and the *Pnei Mosheh*. See also Fox, vol. 2, pp. 138-39.

The fact that Rashi had the reading והו and was able to explain it undoubtedly influenced some of the later Mishnah copyists to adopt this reading. Fox, vol. 2, p. 138. There is also a psychological tendency to credit והו as a legitimate reading because it is followed by a word which begins with the same sound: הושיעה.

One cannot argue that והו must be the correct reading in the Mishnah because it is the reading in the present text of the *hoshanot*. When one looks at the earliest texts of the *hoshanot*, there is much evidence for the reading והוא. See, for example, the late 12th-early 13th century manuscript of *Maḥzor Vitry*, Parma 2574, which consistently utilizes והוא. (This is the second earliest manuscript of this work. I have not been able to check the oldest manuscript, Sasoon 535.) Even earlier, manuscript Oxford 2700, a *siddur* from Palestine probably dating to the 12th century, utilizes והוא on p. 60b, and והו and והוא on p. 61a. But there is a dot on the last *vav* of the והו, perhaps indicating that it was meant as an abbreviation for והוא. This manuscript can be viewed on line at the Bodleian Library site; it is MS Heb g 2.

Some communities today vocalize the last *vav* of והו with a *shuruk* (as does *The Koren Siddur*, American edition, Jerusalem and New Milford, 2009, pp. 854-63). Probably, this vocalization originated with texts that spelled the word והוא.

arose as an abbreviated form of והוא.[20] Since our first evidence for the reading והו is Rashi, it is possible that this reading only arose in his time.[21]

So we must now reformulate our original question and determine instead the meaning of R. Judah's cryptic alternative statement אני והוא הושיעה נא.

R. Hai records a tradition that it is a petition that both oneself (אני) and the altar (הוא) be saved.[22] Rambam writes that the phrase is an allusion to the promise of healing and salvation at Deut. 32:39: ראו עתה כי אני אני הוא.[23] Rambam also refers to earlier commentators on the Talmud (not mentioning them by name) who expressed the view that both אני and והוא were Divine names.[24] Alternatively, as in the case of אני והו, it has been suggested that R. Judah was not disagreeing with the anonymous Tanna; he was merely making a statement about how אנא ה' was actually pronounced or should be pronounced in the ritual.[25] Finally, some scholars have made the creative suggestion that the anonymous Tanna and R. Judah were arguing about which *piyyut* was to be recited

20. Fox, vol. 2, p. 138. He points out that the word שהוא is also sometimes spelled without an *aleph* in this tractate. Perhaps the והו originally had a dot or apostrophe on it to symbolize that it was an abbreviation, and the dot or apostrophe was then overlooked by later copyists.

21. It is remotely possible that some rabbinic figure with a leaning towards mysticism, living shortly before the time of Rashi, was faced with the reading והוא and decided instead to introduce the reading והו; in this way, the 72 three-letter Divine name tradition, well-known in his time, could be referred to in the Mishnah. But more likely, the reading והו first arose as an abbreviated form of והוא, and was then eagerly accepted by Rashi or some of his mystical predecessors, who were happy to be able to read the 72 three-letter Divine name tradition into our Mishnah.

22. Lewin, *Otzar ha-Geonim, Sukkah*, p. 66. R. Hai continues with another explanation similar to the one provided in the Jerusalem Talmud.

23. Rambam, comm. on Mishnah *Sukkah* 4:5. The balance of the verse is: ואין א-להים עמדי אני אמית ואחיה מחצתי ואני ארפא ואין מידי מציל. Rambam writes that the implication of R. Judah's statement is, "Save us, as you have promised in this verse." (Some manuscripts of Mishnah *Sukkah* 4:5 read אני הוא, but these are only a small percentage. The text of the Mishnah utilized by Rambam read אני והוא.)

24. Rambam also refers, in the name of the Geonim, to an explanation similar to the one found in the Jerusalem Talmud.

25. Rubinstein, p. 112.

in this ritual; they were each referring to a different ancient *piyyut!*[26]

An interpretation of the passage is provided in a brief passage in the Jerusalem Talmud:

א"ר אבהו ולכה לישועתה לנו. לך יודייה.[27]

This statement explains the Mishnah by analogizing it to a phrase in Psalms 80:3, interpreted homiletically. This phrase in Psalms 80:3, ולכה לישועתה לנו, literally means that God should go (לכה) to save Israel. But interpreted homiletically, treating לכה as if it were written לך (to You), it means that a salvation to Israel is also a salvation to God (since God shares in the suffering of Israel).[28] The implication is that the expression

26. See Fox, vol. 2, pp. 135-36. In the Kaufmann manuscript of the Mishnah (and some other sources), the reading in the statement of R. Judah is: אני והוא והושיעה נא. There is also much evidence in the anonymous Tanna for the reading אנא הושיעה נא. These readings help support the ancient *piyyut* theory. See Fox, ibid. But I do not find this theory convincing. Neither does Rubinstein. See Rubinstein, p. 111, n. 25.

Another interesting interpretation offered is that R. Judah agrees with Abba Shaul that one is supposed to model one's behavior after the Divine (see *Shabbat* 133b: ואנוהו הוי דומה לו מה הוא חנון ורחום אף אתה היה חנון ורחום). Then the import of R. Judah's statement can be: I make the effort to model myself after You; therefore, I merit being saved. See R. Shemtob Gaguine, *Keter Shem Tov* (Kėdainiai, 1934), vol. 7, p. 120.

אנא means אני in Aramaic. Based on this, Fox (p. 138) raises the possibility that R. Judah can be viewed as translating אנא into Hebrew, and then using הוא as a Divine name to parallel 'ה. R. Judah's statement would then be a rough equivalent of the statement of the anonymous Tanna. But the *vav* of והוא refutes this equivalence theory.

27. The above is the text in the standard printed edition. But there is evidence that the last word was originally וודיה or וודאה, meaning "surely" (i.e., surely a salvation to Israel is also a salvation to God). See, e.g., Epstein, p. 276, n. 5, and Fox, vol. 2, p. 137.

28. A similar idea, that God goes into exile with Israel, is found in many sources. See, e.g., *Megillah* 29a, J. *Taanit* 1:1 (64a), *Mekhilta, Bo* 14, *Sifrei, Behaalotekha* 84, *Sifrei: Masei* 161, and *Pesikta Rabbati* 31.

See also the *vayosha/vayivasha* and *etkhem/itkhem* lines in the כהושעת אלים attributed to R. Eleazar ha-Kallir. I would like to thank R. Stephen Knapp for this reference.

A statement by R. Abbahu similar to the one in the Jerusalem Talmud is found at *Lev. Rabbah* 9:3.

אני והוא הושיעה נא is similarly a request that the person reciting it (אני) should be saved so that there be a salvation for God (הוא).[29]

How are we to evaluate these suggestions? Is the interpretation expressed in the Jerusalem Talmud necessarily the correct one?

It has been suggested that the word הוא is used as a Divine name, or at least hints to a Divine name, in many Biblical passages, particularly in the book of Isaiah.[30] Most striking is לכן יתן אדנ-י הוא לכם אות (Is. 7:14). Some other examples:

- Exod. 34:14: ה' קנא שמו א-ל קנא הוא.
- Is. 42:8: ...אני ה' הוא שמי.
- Is. 43:25 ... אנכי אנכי הוא ... (compare 43:11...אנכי אנכי ה')
- Jer. 10:10 ...וה' א-להים אמת הוא א-להים חיים.

There are many more.[31] Also, the phrase אני הוא is found in several

29. Tosafot gives a similar explanation, even though Tosafot seems to assume that אני והו is the correct text. According to Tosafot, R. Judah is referring to the ואני of Ezek. 1:1 and the והוא of Jer. 40:1. The meaning is that God is in exile with Israel and therefore needs to save Himself with Israel. (Tosafot is basing this interpretation on *Eikhah Rabbah, petiḥta*, sec. 34. Similar is *Pesikta de-Rav Kahana*, sec. 13, not cited by Tosafot.) But it seems highly unlikely that a ritual of the altar in Temple times would be alluding to Biblical verses about exile.

R. Ḥananel and the *Arukh* explain the Mishnah in a way similar to R. Abbahu. R. Ḥananel cites to Is. 63:9 (בכל צרתם לא צר, the *keri* here being לו). The *Arukh* cites to Is. 63:9 and Ps. 91:15 (עמו אנכי בצרה).

30. See, e.g., *The Brown-Driver-Briggs Hebrew and English Lexicon* (Boston: 1906), p. 216, Moshe David Cassuto in *Encyclopedia Mikrait* (Jerusalem: 1950), vol. 1, p. 312, E.C.B. MacLaurin, "The Origin of the Tetragrammaton," *Vetus Testamentum* 12 (1962), pp. 439-63 (455-56), Julian M. Morgenstern, "Deutero-Isaiah's Terminology for 'Universal God,'" *JBL* 62 (1943), pp. 269-80, and James A. Montgomery, "The Hebrew Divine Name and the Personal Pronoun HŪ," *JBL* 63 (1944), pp. 161-63. MacLaurin notes that the third person personal pronoun also served as name for the Deity in Old Babylonian and in Mari. See also Montgomery, p. 163.

31. The following are some other examples:

- Gen. 24:7: ...ה' א-להי השמים... הוא ישלח מלאכו לפניך
- Deut. 32:6: הלוא הוא אביך קנך הוא עשך ויכננך

passages in Isaiah.[32] Moreover, many scholars have suggested that the הוא in Biblical names such as אליהוא and אביהוא reflects the use of הוא as a Divine name.[33]

הוא (spelled הואהא) also seems to be used as a substitute for the Divine name in a passage in the Dead Sea Scrolls. Isaiah 40:3 includes the words: ...במדבר פנו דרך ה'. When this is paraphrased in the *Manual of Discipline* (8:13), the text reads:

ללכת למדבר לפנות שם את דרך הואהא ....[34]

- Deut. 32:39: ...ראו עתה כי אני אני הוא ואין א-להים עמדי (compare Is. 43:11)
- Is. 41:4: אני ה' ראשון ואת אחרנים אני הוא
- Is. 43:10: כי אני הוא לפני לא נוצר א-ל ואחרי לא יהיה
- Is. 43:13: ...גם מיום אני הוא ואין מידי מציל
- Is. 46:4: ...ועוד זקנה אני הוא
- Is. 48:12: אני הוא אני ראשון אף אני אחרון
- Jer. 5:12: כחשו בה' ויאמרו לוא הוא
- Jer. 25:31: ... כי ריב לה' בגיום נשפט הוא לכל בשר
- Ps. 100:3 ... דעו כי ה' הוא א-להים הוא עשנו ולא [קרי: ולו] אנחנו
- Ps. 102:28: ואתה הוא ושנותיך לא יתמו

See also 2 Kings 2:14 and Montgomery, p. 161.

Morgenstern writes: "it is now equally clear... that Deutero-Isaiah and other prophetic writers immediately influenced by him employed הוא as a synonym of [the four-letter Divine name] to designate the Deity in the all-important role... as the eternally existent One, the God of time and history." Morgenstern often points to the absence of the four-letter Divine name in the immediately surrounding verses. This is what enables him to argue that the הוא's that he identifies are not referring to earlier or later references to God, but are their own independent statements of the Divine name.

32. See Is. 41:4, 43:10, 43:13, 46:4, and 48:12. It is also found at Deut. 32:39.

33. See, e.g., Montgomery, p. 162, Moshe Greenberg, "The Hebrew Oath Particle ḤAY/ḤĒ," *JBL* 76 (1957), pp. 34-39 (38), and Samuel I. Feigin, *Mi-Sitrei he-Avar* (New York: 1943), p. 430. (Feigin also points out that the name שלמה is probably a contraction of שלום and הוא.)

34. See Greenberg, p. 38, and Joseph M. Baumgarten, "A New Qumran Substitute for the Divine Name and Mishnah Sukkah 4:5," *JQR* 83 (1992), pp. 1-5 (2). הוא is often spelled הואה in the Dead Sea texts. It has been suggested that the additional א at the end here is intended to call attention to the special use of the word as a surrogate for the Divine name. *The Dead Sea Scrolls Concordance*, ed. Martin G. Abegg, Jr. (Leiden: 2003) puts

הוא has also been interpreted as an allusion to the Divine name in at least two passages in Amoraic literature:

- *Niddah* 31a: The Palestinian amora R. Yoḥanan makes the following comment on the הוא of Genesis 30:16:[35] מאי דכתיב וישכב עמה בלילה הוא מלמד שהקב"ה סייע באותו מעשה.
- *Pesikta de-Rav Kahana* 13:[36] The following comment is made on a passage in Jeremiah 40:1 (והוא אסור באזקים בתוך כל גלות ירושלם ויהודה):

---

this הואהא in the entry with all the Tetragrammatons. (This is the only time הואהא appears in the Dead Sea texts discovered to date.)

MacLaurin points to other passages in the *Manual of Discipline* where הוא may allude to the Deity: 3:17, 3:25, 4:25, and 10:18.

Baumgarten points to a Dead Sea text (4Q266) where אנ הו seems to be used as a surrogate for the Divine name. But since the text of the Mishnah in *Sukkah* seems to have been אני והוא, and not אני והו, I do not think that his text is relevant.

Scholars often point to another Dead Sea text with a claim that הוא is being used as a substitute for the Divine name. The second half of Nah. 1:2 reads: נקם ה' לצריו ונוטר הוא לאיביו. When this passage is quoted in the Damascus Document (9:5), the text reads: נוקם הוא לצריו ונוטר הוא לאויביו. Louis Ginzberg initially made the claim in 1922 that this Dead Sea text was using הוא as a substitute for the Divine name, and he related it to R. Judah's use of הוא. See his *An Unknown Jewish Sect* (New York: 1976, Eng. translation), p. 40. However, נוקם הוא לצריו ונוטר הוא לאיביו seems just to have been a variant reading of Nah. 1:2. It is the reading in the standard printed edition at *Genesis Rabbah* 55:3 when Nah. 1:2 is quoted, and in one manuscript of *Genesis Rabbah* (from Yemen). See the critical edition of *Genesis Rabbah* by Yehudah Theodor and Ḥanokh Albeck (Jerusalem: 1965), vol. 2, p. 586. (All manuscripts have לאויביו.) Ginzberg himself retracted his argument in his same work when he discovered the passage in the printed edition of *Genesis Rabbah*. See Ginzberg, p. 163, n. 64. Scholars repeatedly cite to Ginzberg and his initial claim but overlook the passage in *Genesis Rabbah* and Ginzberg's retraction! (I only became aware of these because the 1976 translation, in an editors' note on p. 40, points to Ginzberg's retraction.)

35. The context is the conception of Issachar. As to how God helped, see *Genesis Rabbah* 99:10. (God caused Jacob's donkey to bray, leading Leah to realize that Jacob was there.)

36. Ed. Dov Mandelbaum, (New York: 1962), p. 232. See also *Eikhah Rabbah, petiḥta* 34.

מהו "והוא"? א"ר אחא כביכול הוא והוא (=It is as if both Jeremiah and God were bound in chains).

- Finally, the following passage is found in *Midrash ha-Gadol*: והוא שמו ושמו הוא דכתיב אני ה' הוא שמי (Is. 42:8).[37]

Based on all of the above, a strong argument can be made that הוא is a reference to a Divine name in the statement by R. Judah in our Mishnah.[38]

Regarding the word אני, one can argue that it alludes to a Divine name in certain verses in the Bible.[39] It certainly refers to God and perhaps alludes to a Divine name in statements attributed to Hillel (first century C.E.) at *Sukkah* 53a: [40]

> אמרו עליו על הלל הזקן כשהיה שמח בשמחת בית השואבה אמר כן **אם אני כאן הכל כאן** ואם איני כאן מי כאן. הוא היה אומר כן למקום שאני אוהב שם רגלי מוליכות אותי אם תבא אל ביתי **אני** אבא אל ביתך אם אתה לא תבא אל ביתי **אני** לא אבא אל ביתך שנאמר "בכל המקום אשר אזכיר את שמי אבא אליך וברכתיך" (שמות כ: כ).

In light of these statements by Hillel, his statement אם אין אני לי מי לי (first chapter of *Avot*) also perhaps should be interpreted as one which alludes to אני as a Divine name.[41]

---

37. *Midrash ha-Gadol, Va-Yigash* (ed. Mordecai Margaliot, Jerusalem, 1997), p. 773. Although *Midrash ha-Gadol* is a thirteenth-century work emanating from Yemen, the traditions included in the work largely date to the Talmudic period. See *Encyclopaedia Judaica* (Jerusalem: 1972) 11:1515.

38. It is also possible to speculate that the הוא in the phrase *ha-kadosh barukh hu*, a term found many times in the Mishnah, is an allusion to the Divine name הוא.

Interestingly, the Septuagint translates פיהו, at Prov. 24:7, as ςτόματος κυρίου (=the mouth of God). See Ginzberg, p. 41.

39. See, for example, the many Biblical verses that include the phrase אני ה', such as Ex. 12:12 and Is. 42:8. Greenberg, pp. 38-39, suggests that when the Bible describes God as taking an oath with the phrase חי אני, the latter is being used as a Divine name.

40. Many adopt this interpretation. See, e.g., *Encyclopaedia Judaica* 7:684, Baumgarten, p. 3, n. 11, Rubinstein, p. 113, n. 35, and R. Barukh Epstein, *Barukh She-Amar*, comm. to *Avot* 1:14.

41. R. Epstein is one who takes this position.

Based on all of the above, most likely אני and הוא were meant as Divine names in our Mishnah in *Sukkah*, and R. Judah was merely advocating for an *aravah* ritual that included the recitation of these names.[42] As mentioned above, Maimonides mentions such an interpretation in the name of "commentators on the Talmud." Perhaps the amoraim of the Jerusalem Talmud knew that אני and הוא were meant as Divine names by R. Judah, and R. Abbahu was merely trying to provide an additional, more homiletic, interpretation. It has been observed that the explanation offered by R. Abbahu sounds more like rabbinic theology than an explanation of a ritual in the Temple.[43] The fact that R. Judah has made mystical statements elsewhere provides some support for our view that he is advocating a somewhat mystical approach in our Mishnah.[44]

◆ ◆ ◆

The realization that הוא sometimes served as a Divine name in the Tannaitic period has many implications for our prayers and other texts. Consider the following passages from prayers and other texts that likely date to the Tannaitic period or the few centuries thereafter:

- The statement of R. Eleazar ha-Kappar in Mishnah *Avot* (end of the fourth chapter):

  שהוא א-ל הוא היוצר הוא הבורא הוא המבין הוא הדין הוא העד הוא בעל דין הוא עתיד לדון ברוך הוא... ועל כרחך אתה עתיד לתן דין וחשבון לפני מלך מלכי המלכים הקדוש ברוך הוא

- The statement in *Modim*:[45] שאתה הוא ה' א-להינו...

42. After reviewing much of the scholarship on this issue, Rubinstein (pp. 112-13) adopts this position. So too does Greenberg, p. 39.

Admittedly, הוא and אני are not among the Divine names mentioned at *Shavuot* 35a and JT *Megillah* 1:11 (71d).

43. Rubinstein, p. 112.

44. See, e.g., Mishnah *Megillah* 4:10 (R. Judah permits the reading of the *merkavah* as a *haftarah*), and Tosefta *Berakhot*, first chapter (he advocates for the recitation of *kadosh, kadosh, kadosh*… and *barukh kevod*…).

45. Admittedly, אתה הוא ה' א-להינו is borrowed from Jer. 14:22. Very likely, אתה, not שאתה, is the original reading in *Modim*. See Uri Ehrlich, "*Tefillat Shemoneh Esreh Shelemah Al Pi Minhag Eretz Yisrael*," *Kobetz Al Yad* 18 [2005], pp. 1-22 (21).

- The statement in *Aleinu*: ... הוא א-להינו אין עוד.[46]
- The passage at *Rosh Hashanah* 17b, commenting on the thirteen *middot* (Ex. 34:6-7): ... ה' ה' אני הוא קודם שיחטא האדם ואני הוא לאחר שיחטא האדם.
- The line in the *Kedushah* prayer for *Musaf* of *Shabbat*: הוא א-להינו הוא אבינו הוא מלכנו הוא מושיענו והוא ישמיענו...
- The *piyyut* *Adir Hu*: אדיר הוא בחור הוא גדול הוא. [47]
- The lines in *Tefillat Geshem* and *Tefillat Tal* by R. Eleazar ha-Kallir:[48] שאתה הוא ה' א-להינו משיב הרוח ומוריד הגשם/הטל
- The line in the blessing *yotzer ha-meorot*: כי הוא לבדו פועל גבורות.

Most likely, הוא served as an allusion to the Divine name in some (or perhaps even all!) of these texts. [49]

Finally, most interesting is a close examination of the prayer יהי כבוד.[50] This prayer is composed of eighteen sentences, sixteen of which include the four-letter Divine name. The two sentences that do not

---

46. *Aleinu* was not composed by Joshua. It is practically a certainty that it was composed in the Tannaitic or early Amoraic period. See my article on *Aleinu* in the present volume.
47. See Meir Bar-Ilan, "*Mi-Piyyutei ha-Haggadah: 'Adir Hu' ve-'Adir bi-Melukhah*,'" in *Masoret ha-Piyyut* 4 (2008), pp. 37-60. Bar-Ilan argues convincingly that the main part of this *piyyut* (words beginning with each letter of the alphabet, followed by הוא) originated in *heikhalot* literature, even though our earliest sources for this *piyyut* are only from the time of the Rishonim. Bar-Ilan points to parallels to *Adir Hu* in other *piyyutim* from *heikhalot* literature. *Adir Hu* uses much of the same terminology as *Adir bi-Melukhah* but Bar-Ilan dates the latter to between the 6th and 9th centuries.
48. Kallir's lifespan has been estimated as 570-640 C.E. See Ezra Fleischer, "*Le-Pitron She'elat Zemano u-Makom Pe'iluto Shel R. Eleazar be-Rabbi Kallir*," *Tarbiz* 54 (1985), pp. 383-427.
49. Also deserving of mention is the statement in the Haggadah: אני הוא לא אחר (commenting on the אני ה' of Ex. 12:12). But this seems to be a late addition to the Haggadah. See Shmuel and Ze'ev Safrai, *Haggadat Ḥazal* (Jerusalem: 1998), p. 140 and Menaḥem M. Kasher, *Haggadah Shelemah* (Jerusalem: 1967, third edition), p. מה.
50. This prayer is referred to at *Soferim*, chap. 17, *Siddur Rav Saadiah Gaon*, eds. Israel Davidson, *Simḥah Assaf and Yissakhar Joel* (Jerusalem: 1941), p. 33, and *Seder Rav Amram Gaon*, ed. Daniel Goldschmidt, (Jerusalem: 1971), p. 9. It is not unreasonable to take the position that it may have been composed centuries earlier.

are: כי הוא אמר ויהי הוא צוה ויעמד (Psalms 33:9) and ... והוא רחום לכפר עון (Psalms 78:38). Is it coincidence that both of these include the word הוא, prominently placed? Almost certainly, the author of this collection viewed הוא as a Divine name.[51]

Conclusion

Most likely, R. Judah was advocating for an *aravah* ritual that included the recitation of אני and הוא as Divine names. Perhaps the amoraim of the Jerusalem Talmud knew this, and R. Abbahu was merely trying to provide an additional, more homiletic, interpretation to the Mishnah.

There is a rabbinic tradition that the verses at Ex. 14:19-21 serve as a source for the derivation of 72 three-letter Divine names.[52] But this tradition has nothing to do with our Mishnah which had the original reading והוא.

Many prayers and other texts can now be explained with our new insight into the word הוא.

I will close with the declaration that is customarily made at the close of the Yom Kippur service, which we may now appreciate even further: ה' הוא הא-להים![53]

51. Perhaps the allusion to the Divine name in the verse ... והוא רחום was one of the factors that led it to be chosen to open the daily *Maariv* prayer. It already served this role in Geonic times. See *Seder Rav Amram Gaon*, p. 51, and the Geonic responsum cited in *Siddur Otzar ha-Tefillot* (Vilna: 1914), vol. 1, p. 533. (But it does not open the *Maariv* in the *Siddur Rav Saadiah Gaon.*) Perhaps it was chosen to open the *Taḥanun* prayer for the same reason. Ps. 78:38 is the most recited verse from Psalms in the prayers each week. See Hillel Fendel, *Aḥat Shaalti* (Jerusalem: 1993), p. 82.

52. I discuss the origin of this tradition in the appendix to this article.

As mentioned earlier, the practice of representing the Divine name with two *yods* is probably an offshoot of the practice of representing the Divine name with three *yods*, and the latter probably arose because it was one of the 72 Divine names derived from our three verses.

53. Even though this phrase was almost certainly introduced at the conclusion of the Yom Kippur service because of its role in the culmination of the story at 1 Kings 18, I cannot help but wonder if those who introduced it may also have been aware of the allusion to the Divine name in the word הוא. The earliest source we have for its recital at the conclusion of the Yom Kippur service is from the twelfth century. See *Beit Yosef, OH* 624. For a reference to an earlier custom of reciting this phrase, not in connection with the conclusion of the Yom Kippur service, see *Soferim* 14:13 (14:7 ed. Higger).

Appendix: Note on the Origin of the 72 Three-Letter Divine Name Tradition

As mentioned at the outset, Rashi knew of a tradition that 72 three-letter Divine names can be derived from the verses at Ex. 14:19-21.[54] One source prior to Rashi that clearly refers to this tradition is a work known as *Sefer ha-Yashar*.[55] This is a mystical work, now lost, that is cited by R. Hai Gaon.[56] It is cited even earlier by the late ninth century Karaite Daniel Al-Qumisi.[57]

Naphtali Wieder discusses a custom in the period of the Rishonim of the congregation raising its voice in the High Holiday *Aleinu* when reciting the phrase הוא אלקינו . See his *Hitgabshut Nusaḥ ha-Tefillah be-Mizraḥ u-be-Maarav* (Jerusalem: 1998), pp. 395- 439. As Wieder suggests (pp. 402-03), this custom may have its origin in the allusion to the Divine name in the word הוא.

54. The Talmud (*Kiddushin* 71a) refers to a 12-letter Divine name and a 42-letter name Divine name, but has nothing about a 72-letter Divine name nor 72 three-letter Divine names.

Traditions of 70 Divine names (completely unrelated to Ex. 14:19-21) are found in several post-Talmudic sources. See, e.g., *Aggadat Shir ha-Shirim* (ed. S. Schechter, London: 1896), p. 9, *Numbers Rabbah* 14:12, *Midrash ha-Gadol, Va-Yigash*, pp. 773-774 (ed. Margaliot), and *Otiyyot de-Rabbi Akiva* in Shelomoh Wertheimer, *Battei Midrashot*, vol. 2 (Jerusalem: 1968), pp. 350-51.

55. Quoted in R. Tobiah b. Eliezer, *Lekaḥ Tov* (*Pesikta Zutarti*) to Ex. 14:21. After Rashi, the tradition that 72 three-letter Divine names can be derived from these three verses is found in sources such as *Sefer ha-Bahir*, *Sefer Raziel*, *Zohar*, Ibn Ezra (shorter comm. to Ex. 3:13, longer comm. to Ex. 14:19 and 33:21, *Sefer ha-Shem*, fifth section, and *Shirei ha-Kodesh Shel Avraham Ibn Ezra*, ed. Yisrael Levin, Jerusalem, 1975, vol. 1, p. 136, poem #74), and Naḥmanides (intro. to his Torah commentary). For more details, see Menaḥem M. Kasher, *Torah Shelemah* (New York and Jerusalem: 1949-74) vol. 14, pp. 284-86, and Ephraim Kanarfogel, *Peering Through the Lattices* (Detroit: 2000), p. 144, n. 28. See also Simḥah Assaf, *Mi-Sifrut ha-Geonim* (Jerusalem: 1933), p. 215, Menashe Grossberg, *Sefer ha-Atzamim* (London: 1901), p. 53 and *Sefer ha-Maasim*, ed. Toisik, p. 72, quoted in Lewin, Iggeret R. Sherira Gaon, pp. xxxi-xxxii.

56. See Lewin, *Otzar ha-Geonim, Hagigah*, p. 20 (and n. 11), and *Simḥah Emanuel*, ed., *Teshuvot ha-Geonim ha-Ḥadashot* (Jerusalem: 1995), p. 131, n. 60.

57. Emanuel, ibid.

R. Saadiah Gaon (d. 942) refers to only one Divine name of 72 letters included in three adjacent verses:[58]

ותיכון[59] השם שבעים ושתים אותיות הוא חקוק ובשלש מקראות בתורה זה אחר זה הוא כמוס וכל אחד שבעים ושתים אותיות הוא חקוק....

Similar is a statement of R. Hai (d. 1038):[60]

והשם האחד הגדול שהוא בן שבעים ושתים אותיות הוא לקוח משלש מקראות שבתורה ואין אותיותיו ידועות.

Presumably, both are referring to our three verses at Exodus 14:19-21, but it seems that they are unaware of the tradition of 72 three-letter Divine names.

Many early sources refer to one 72-letter Divine name, without any reference to Ex. 14:19-21. See, e.g., *Avot de-R. Natan* 13, *Tanḥuma Va-Yera* 4, *Pesikta de-Rav Kahana* 5, *Pesikta* 15, *Genesis Rabbah* 44:19, *Leviticus Rabbah* 23:2, and *Deuteronomy Rabbah* 1:10.[61] It is an interesting question how a tradition of a 72-letter Divine name, without any connection to Ex. 14:19-21, would ever have arisen. Most likely, the number 72 came to be viewed as significant because it is the sum of *yod* (10), *yod he* (15), *yod he vav* (21), and *yod he vav he* (26).[62]

58. See Menaḥem Zulay, *Ha-Askolah ha-Paytanit Shel Rav Saadiah Gaon* (Jerusalem: 1964), p. 224.

59. Zulay suggests an emendation of this word to ותוכן. Another manuscript reads וסכום.

60. Lewin, *Otzar ha-Geonim, Ḥagigah*, p. 23, and Emanuel, p. 134.

61. Many interpret these passages as referring to the 72 three-letter Divine names derived from Ex. 14:19-21, but this is probably not correct. These passages seem to refer only to one Divine name with 72 אותיות. Admittedly, at *Shir Ha-Shirim Rabbah* 2:2, the reading is שמו של הקב"ה שבעים ושתים שמות הן, but probably this passage too originally read אותיות.

62. See the statement of Ibn Ezra in *Sefer ha-Shem*, fifth section, quoted at *Torat Ḥayyim*, Ex. 14:19, n. 53 to his longer commentary. (I am following the first of the two explanations of Ibn Ezra's statement provided there. This one seems much more likely.) See similarly Ibn Ezra's *Yesod Mora ve-Sod Torah*, eds. Yosef Cohen and Uriel Simon (Ramat Gan: 2007, 2d. ed.), chap. 9, p. 197 and the editors' note to line 104. For a different explanation of the significance of the number 72, see Ephraim E. Urbach, *Ḥazal: Pirkei Emunot ve-Deot* (Jerusalem: 1982), p. 111.

The tradition of one 72-letter Divine name helps explain the origin of our 72 three-letter Divine name tradition. Once the number 72 was viewed as an allusion to a Divine name, it must have been viewed as extremely significant when three verses in a row were discovered to include exactly 72 letters. Since these verses also described a profound act of Divine power, the allusion to Divine names was then attributed to them.[63]

Ibn Ezra mentions that Ezek. 1:1 has 72 letters. See his standard commentary to Ex. 14:19 and his shorter commentary to Ex. 3:13. (Although this verse has 74 letters in our texts, it had 72 letters in the text in front of Ibn Ezra. See *Torat Ḥayyim*, Ex. 14:19, n. 56 to the longer commentary. See also Asi Farber-Ginat and Daniel Abrams, *Peirushei ha-Merkavah le-R. Eleazar mi-Worms u-le-R. Yaakov Ben Yaakov Hakohen*, Los Angeles, 2004, p. 83, text and comm. of R. Yaakov.)

63. See similarly Meir Bar-Ilan, *Numerologiah Bereshitit* (Reḥovot: 2003), p. 181. But it still requires explanation why someone would decide that the derivation from the second verse proceeds in the reverse order.

4

What is the Meaning of "Maccabee"?[1]

The name "Maccabee" is not found in classical Tannaitic or Amoraic literature.[2] But this is not surprising. The name was originally an additional name for Judah only, and there are no references to Judah by name in classical Tannaitic or Amoraic literature.[3]

The earliest sources that include the name in some form are works preserved by the Church: 1 & 2 Maccabees. (These are not the original

---

1. An earlier version of this article was published at seforim.blogspot.com (Dec. 20 2011): "The Meaning of the Name 'Maccabee.'"

All translations from 1 & 2 Maccabees are from the editions of Jonathan A. Goldstein (Anchor Bible, vols. 41 and 41A, Garden City: 1976 and 1983). All citations to the *Encyclopaedia Judaica* are to the original edition (Jerusalem: 1972).

2. I am not considering *Megillat Antiochus* ("MA") to be within "classical rabbinic literature." I will discuss this unusual work at the end.

3. Aside from the references in MA, the earliest reference to Judah by name in rabbinic literature is a reference in *Mishnat R. Eliezer*. See below, n. 58. *Mishnat R. Eliezer* is perhaps an eighth-century work.

Judah is also referred to by name in two of the three *midrashim* on Hanukkah published by Adolf Jellinek in the mid-19th century, and republished by Judah David Eisenstein in his *Otzar Midrashim* (New York: 1915). See Eisenstein, pp. 190 and 192. These *midrashim* are estimated to date to the 10th century. See *Encyclopaedia Judaica* 11:1511.

The story of Judah defeating the Syrian military commander Nikanor is found in both the Jerusalem and Babylonian Talmuds, but Judah is not referred to by name in these passages. In the passage at J. *Taanit* 2:12 (2:13, 66a), the reference is to *eḥad mi-shel beit Ḥashmonai*. In the passage at J. *Megillah* 1:4 (1:6, 70c), the reference is to *eḥad mi-shel Ḥashmonai*. In the Babylonian Talmud, *Taanit* 18b, the name of the victor is given more generally as *malkhut beit Ḥashmonai*. Also, the scholium to the Day of Nikanor holiday in *Megillat Taanit* (13th of Adar) does not mention Judah by name.

titles of these works.) 1 Maccabees was originally written in Hebrew,[4] but what has survived is only a Greek translation from the Hebrew (and ancient translations made from this Greek translation). 2 Maccabees, an entirely different work, was written in Greek. In the early Church, 1 & 2 Maccabees were considered part of the Bible.[5]

4. There are many factors that point to the fact that the Greek is only a translation. See, e.g., *Encyclopaedia Judaica* 11:657, and Goldstein, *I Maccabees*, p. 14. For example, many Hebrew idioms are used. The church father Jerome (4th cent.) clearly implies that the Greek version of 1 Maccabees is only a translation. He writes, "I have found the First Book of Maccabees in Hebrew; the Second is a Greek book as can also be proved from considerations of style alone" (Goldstein, *I Maccabees*, p. 16.) An earlier church father Origen (3rd cent., quoted in Eusebius) mentions an extra-Biblical book used by the Jews which is a "Maccabean History which bears the title '*sarbêthsabanaiel*.'" Since this title is in Hebrew or Aramaic, this suggests that the book he is referring to, almost certainly 1 Maccabees, was composed in Hebrew or Aramaic. As to the meaning of this title, see Goldstein, *I Maccabees*, pp. 16-21 and J. *Taanit* 4:5 (4:7, 68d). Jerome is the last individual to refer to the original Hebrew of 1 Maccabees.

Neither 1 nor 2 Maccabees is referred to or alluded to in either Talmud. But some of the language in *Al ha-Nissim* does resemble language in 1 and 2 Maccabees. See particularly 1 Macc. 1:49, 3:17-20, 4:24, 4:43, 4:55, and 2 Macc. 1:17 and 10:7. See also perhaps 1 Macc. 4:59. Of course, the resemblances may be only coincidental.

Unfortunately, no Hebrew text of 1 Maccabees was found among the Dead Sea Scrolls, perhaps due to the strong anti-Hasmonean stance of the Qumran sectarians. See Lawrence H. Schiffman, *Qumran and Jerusalem* (Grand Rapids: 2010), p. 62.

5. For example, they were included in codices of the Septuagint. Judah and his brothers were seen as heroes by the early church. Centuries later, the Protestant church denied the sanctity of 1 and 2 Maccabees and of all the other books known today as the Apocrypha. But the Apocrypha are still part of the canon of the Roman Catholic and Greek Orthodox churches.

The Biblical canon may have been considered closed by Jewry even before 1 Maccabees was composed. See Sid Z. Leiman, *The Canonization of Hebrew Scripture* (New Haven: 1976), pp. 29-30 and 131-32. Even if the canon was still open (see, e.g., Lawrence H. Schiffman, *Reclaiming the Dead Sea Scrolls*, Philadelphia: 1994, pp. 162-169, and M. *Yadayim* 3:5 and M. *Eduyyot* 5:3), a strong argument can be made that 1 Maccabees was never a candidate for canonization since it did not claim to be a book composed before the period of prophecy ended. 2 Maccabees would never have been a candidate for canonization since it was composed in Greek.

1 Maccabees (2:2-5) tells us that Mattathias (Matityahu) had five sons, and that each had another name. For Joudas (Judah), the name was Makkabaios (Gr: Μακκαβαῖος.)[6] The additional names were probably given to the sons to help distinguish them from others with the same name.[7] In 1 Maccabees, Makkabaios is used for Judah six times. In 2 Maccabees, it is used for him twenty-three times.[8]

To determine whether the earliest spelling of the name in Hebrew was with a כ or a ק, one must guess from the double *kappa* in Makkabaios what the original Hebrew letter (or letters) would have been.

Fortunately, this is not hard. Although there are exceptions, there is a general pattern in the Greek translation of the Bible of transliterating כ with *chi* (χ), and ק with *kappa* (k).[9] Usually ק is transliterated with one *kappa*, but sometimes two *kappas* are used.[10] A transliteration of כ with two *kappas* is very rare.[11]

These same patterns hold true in 1 and 2 Maccabees. For example, if we focus on 1 Maccabees,[12] and look at the Greek transliteration of names, places, and months whose Hebrew spelling is known from the Bible, we find:

---

6. As is evident from the names Mattathias, Joudas, and Makkabaios, Greek often adds an "s" at the end of foreign names. That is why משה became "Moses" in the Septuagint, and why there is an "s" at the end of the name "Jesus."

7. Goldstein, *I Maccabees*, p. 230.

8. In 2 Maccabees, the name is usually used alone, without the name Judah. In 1 Maccabees, the name is used alone one time.

Although the name is spelled with two *kappas* each time, the "s" at the end is not there each time. In Greek, the ending of the name varies depending on the how the name is being used in the sentence.

9. *The First Book of Maccabees*, tr. by Sidney Tedesche, intro. and comm. by Solomon Zeitlin (New York: 1950), p. 250, and Samuel Ives Curtiss, Jr., *The Name Machabee* (Leipzig: 1876), p. 8.

10. See, e.g., the transliteration of the name בקי at Ezra 7:4, and the transliteration of the city עקרון (many times).

11. Curtiss, who seems to have gone through the Septuagint very carefully, can cite only one such case: תכן at 1 Ch. 4:32. See Curtiss, p. 9. But even here, there is another reading in which the transliteration is with two *chis*.

12. In 2 Maccabees, the occurrence of names and places whose Hebrew spelling is known from the Bible is very limited. (Unlike 1 Maccabees, 2 Maccabees does not provide many geographic details.) In 2 Maccabees, transliterated with *chi* are כסלו and מרדכי. Transliterated with *kappa* are יעקב, חזקיה and קרנים.

- transliterated with χ are: כלב, זכריה, מכמש, כתים, and כסלו;
- transliterated with one *kappa* are: יעקב, עקרבים, תקוע, אשקלון, קדש, and קרנים;
- transliterated with two *kappas* are: עקרון[13] and הקוץ[14].

At no time in 1 Maccabees is כ transliterated with *kappa*.[15]

Thus, the spelling of Makkabaios with two *kappas* points strongly to a ק in the original Hebrew or Aramaic,[16] and does not mandate assuming a קק. Moreover, an original מקקב would be extremely unlikely. Hebrew and Aramaic words do not ordinarily have four-letter roots. If we make the alternative assumption that the initial *mem* was not a part of the root, this does not help either. There is no root קקב in either Hebrew or Aramaic.[17] The double *kappa* just confirms our supposition that the original reading was ק, and not כ.[18] Based on this spelling, it seems reasonable to agree with the oft-proposed suggestion that the name is related to the Hebrew and Aramaic words מקבת and מקבא, which mean, "hammer."[19]

---

13. 1 Macc. 10:89.
14. 1 Macc. 8:17: "Judah chose Eupolemus son of John of the clan of Hakkoz…" I am making the reasonable assumption that Hakkoz is the same as the priestly clan הקוץ mentioned at 1 Ch. 24:10. (Although the reading of the majority of Septuagint manuscripts is Ακκως, there is another reading: ακχως.)
15. This is true in 2 Maccabees as well. Admittedly, in most of the instances I have listed, the authors of 1 & 2 Maccabees were not deciding on their own how to transliterate these names and places, but were following already established conventions.
16. The name could be an Aramaic one, even assuming that 1 Maccabees was composed in Hebrew.
17. Semitic languages (other than Akkadian) do not have roots with identical consonants in the first two positions. Eduard Yechezkel Kutscher, *A History of the Hebrew Language* (Jerusalem: 1984, 2d ed.), p. 7.
18. The Syriac translation of 1 Maccabees also spells the name with a ק. The Syriac translation of the Bible was generally based on the Greek translation, but it has been argued that sometimes the translators consulted the original Hebrew and that perhaps the Hebrew original was consulted here. See Felix Perles, "The Name ΜΑΚΚΑΒΑΙΟΣ," *JQR* 17 (1926-27), pp. 404-405.
19. See, e.g., Emil Schürer, *The History of the Jewish People in the Age of Jesus Christ*, revised and edited by Geza Vermes, Fergus Millar, and

As to why Judah was called by this name, one view is that the name alludes to his physical strength or military prowess.[20] But a מקבא/מקבת is not a military weapon; it is a worker's tool.[21] Therefore, it has been suggested alternatively that the name reflects that Judah's head or body had the physical appearance of a hammer.[22] Interestingly, the Mishnah

---

Matthew Black, vol. 1 (Edinburgh: 1973), p. 158, Zeitlin, pp. 250-52, Nosson Dovid Rabinowich, *Binu Shenot Dor va-Dor* (Jerusalem: 1985), pp. 184-87, and Ernest Klein, *A Comprehensive Etymological Dictionary of the Hebrew Language for Readers of English* (New York: 1987), p. 377. For references to earlier scholars who argued for this approach, see Curtiss, pp. 18-20 and Ralph Marcus, "The Name ΜΑΚΚΑΒΑΙΟΣ" in *The Joshua Starr Memorial Volume* (New York: 1953), p. 62.

מקבת is found in the *Tanakh* at Judg. 4:21. (See also Is. 51:1.) It is also found in *Tanakh* in the plural מקבות, at 1 Kings 6:7, Jer. 10:4, and Is. 44:12. It is usually viewed as deriving from the root נקב, since it is a tool which penetrates.

20. There are various ways of understanding the metaphor. Some reasonable suggestions are: 1) he was as strong as a hammer, 2) he dashed the enemy into pieces, and 3) he penetrated the enemies' forces.

As many scholars have noted, another historical figure with such an additional name was Charles Martel, ruler of the Franks in the eighth century. Martel is French for "hammer." He was given this additional name following his victory over the invading Muslim army at Tours in 732 C.E. This victory halted northward Islamic expansion in Western Europe.

Judah is described by the name Makkabaois before he battled the forces of Antiochus IV. But this is not a difficulty. According to 1 Macc. 2:66, he was "a mighty warrior from his youth."

21. See, e.g., M. *Kelim* 29:5 and 29:7 (referring to a מקבת used by stonecutters). See also M. *Parah* 3:11 and Tosefta *Shabbat* 13:17 (ed. Lieberman).

Marcus (p. 63, n. 3) notes that at *Berakhot* 28b, when one of the Sages is called a "strong hammer" (*patish ha-ḥazak*), it is the word פטיש, and not מקבת, that is used.

22. See, e.g., Schürer, vol. 1, p. 158 and Zeitlin, pp. 250-252. Exactly how to understand this is open to interpretation. Was it the shape of his skull that looked like a hammer? Something about his face? Something about his neck? Something about his body? Something about the relationship of these objects to one another? For some possible understandings of the term in the Mishnah, see Rashi to *Bekhorot* 43b, and the commentaries to M. *Bekhorot* 7:1 of Rambam and *Tiferet Yisrael*. It has also been suggested that the reference to a hammer alludes to Judah's having an occupation as

at *Bekhorot* 7:1 lists one of the categories of disqualified priests as המקבן, and the term is explained in the Talmud as meaning one whose head resembles a מקבא.[23] Naming men according to physical characteristics was common in the ancient world.[24]

Is it possible that Makkabaios and the other four names were Greek names?[25] The additional names for the other sons were: Gaddi (Γαδδι), Thassi (Θασσι), Auaran (Αυαραν) and Apphous (Απφους).[26] Perhaps it would have been beneficial for a Jew even as early as the age of Mattathias to have had an additional name in the Greek language. It is seen from the reference to Antigonus at Mishnah *Avot* 1:3 that a "traditional" Jew circa 200 B.C.E. could have borne a Greek name. (In

---

a blacksmith. It has also been observed that מקבא means "nostril" in Syriac and that perhaps Judah possessed uncommon nostrils. Perles, p. 405.

Bezalel Bar-Kochva, *Judas Maccabaeus* (Cambridge and New York: 1989), p. 147, attempts to support the view that the name refers to some flaw in Judah's physical appearance by noting that 1 & 2 Maccabees nowhere laud Judah's physical stature or beauty.

23. *Bekhorot* 43b. Although the printed edition of the Talmudic passage reads למקבן here (just like the word in the Mishnah), Rashi's text read למקבא. This would seem to be the correct reading.

24. See Zeitlin, *The Rise and Fall of the Judaean State* (Philadelphia: 1962), vol. 1, p. 96 for some examples. Josephus tells us (*Life*, para. 3) that one of his ancestors (a contemporary of John Hyrcanus) was called "Simon Psellus,"—Simon, the stammerer.

25. This suggestion is made at *Encyclopaedia Judaica* 12:808.

26. These are the additional names for John, Simon, Eleazar, and Jonathan, respectively. Of the four names above, Gaddi is the easiest to relate to a known Hebrew or Aramaic word. It can be related to the Hebrew and Aramaic word גד, "fortune" (see, e.g., Gen. 30:11). For some attempts to give meaning in Hebrew or Aramaic to the other names, see Goldstein, *I Maccabees*, p. 231, Rabinowich, p. 186, and Ralph Marcus, *Josephus* (Loeb Classical Library), vol. VII (*Jewish Antiquities*, Books XII-XIV, Cambridge, Mass. and London: 1936), p. 139 (notes).

1 Macc. 2:2-4 states explicitly that Mattathias had five sons: John, Simon, Judah, Eleazar and Jonathan. Interestingly, another brother, Ιωσηπον (Joseph), is mentioned as a commander of a regiment at 2 Macc. 8:22. But it has been suggested that the original reading here was Ιωαννης (John), or that Joseph was only a half-brother, or that the author of Maccabees erred, having been led astray by the knowledge that most of the commanders were Judah's brothers. For the last suggestion, see Daniel R. Schwartz, *2 Maccabees* (Berlin: 2008), p. 340.

the period after Judah, we know of many prominent Jews who had both a Hebrew/Aramaic name and a Greek name.[27] For example, Simon's son John was also called Hyrcanus,[28] John's son Judah was also called Aristobulus,[29] John's son Yannai was also called Alexander,[30] and Yannai's wife Shelomtziyon was also called Alexandra.[31])

But the letters μ,κ,β or μ,κ,κ,β, with any combination of vowels in between them, do not seem to correspond to any known word in ancient Greek.[32] Moreover, the two *kappas* also suggest that the name

27. For an extensive discussion, see Tal Ilan, "The Greek Names of the Hasmoneans," *JQR* 78 (1987), pp. 1-20.
28. Josephus, *Antiquities*, XIII, para. 228.
29. Ibid., XX, para. 240.
30. Ibid., XIII, para. 320.
31. Ibid. Perhaps she was given this name after her marriage to Alexander. The Hebrew name of Yannai's wife was transmitted in rabbinic sources in various forms. See Schürer, vol. 1, p. 229, n. 2 and Ilan, p. 7, n. 28. That the original Hebrew form was שלמציון has now been shown by two Dead Sea texts: 4Q331 and 4Q332. See *DJD* XXXVI (Oxford: 2000), pp. 277 and 283.
32. I make this statement based on my examination of the following work: *An Intermediate Greek-English Lexicon*, founded upon the seventh edition of Liddell and Scott's *Greek-English Lexicon* (Oxford: 1889). In contrast, many Greek words related to fighting begin with "μαχ." Also, the Greek word for "knife" or "dagger" begins with these letters. (Rashi mentions this at Gen. 49:5, מכרתיהם, citing *Midrash Tanḥuma*.)

Even though the letters μ,κ,β or μ,κ,κ,β do not seem to correspond to any known word in ancient Greek, we do find Azariah de Rossi (16th cent.), in his *Meor Einayim, Imrei Binah*, chap. 21, adopting the suggestion of a sixteenth-century monk that the name is a Greek one and that the meaning is the equivalent of the Italian *paladino*, "hero, champion." Also, R. David Ganz (16th cent.), *Tzemaḥ David*, p. 69 (ed. Breuer), writes that מכבאי in the Greek language is a *gibbor* and *ish milḥamah*.

Of course, it is possible that the names of Judah and of some of the other brothers were Greek and what are recorded in 1 Maccabees are only shortened forms of names that originally combined two Greek words. Also, if the additional names originated as affectionate nicknames, whether in Greek, or in Hebrew/Aramaic, such names are often substantially altered forms of the original proper name. (In English, note Dick for Richard, Jack for John, and Billy for William.)

Most likely, *Ḥashmonai* was the additional name of Mattathias. (See M. *Middot* 1:6, Goldstein, *I Maccabees*, pp. 18-19, and Chapter 5 of this

is not Greek. Two consecutive *kappas* are not typical in a Greek word.[33] Finally, there are no non-Jewish figures from this period or any earlier period with a name like *Makkabaios*. This is strong evidence that the name is not a Greek one.

However, our task of determining the original spelling and meaning of the additional name of Judah is not that simple. Two further issues present themselves. First, assuming that *Makkabaios* is a Greek representation of a Hebrew or Aramaic name, we still do not know whether the authors of 1 & 2 Maccabees knew how Judah himself, who died in approximately 160 B.C.E., spelled the name. 1 Maccabees, which covers the period 175-134 B.C.E., was probably composed after the death of John Hyrcanus in 104 B.C.E., or at least when his reign was well advanced. This is seen from the last two sentences of the work.[34] After describing the murder of Simon and the attempted murder of Simon's son John, the book closes with the following statement (16:23-24):

> As for the remainder of the history of John, his wars and his valorous deeds and his wall building and his other accomplishments, all these are recorded in the chronicle of his high priesthood, from the time he succeeded his father as high priest.[35]

---

volume. At *Antiquities* XII, 265, Josephus states that *Ḥashmonai* was the name of the great-grandfather of Mattathias, but this was probably just a conjecture.) *Ḥashmonai* sounds like a Hebrew or Aramaic name. See Josh. 15:27, Num. 33:29-30, and Ps. 68:32.

33. Curtiss, pp. 8-9, theorizes that the original Greek spelling was with only one *kappa*. He writes that letters which are single in earlier Greek manuscripts often end up being doubled in later ones. Curtiss, p. 9, n. 1.

34. It has been suggested that the last three chapters of 1 Maccabees were added later, because Josephus never uses them. But the failure of Josephus to use these chapters can be explained in other ways. See, e.g., Marcus, *Josephus*, vol. VII, pp. 334-335.

35. Goldstein, *I Maccabees*, p. 62. There is another comment which perhaps suggests that the book was composed long after the events described. 1 Macc. 13:30 reads: "This tomb, which he [Simon] erected in Modeïn, still exists today." Despite verses 16:23-24, some scholars take the position that 1 Maccabees may have been composed closer to the beginning of the reign of John Hyrcanus. Both views are briefly summarized at Schwartz, p. 15, n. 32.

The reign of John Hyrcanus began in 135/134 B.C.E.

With regard to 2 Maccabees, we are told by the unknown author that it is an abridgment of an earlier work by someone named Jason of Cyrene. Cyrene is a city on the northern coast of Libya.[36] This Jason is otherwise unknown. The generally accepted view is that Jason wrote very close in time to the events he described.[37] The narrative in 2 Maccabees ends with Judah's victory over the general Nicanor in 161 B.C.E. Perhaps Jason's work ended around this time as well.[38]

It is possible that Jason was born and raised in Cyrene but spent the rest of his adult life in Jerusalem. Or perhaps he was a lifetime resident of Cyrene who spent some intervening years in Jerusalem. Finally, perhaps he was a lifetime resident of Jerusalem who retired to Cyrene to write his work. No one knows.[39] Even if Jason wrote very close in time to the events he described, it is still possible that Jason did not know how Judah himself spelled the name.[40] We are never told in 2 Maccabees that Jason had a close relationship with Judah.[41]

The positive attitude towards the Roman Empire in the book strongly suggests that the book was composed before 63 B.C.E. See, e.g., 1 Macc. 8:1: "Judas had heard about the Romans: that they were a great power who welcomed all who wished to join them and established ties of friendship with all who approached them."

36. The reference can also be not to the city but to the whole region.

37. Schwartz, p. 15. For example, Victor Tcherikover, *Hellenistic Civilization and the Jews* (Philadelphia: 1959), p. 385, writes: "[I]t may be concluded—if not with absolute assurance, at least with a very high degree of certainty—that Jason of Cyrene was a contemporary of Judah the Maccabee and saw most of the events which he described with his own eyes."

38. But Goldstein argues (*I Maccabees*, p. 5) that if the abridger had followed Jason to the end, the abridger would have ended with something like: "Since Jason ended his work at this point, my work, too, is done." Instead the abridger ends: "Such was the outcome of the affair of Nicanor. From that time on, the city has been held by the Hebrews. Therefore, I myself shall bring my account to a stop at this very point...."

39. See further Schwartz, p. 175 and Tcherikover, pp. 386-87.

40. I am making the likely assumption that the author of 2 Maccabees followed the spelling used by Jason. It is not known for certain that Jason composed his work in Greek, but this seems very likely. 2 Maccabees begins with an introduction, and the author did not say anything here about changing the language of Jason's work.

41. Admittedly, it has been suggested that Jason is to be identified with

There are also those who take the position that Jason did not write very close in time to the events he described. For example, it has been argued that Jason composed his work between 90-86 B.C.E. as a response to 1 Maccabees.[42] If so, Jason's reliability on the spelling of "Maccabee" is much more questionable.

The second issue that presents itself arises from the fact that the name is written "Machabaeus" in the Latin translation of 1 & 2 Maccabees composed by the church father Jerome (c. 400 C.E.).[43] There is a question whether this spelling reflects Jerome's own spelling choice, which was perhaps made after he consulted the original Hebrew of 1 Maccabees,[44] or whether this was the conventional spelling of the name in the earlier Latin translations made from the Greek, which Jerome simply let stand. If this spelling was Jerome's own and he made it after consulting with the original Hebrew of 1 Maccabees,[45] this would strongly suggest that the Hebrew text that he had before him spelled the name with a כ. In his translation of the Bible into Latin, Jerome almost uniformly used "ch" to represent כ.[46]

Jason son of Eleazar, mentioned at 1 Macc. 8:17 as having been sent by Judah on a mission to Rome. But this identification is only conjecture.

42. This is the view of Goldstein. See his *I Maccabees*, pp. 62-89 and *II Maccabees*, pp. 82-83. If this theory would be correct, we cannot view the similar spelling, *Makkabaios*, as an independent confirmation of this spelling, since perhaps the later work merely adopted the spelling of the work that it was responding to.

43. Curtiss, p. 7.

44. Throughout his Latin translation of the Bible, Jerome seems to have consulted the Hebrew and corrected earlier erroneous transliterations found in the Greek translation (Curtiss, pp. 6 and 31). Jerome was more advanced in Hebrew than of any of the other Church fathers.

45. It is only speculation that Jerome consulted the original Hebrew of 1 Maccabees here. Even though Jerome refers to this work (see above, n. 4), he may not have had access to it and may not have remembered all of its spellings at the time he composed his Latin translation of 1 Maccabees. It sounds like he was referring to a work that was rare and not easily accessible.

46. Curtiss, p. 7. Jerome transliterated ק with "c" or "cc" 188 times. There were only two occasions when Jerome transliterated ק with "ch." (Curtiss attempts to explain what led Jerome to make exceptions in these instances. See pp. 7 and 32.)

Alternatively, if the "ch" spelling originated in the Latin translations before Jerome, or if it originated with Jerome, but not in consultation with the original Hebrew of 1 Maccabees, it would seem to be based on a Greek text which spelled the name with *chi*. This too would seem to reflect an original Hebrew spelling of the name with a כ.

Thus, although we saw earlier that the double *kappa* in the Greek translation of 1 Maccabees suggests a ק in the original Hebrew, the evidence from Jerome's Latin translation points in the opposite direction. Perhaps already in an early stage there were two different Hebrew spellings of the name.[47] If the Hebrew name was spelled with a כ, the meaning that suggests itself is "the extinguisher."[48]

◆ ◆ ◆

The spelling of "Maccabee" with a כ that is prevalent in Jewish sources today is not evidence of an original כ spelling. It is only the consequence of the spelling found in *Yosippon*, a medieval Jewish historical work.[49] One of the sources utilized by this work was a Latin translation of 1 & 2 Maccabees.[50] There, Judah's additional name was spelled "Machabaeus." Based on this, the name was spelled מכביי in *Yosippon*.[51] This spelling of the name with a כ was followed by the Rishonim.[52]

---

47. Curtiss (pp. 8-9) tries to get around this scenario by postulating that the original Greek text only had one *kappa*, and that it was only later that the *kappa* was doubled. An original כ could have been transliterated with one *kappa*.

48. See, e.g., Curtiss, pp. 25-29.

49. David Flusser, in his extensive study of this work, argued that it was by one author and composed in 953 C.E. See his *Sefer Yosippon*, vol. 2 (Jerusalem: 1980), p. 83. More recent scholarship suggests that the work originated earlier and evolved, and should be viewed as a composite work. See Shulamit Sela, *Sefer Yosef ben Gorion ha-Aravi*, vols. I and II (Jerusalem and Tel Aviv: 2009).

50. The author or authors of *Yosippon* could not read Greek.

51. Flusser, *Sefer Yosippon*, vol. 1 (Jerusalem: 1978), pp. 79 and 80. Flusser writes that this is the reading in the better manuscripts of *Yosippon*. Much later in the work, in a different context, the group is called המקווים. See Flusser, vol. 1, p. 342.

The spelling מכביי is also found in a medieval Hebrew translation and adaptation of 1 & 2 Maccabees which Flusser believes was authored by the author of *Yosippon*. See Flusser, *Sefer Yosippon*, vol. 2, p. 132.

52. Flusser, vol. 1, p. 79, note to line 56.

There never was a group by the name "Maccabees" in ancient times. How did the references to this non-existent group ever arise and how did the books get their titles? 2 Maccabees focuses in large part on Judah. Jonathan Goldstein explains further:[53]

> Clement of Alexandria and Origen, the earliest of the Church Fathers to mention the books by name, call them *Ta Makkabaïka*, "Maccabaean Histories," from which title persons who spoke loosely probably turned to call all the heroes in the stories "Maccabees."[54]
>
> The first datable occurrence of such use of "Maccabees" for the heroes is in Tertullian...ca. 195 C.E.[55]

Finally, it must be pointed out that מקבי seems to be the original reading in the work now commonly referred to as *Megillat Antiochus*.[56] But this work is replete with errors:

- It reports that Antiochus decided to persecute the Jews in the 23rd year of his reign. But Antiochus IV, the one who persecuted the Jews, only reigned 11 years.
- It associates the name מקבי with Yoḥanan (John), while according to 1 & 2 Maccabees, this name is only associated with Judah.

---

53. Goldstein, *I Maccabees*, pp. 3-4.
54. A similar development seems to have occurred with the name *Ḥashmonai*, which probably originated as the additional name of Mattathias alone. See Chapter 5 in this volume.
55. Goldstein, *I Maccabees*, p. 4, n. 1, also suggests a possible earlier occurrence.
56. Some manuscripts of MA read מכבי. But the Yemenite manuscripts of MA, which reflect ancient traditions, read מקבי. If we look at the three oldest manuscripts of MA (Turin 111, Huntington 399, and Paris 20, all of which date from around 1300 and none of which are Yemenite manuscripts), two read מקבי and one reads מקוי. See Menaḥem Tzvi Kadari, "*Megillat Antiochus ha-Aramit*," *Bar Ilan* 1 (1963), pp. 81-105 (93), and Curtiss, pp. 37-41. (There are also a few manuscripts of MA in which the word is omitted.) In the manuscripts of MA, the term מכבי/מקבי is usually followed by words like קטלא תקיפין (killer of strong men), perhaps implying that the author of MA viewed this as its definition.

- It describes Yoḥanan as killing the general Nikanor in a private encounter in the area of the Temple. But according to 1 & 2 Maccabees, Nikanor was killed by Judah and his forces in a battle that took place outside of Jerusalem.
- It describes Judah as being killed before the Temple was retaken and describes Mattathias as stepping in to fight with the other brothers. But according to 1 Maccabees, Mattathias died before the Temple was retaken and Judah led the brothers in battle. 2 Maccabees does not even mention Mattathias and describes Judah as leading the brothers in battle.
- In its dating of the story of Hanukkah, it erroneously assumes that the retaking of the Temple coincided with the beginning of Hasmonean rule in Palestine. But over two decades separated these events.

Because of these and other errors, it is hard to treat this work as a reliable historical source on any issue.[57] It is not referred to in either the Babylonian or Jerusalem Talmuds, and most likely was composed in the Geonic period.[58]

---

57. I would not have phrased it in this manner, but the *Encyclopaedia Judaica* entry "Scroll of Antiochus" (14:1046-47) includes the following statement: "[T]he author was totally ignorant of the historical circumstances at the time of the Maccabees and made no use of any reliable sources on the period."

58. See Aryeh Kasher, "The Historical Background of Megillath Antiochus," *Proceedings of the American Academy for Jewish Research* 48 (1981), pp. 207-30, and Ze'ev Safrai, "The Scroll of Antiochus and the Scroll of Fasts," in *The Literature of the Sages*, vol. 2, eds. Shmuel Safrai, Ze'ev Safrai, Joshua Schwartz, and Peter J. Tomson (Assen, Netherlands, and Philadelphia: 2006), pp. 238-41. According to Safrai, linguistic analysis of the Aramaic indicates that the scroll dates from sometime between the 6th and 8th centuries, and the Aramaic is Babylonian for the most part.

The Palestinian *paytannim* of the 6th through 8th centuries do not seem to have had MA. See Shulamit Elitzur, *Piyyutei ha-Ḥanukkah: Semel Mul Realiyah*, in David Amit and Ḥanan Eshel, eds., *Yemei Beit Ḥashmonai* (Jerusalem: 1995), p. 309.

Mishnat R. Eliezer, ed. Hillel Gershom Enelow (New York: 1934), p. 103, refers to four sons of *Ḥashmonai* after Judah, the eldest, was killed. These details match the scenario depicted in MA. But this does not prove that MA was known to the author or final editor of *Mishnat R. Eliezer*.

◆ ◆ ◆

Some of the other more remote possibilities for the origin of the name "Maccabee" are: a derivation from מקוה (hope),[59] from מחבה (one who hides),[60] or from מכאב (one who causes grief).[61] The name has also been interpreted in various ways as an acrostic.[62]

(*Mishnat R. Eliezer* perhaps dates to 8th century Palestine. See *Encyclopaedia Judaica* 16:1515.) *Mishnat R. Eliezer* may merely have been recording a tradition similar to one that made its way into MA. (*Mishnat R. Eliezer* is also known as *Midrash Agur* and *Midrash Sheloshim u-Shetayim Middot*.)

One of the *midrashim* on Hanukkah first published by Jellinek (see above, n. 3) is clearly based on MA but the *midrashim* published by Jellinek are estimated to date to the 10th century. See *Encyclopaedia Judaica* 11:1511. (The *midrash* that is based on MA is the one that Eisenstein refers to as *Maaseh Ḥanukkah Nusaḥ* 'ב.)

Some editions of the *Halakhot Gedolot*, a work authored in the early or middle 9th century, include a statement that *Megillat Beit Ḥashmonai* was composed by the elders of Beit Shammai and Beit Hillel. Many have argued that the reference here is to MA. But most likely, the correct reading in the passage is not *Megillat Beit Ḥashmonai* but *Megillat Taanit*. See *Vered Noam, Megillat Taanit* (Jerusalem: 2003), pp. 383-35 and *Shabbat* 13b.

MA was originally composed in Aramaic. The widely known Hebrew version (included, for example, in the *Siddur Avodat Yisrael*, the *Siddur Otzar ha-Tefillot*, and the Birnbaum Siddur) is only a later translation. In the 10th century, R. Saadiah Gaon translated MA from Aramaic into Arabic.

59. Marcus, pp. 64-65. His suggestion is that Judah was thought of as living proof that God was Israel's hope. Marcus makes the interesting argument that if the name was derived from the Hebrew מקבן, the Greek form could have been Μακκβάν. There would have been no reason for the Greek form to have changed the ending, since names can end with "an" in Greek. The additional name of Eleazar was Auaran (Αυαραν). The problem with Marcus' suggestion is that the Greek letter *beta* usually corresponds to ב. But Marcus finds some examples of *beta* being used to transliterate *vav*.

Marcus did not realize it, but he was preceded in his attempted solution by the book of *Yosippon*. There is one place where the book of *Yosippon* calls the group המקווים. See Flusser, vol. 1, p. 342.

60. Curtiss, p. 13 and *Jewish Encyclopedia* (New York: 1901-06), "The Maccabees." Mattathias and his sons had fled and hid in the mountains during the period of persecution by Antiochus IV. But Judah seems to have had this name even before the persecution by Antiochus IV.

61. Curtiss, p. 13 and Ezek. 28:24.

62. Curtiss, pp. 14-17.

Finally, on a lighter note, the suggestions of Franz Delitzsch and Filosseno Luzzatto (son of Samuel David Luzzatto) deserve mention. Delitzsch suggests that the name is a contraction of the exclamation *mah ke-avi!* ("who is comparable to my father!")[63] Luzzatto observes that there is a Greek term βιαιο-μάχας (*biaio-machas*) which means "fighting violently."[64] If one places these words in reverse order, one gets something close to Judah's additional name![65]

Conclusion

The two *kappas* in the name in the Greek translation of 1 Maccabees suggest that the original Hebrew from which this translation was made spelled the name with a ק. That the two *kappas* stem from an original כ is extremely unlikely.

A ק spelling would suggest that the name is related to the Hebrew and Aramaic words מקבת and מקבא, and that the name was assigned to Judah based on either his physical strength/military prowess or his physical appearance.

But it is also possible that neither the author of 1 Maccabees nor Jason (nor the author of 2 Maccabees) knew how Judah spelled the name. Also, the fact that the name is spelled with a "ch" in Jerome's Latin translation suggests that there may also have been a Hebrew version of 1 Maccabees that spelled the name with a כ.

◆ ◆ ◆

1 Macc. 13:27-30 includes a description of the tombs of Judah and his family:

> Over the tomb of his father and his brothers Simon constructed a monument impressive for its height, built of hewn stone on both its front and rear sides. He set up seven pyramids, one in front of the other, for his father, his mother, and his four brothers. For the pyramids he contrived an elaborate setting: he surrounded them with massive pillars on which he placed full suits of armor as a perpetual memorial; besides the full

63. Curtiss, p. 23.
64. See, e.g., *An Intermediate Greek-English Lexicon*, p. 150.
65. Curtiss, p. 14.

> suits of armor, there were carved ships, intended to be seen by all who sailed the sea. This tomb, which he erected in Modeïn, still exists today.[66]

The search for the village of Modein and for this burial site continues to this day.[67] If Modein is ever located and an inscription with Judah's additional name is found, the issue of the original spelling of the name Maccabee can finally be resolved!

---

66. Josephus, *Antiquities*, XIII, paras. 211-12, mentions these structures as having still been in existence in his own time (late 1st century C.E.).
67. See most recently Shlomit Weksler-Bdolah and Alexander Onn, "Modi'in: Hometown of the Maccabees," *BAR* March-April 2014, pp. 52-58 and 70.

5

What is the Meaning of *Ḥashmonai*?[1]

The name *Ḥashmonai* appears many times in the Babylonian Talmud, but usually the references are vague. The references are either to *beit Ḥashmonai, malkhut Ḥashmonai, malkhut beit Ḥashmonai, malkhei beit Ḥashmonai,* or *beit dino shel Ḥashmonai.*[2] One time (*Megillah*

---

1. An earlier version of this article was published at seforim.blogspot.com (Nov. 27 2013).

I will spell the name *Ḥashmonai* throughout, as is the modern convention, even though the *vav* has a *shuruk* in the Kaufmann manuscript of the Mishnah and *Ḥashmunai* may be the original pronunciation

2. The references to *beit dino shel Ḥashmonai* are at *Sanhedrin* 82a and *Avodah Zarah* 36b.

The balance of the references are at: *Shabbat* 21b, *Menaḥot* 28b and 64b, *Kiddushin* 70b, *Sotah* 49b, *Yoma* 16a, *Rosh Hashanah* 18b and 24b, *Taanit* 18b, *Megillah* 6a, *Avodah Zarah* 9a, 43a, and 52b, *Bava Kamma* 82b, and *Bava Batra* 3b. For passages in classical midrashic literature that include the name *Ḥashmonai*, see, e.g., *Bereshit Rabbah* 99:2, *Bereshit Rabbah* 97 (ed. Theodor-Albeck, p. 1225), *Tanḥuma Vayeḥi* 14, *Tanḥuma Vayeḥi*, ed. Buber, p. 219, *Tanḥuma Shofetim* 7, *Pesikta de-Rav Kahana* 5 (ed. Mandelbaum, p. 107), and *Pesikta Rabbati* 5a and 23a (ed. Ish Shalom). See also *Midrash ha-Gadol* to Genesis 49:28 (p. 866). The name is also found in the Targum to 1 Sam. 2:4 and Song of Songs 6:7.

The name is also found in sources such as *Al ha-Nissim*, the scholion to *Megillat Taanit*, *Soferim*, *Seder Olam Zuta*, and *Midrash Tehillim*. These will be discussed further below.

The name is also found in *Megillat Antiochus*. This work, originally composed in Aramaic, seems to refer to *benei Ḥashmunai* and/or *beit Ḥashmunai*. See Menaḥem Tzvi Kadari, "*Megillat Antiochus ha-Aramit*," *Bar Ilan* 1, pp. 81-105 (1963), p. 100, verse 61 and notes, and p. 101, verse 64 and notes. There is also perhaps a reference to the individual. See the added paragraph at p. 101 (bottom). This work is generally viewed as very

11a) the reference is to an individual named *Ḥashmonai*, but neither his father nor his sons are named.

The term *Ḥashmonai* (with the spelling חשמוניי) appears two times in the Jerusalem Talmud, once in the second chapter of *Taanit* and the other in a parallel passage in the first chapter of *Megillah*.[3] Both times the reference is to the story of Judah defeating the Syrian military commander Nicanor,[4] although Judah is not mentioned by name. In the passage in *Taanit*, the reference is to *eḥad mi-shel beit Ḥashmonai*.[5] In the passage in *Megillah*, the reference is to *eḥad mi-shel Ḥashmonai*. Almost certainly, the passage in *Taanit* preserves the original reading.[6] If so, the reference is again vague.

---

unreliable. See, e.g., *Encyclopaedia Judaica* (Jerusalem: 1972) 14:1046-47. Most likely, it was composed in Babylonia in the Geonic period. See Aryeh Kasher, "The Historical Background of *Megillath Antiochus*," *Proceedings of the American Academy for Jewish Research* 48 (1981), pp. 207-30, and Ze'ev Safrai, "The Scroll of Antiochus and the Scroll of Fasts," in *The Literature of the Sages*, vol. 2, eds. Shmuel Safrai, Zeev Safrai, Joshua Schwartz, and Peter J. Tomson (Assen, The Netherlands: 2006). A Hebrew translation of *Megillat Antiochus* was included in sources such as the *Siddur Otzar ha-Tefillot* and in the Birnbaum Siddur.

3. *Taanit* 2:12 (2:8, 66a) and *Megillah* 1:4 (1:3, 70c).

4. This took place in 161 B.C.E. On this event, see 1 Macc. 7:26-49, 2 Macc. 15:1-36, and Josephus, *Antiquities* XII, 402-412. The story is also found at *Taanit* 18b, where the name of the victor is given more generally as *malkhut beit Ḥashmonai*.

5. *Mi-shel* and *beit* are combined and written as one word in the Leiden manuscript. Also, there is a *ḥirik* under the *nun*. See Yaakov Zusman's edition of the Leiden manuscript, Talmud Yerushalmi (Jerusalem: 2001), p. 717.

6. The phrase *eḥad mi-shel Ḥashmonai* is awkward and unusual; it seems fairly obvious that a word such as *beit* is missing. Vered Noam, in her discussion of the passages in the Jerusalem Talmud about Judah defeating Nicanor, adopts the reading in *Taanit* and never even mentions the reading in *Megillah*. See her *Megillat Taanit* (Jerusalem: 2003), p. 300.

There are no manuscripts of the passage in *Megillah* other than the Leiden manuscript. There is another manuscript of the passage in *Taanit*. It is from the Genizah and probably dates earlier than the Leiden manuscript (copied in 1289). It reads *eḥad mi-shel-beit Ḥashmonai*. See Levi (Louis) Ginzberg, *Seridei ha-Yerushalmi* (New York: 1909), p. 180.

Mi-shel and *Ḥashmonai* are combined and written as one word in the Leiden manuscript of the passage in *Megillah*, and there is no vocalization under the *nun* of *Ḥashmonai* there.

Critically, the name *Ḥashmonai* is not found in any form in 1 or 2 Maccabees, our main sources for the historical background of the events of Hanukkah.[7] But fortunately the name does appear in two sources in Tannaitic literature.[8] It is only through one of these two sources that we can get a handle on the identity of *Ḥashmonai*.

◆ ◆ ◆

Already in the late first century, the identity of *Ḥashmonai* seems to have been a mystery to Josephus. (Josephus must have heard of the name from his extensive Pharisaic education, and from being from the family.) In his *Jewish War*, he identifies *Ḥashmonai* as the father of Mattathias.[9] Later, at XII, 265 of his *Antiquities*, he identifies *Ḥashmonai* as the great-grandfather of Mattathias.[10] Probably, his approach here is

7. 1 Maccabees was probably composed after the death of John Hyrcanus in 104 B.C.E., or at least when his reign was well advanced. See 1 Macc. 16:23-24. 2 Maccabees is largely an abridgment of the work of someone named Jason of Cyrene. This Jason is otherwise unknown. Most scholars believe that he was a contemporary of Judah. Mattathias is not mentioned in 2 Maccabees. The main plot of the Hanukkah story (the persecution of the Jews by Antiochus IV and the Jewish rededication of the Temple) took place over the years 167-164 B.C.E.

8. M. *Middot* 1:6 (*benei Ḥashmonai*) and *Seder Olam* 30 (*malkhut beit Ḥashmonai*).

9. I, 36. This view is also found in *Seder Olam Zuta* 8.

Josephus wrote in *Jewish War* I, 19, that Antiochus Epiphanes was expelled by 'Ασαμωναίου παίδων ("the sons of" Ḥashmonai; see the Loeb Classical Library edition, p. 13, note a.). This perhaps implies an equation of *Ḥashmonai* and Mattathias, But παίδων probably means "descendants of" here.

10. XII, 265. Jonathan Goldstein in his *I Maccabees* (Garden City: 1976), p. 19, prefers a different translation of the Greek here. He claims that, in this passage, Josephus identifies *Ḥashmonai* with Simon. But Goldstein's translation of this passage is not adopted by most scholars.

There are also passages in *Antiquities* that could imply that *Ḥashmonai* is to be identified with Mattathias. See XX, 190, 238, and 249. But παίδων probably has the meaning of "descendants of" (and not "sons of") in these passages, and there is no such identification implied.

The ancient table of contents that prefaces book XII of *Antiquities* identifies *Ḥashmonai* as the father of Mattathias. See *Antiquities*, XII, pp. 706-07, Loeb Classical Library edition. (This edition publishes these tables

the result of his knowing from 1 Macc. 2:1 that Mattathias was the son of a John who was the son of a Simon, and deciding to integrate the name *Ḥashmonai* with this data by making him the father of Simon.[11] It is very likely that Josephus had no actual knowledge of the identity of *Ḥashmonai* and was just speculating. It is too coincidental that he places *Ḥashmonai* as the father of Simon, where there is room for him. If Josephus truly had a tradition from his family about the specific identity of *Ḥashmonai*, it would already have been included in his *Jewish War*.

The standard printed text at *Megillah* 11a implies that *Ḥashmonai* is not Mattathias: *she-he'emadeti lahem Shimon ha-Tzaddik ve-Ḥashmonai u-vanav u-Matityah kohen gadol*.... This is also the implication of the standard printed text at *Soferim* 20:8, when it sets forth the Palestinian version of the *Amidah* insertion for Hanukkah; the text includes the phrase: *Matityahu ben Yoḥanan kohen gadol ve-Ḥashmonai u-vanav*....[12] There are also *midrashim* on Hanukkah that

---

of contents at the end of each book.) But these tables of contents may not have been composed by Josephus but by his assistants. Alternatively, they may have been composed centuries later.

In his autobiographical work *Life* (paras. 2 and 4), Josephus mentions *Ḥashmonai* as his ancestor. But the statements are too vague to determine his identity. This work was composed a few years after *Antiquities*.

11. Goldstein suggests (pp. 60-61) that Josephus did not have 1 Macc. in front of him when writing his *Jewish War*, even though Goldstein believes that Josephus had read it and was utilizing his recollection of it as a source. Another view is that Josephus drew his sketch of Hasmonean history in his *Jewish War* mainly from the gentile historian Nicolaus of Damascus.

Most likely, even when writing *Antiquities*, Josephus did not have 2 Maccabees or the work of Jason of Cyrene. See, e.g., Daniel R. Schwartz, *2 Maccabees* (Berlin: 2008), pp. 86-87, Isaiah M. Gafni, "Josephus and I Maccabees," in *Josephus, the bible, and history*, eds. Louis H. Feldman and Gohei Hata (Detroit: 1989), p. 130, n. 39, and Menaḥem Stern, "*Moto shel Ḥonyo ha-Shelishi*," *Tziyyon* 25 (1960), pp. 1-16 (11).

12. I am not referring to the Palestinian version as *Al ha-Nissim*, since it lacks this phrase. The text of *Al ha-Nissim* in the *Seder Rav Amram Gaon* is the same (except that it reads *Matityah*). See *Seder Rav Amram Gaon*, ed. Daniel Goldschmidt (Jerusalem: 1971), p. 97. See also R. Abraham ha-Yarḥi (12th cent.), *Ha-Manhig*, ed. Yitzḥak Raphael (Jerusalem: 1978), vol. 2, p. 528, which refers to *Matityah kohen gadol ve-Ḥashmonai u-vanav*, and seems to be quoting here from an earlier midrashic source. Finally, see *Midrash Tehillim* 30:6 which refers to *Ḥashmonai u-vanav* and then to

refer to a *Ḥashmonai* who was a separate person from Mattathias and who was instrumental in the revolt.[13]

But the fact that 1 Maccabees does not mention any separate individual named *Ḥashmonai* involved in the revolt strongly suggests that there was no such individual. Moreover, there are alternative readings at both *Megillah* 11a and *Soferim* 20:8.[14] Also, the *midrashim* on Hanukkah that refer to a *Ḥashmonai* who was a separate person from Mattathias are late *midrashim*.[15] In the prevalent version of *Al ha-Nissim* today, *Ḥashmonai* has no *vav* preceding it.[16]

If there was no separate person named *Ḥashmonai* at the time of the revolt, and if the statement of Josephus that *Ḥashmonai* was the great-grandfather of Mattathias is only a conjecture, who was *Ḥashmonai*?

---

benei Matityahu. The passages clearly imply that these are different groups.

13. See the *midrashim* on Hanukkah first published by Adolf Jellinek in the mid-19th century, later republished by Judah David Eisenstein in his *Otzar Midrashim* (New York: 1915). Mattathias and *Ḥashmonai* are clearly two separate individuals in the texts which Einsenstein calls *Midrash Maaseh Ḥanukkah* and *Maaseh Ḥanukkah, Nusaḥ* 'ב. See also Rashi to Deut. 33:11 (referring to twelve sons of *Ḥashmonai*).

14. As I write this, Lieberman-institute.com records four manuscripts that have *Ḥashmonai* with the initial *vav* like the Vilna edition, two manuscripts that have *Ḥashmonai* without the initial *vav* (Goettingen 3, and Oxford Opp. Add. fol. 23), and one manuscript (Munich 95) that does not have the name at all. (Another manuscript does not have the name but it is too fragmentary.) There are three more manuscripts of *Megillah* 11a, aside from what is presently recorded on Lieberman-institute.com. See Yaakov Zusman, *Otzar Kitvei ha-Yad ha-Talmudiyyim* (Jerusalem: 2012), vol. 3, p. 211. I have not checked these.

With regard to the passage in *Soferim* 20:8, there is at least one manuscript that reads חשמונאי (without the initial *vav*). See Michael Higger, ed., *Massekhet Soferim* (New York: 1937), p. 346, line 35 (text). (It seems that Higger printed the reading of ms. ב in the text here.)

15. These *midrashim* are estimated to have been compiled in the 10th century. *Encyclopaedia Judaica* 11:1511.

16. The prevalent version is based on the *Siddur Rav Saadiah Gaon: Matityah ben Yoḥanan kohen gadol Ḥashmonai u-vanav*. See *Siddur Rav Saadiah Gaon*, eds. Israel Davidson, Simḥah Assaf, and Yissakhar Joel (Jerusalem: 1941), p. 255. This version too can be read as reflecting the idea that *Ḥashmonai* was a separate person.

Let us look at our two earliest sources for *Ḥashmonai*. One of these is Mishnah *Middot* 1:6.[17]

> ארבע לשכות היו בבית המוקד... מזרחית צפונית בה גנזו בני חשמוניי את
> אבני המזבח ששיקצום מלכי יוון....[18]

From here, it seems that *Ḥashmonai* is just another name for Mattathias. This is also the implication of *Ḥashmonai* in many of the later passages.[19]

---

17. *Middot* is a tractate that perhaps reached close to complete form earlier than most of the other tractates. See Abraham Goldberg, "The Mishna- A Study Book of Halakha," in *The Literature of the Sages*, vol. 1, ed. Shmuel Safrai (Assen and Philadelphia: 1987).

18. The above is the text in the Kaufmann Mishnah manuscript. Regarding the word *benei*, this is the reading in both the Kaufmann and Parma (De Rossi 138) manuscripts. Admittedly, other manuscripts of Mishnah *Middot* 1:6, such as the one included in the Munich manuscript of the Talmud, read *ganzu beit Ḥashmonai*. But the Kaufmann and Parma (De Rossi 138) manuscripts are generally viewed as the most reliable ones. Moreover, the *beit* reading does not fit the context. Since the references to *Ḥashmonai* in the Babylonian Talmud are often prefixed by the word *beit* and are never prefixed by the word *benei*, we can understand how an erroneous reading of *beit* could have crept into the Mishnah here.

The Mishnah in *Middot* is quoted at *Yoma* 16a and *Avodah Zarah* 52b. At *Yoma* 16a, Lieberman-institute.com presently records five manuscripts or early printed editions with *beit*, and none with *benei*. At *Avodah Zarah* 52b, it records three with *beit* and one with *benei*. (The Vilna edition has *beit* in both places.)

Regarding the spelling חשמוניי in the Mishnah, most likely, this was the original spelling of the name. See the discussion below.

19. See, e.g., *Bereshit Rabbah* 99:2: ביד מי מלכות יון נופלת ביד בני חשמונאי, *Bereshit Rabbah* 97 (ed. Theodor-Albeck, p. 1225): שבני חשמוניי היו משבטו של לוי, *Pesikta Rabbati* 5a, *Tanḥuma Vayeḥi* 14, *Tanḥuma Vayeḥi*, ed. Buber, p. 219, *Pesikta de-Rav Kahana* 5 (p. 107), and *Midrash ha-Gadol* to Gen. 49:28. See also the *midrash* published by Jacob Mann and Isaiah Sonne in *The Bible as Read and Preached in the Old Synagogue*, vol. 2 (Cincinnati: 1966), p. עב.

I also must mention the scholion to *Megillat Taanit*. (I am not talking about *Megillat Taanit* itself. There are no references to *Ḥashmonai* there.) As Vered Noam has shown in her critical edition of *Megillat Taanit*, the two most important manuscripts to the scholion are the Parma manuscript and the Oxford manuscript.

The other Tannaitic source for *Ḥashmonai* is *Seder Olam* 30. Here the language is: *malkhut beit Ḥashmonai meah ve-shalosh*, "the dynasty of the House of *Ḥashmonai*, 103 [years]."[20] Although one does not have to interpret *Ḥashmonai* here as a reference to Mattathias, this interpretation does fit this passage.

Thus a reasonable approach based on these two early sources is to interpret *Ḥashmonai* as another way of referring to Mattathias.[21] But

---

- The Parma manuscript to the scholion to 25 Kislev uses the phrase *nikhnesu benei Ḥashmonai le-har ha-bayit*, implying that the author of this passage viewed *Ḥashmonai* as Mattathias.
- On 14 Sivan, the Oxford manuscript of the scholion tells us that וכשגברה יד חשמונאי, the city of קסרי was conquered. Probably, the author of this passage is referring to the acquisition of Caesarea by Alexander Yannai, and the author is using *Ḥashmonai* loosely. Probably the author meant *beit Ḥashmonai* or *malkhut beit Ḥashmonai*. (One of these may even have been the original text.)
- On 15-16 Sivan, the Parma manuscript of the scholion tells us about the military victory of בני חשמונאי over Beit Shean. We know from Josephus (*Antiquities* XIII, 275-83 and *Jewish War* I, 64-66) that this was a victory that occurred in the time of John Hyrcanus and that his the sons were the leaders in the battle. But it would be a leap to deduce that the author of this passage believed that John was חשמונאי. Probably, the author was using בני חשמונאי loosely and meant *beit Ḥashmonai* or *malkhut beit Ḥashmonai*. Not surprisingly, the Oxford manuscript has *beit Ḥashmonai* here.
- In the balance of the passages in the scholion, if we look only at the Parma and Oxford manuscripts, references to *beit Ḥashmonai* or *malkhut beit Ḥashmonai* are found at 23 Iyyar, 27 Iyyar, 24 Av, 3 Tishrei, 23 Marḥeshvan, 3 Kislev, 25 Kislev, and 13 Adar.

20. This passage is quoted at *Avodah Zarah* 9a. In the Vilna edition, the passage reads *malkhut Ḥashmonai*. The three manuscripts presently recorded at Lieberman-Institute.com all include the *beit* preceding חשמונאי. The other source recorded there is the Pesaro printed edition of 1515. This source reads מלכות חשמוניי.

21. One can also make this argument based on the passage in the first chapter of *Megillah* in the Jerusalem Talmud: ויצא אחד משלחשמוניי. This passage tells a story about Judah (without mentioning him by name). But the parallel passage in the second chapter of *Taanit* reads: ויצא אליו אחד משל בית חשמוניי. As pointed out earlier, almost certainly this is the original reading. Moreover, if a passage intended to refer to a son of *Ḥashmonai*, the reading we would expect would be: ויצא אחד מבני חשמוניי.

we still do not know why these sources would refer to him in this way. Of course, one possibility is that it was his additional name.[22] Just like each of his five sons had an additional name,[23] perhaps *Ḥashmonai* was the additional name of Mattathias.[24] But 1 Maccabees, which stated that each of Mattathias' sons had an additional name, did not make any such statement in the case of Mattathias himself.

Perhaps we should not deduce much from this omission. Nothing required the author of 1 Maccabees to mention that Mattathias had an additional name. But one scholar has suggested an interesting reason for the omission. It is very likely that a main purpose of 1 Maccabees was the glorification of Mattathias in order to legitimize the rule of his descendants.[25] Their rule needed legitimization because the family was

22. Goldstein, p. 19, n. 34, writes that the Byzantine chronicler Georgius Syncellus (c. 800) wrote that Asamónaios was Mattathias' additional name. Surely, this was just a conjecture by the chronicler or whatever source was before him.

23. The additional names for the sons were: Makkabaios (Μακκαβαῖος), Gaddi (Γαδδι), Thassi (Θασσι), Auaran (Αυαραν) and Apphous (Απφους). These were the names for Judah, John, Simon, Eleazar and Jonathan, respectively. See 1 Macc. 2:2-4.

24. See, e.g., Goldstein, pp. 18-19. Goldstein also writes (p. 19):

> Our pattern of given name(s) plus surname did not exist among ancient Jews, who bore only a given name. The names of Mattathias and his sons were extremely common in Jewish priestly families. Where many persons in a society bear the same name, there must be some way to distinguish one from another. Often the way is to add to the over-common given name other names or epithets. These additional appellations may describe the person or his feats or his ancestry or his place of origin; they may even be taunt-epithets.

The names Mattityah and Mattiyahu do occur in *Tanakh*, at 1 Chron. 9:31, 15:18, 15:21, 16:5, 25:3, 25:21, Ezra 10:43, and Neh. 8:4. But to say that that these names were common prior to the valorous deeds of Mattathias and his sons is still conjectural. (Admittedly, the names did become common thereafter.)

25. See, e.g., Schwartz, pp. 54-55, Gafni, pp. 119 and 131 n. 49, and Goldstein, pp. 7 and 12. See particularly 1 Macc. 5:62.

As mentioned earlier, 1 Maccabees was probably composed after the death of John Hyrcanus in 104 B.C.E., or at least when his reign was well advanced. See 1 Macc. 16:23-24.

not from the priestly watch of Yedayah. Traditionally, the high priest came from this watch.[26] 1 Maccabees achieves its purpose by portraying a zealous Mattathias and creating parallels between Mattathias and the Biblical Pinḥas, who was rewarded with the priesthood for his zealousness.[27] Perhaps, it has been suggested, the author of 1 Maccabees left out the additional name for Mattathias because it would remind readers of the obscure origin of the dynasty.[28] (We will discuss why this might have been the case when we discuss the meaning of the name in the next section.)

◆ ◆ ◆

We have seen that a reasonable approach, based on the two earliest rabbinic sources, is to interpret *Ḥashmonai* as another way of referring to Mattathias.

The next question is the meaning of the name. The name could be based on the name of some earlier ancestor of Mattathias. But we have no clear knowledge of any ancestor of Mattathias with this name.[29] Moreover, this only begs the question of where the earlier ancestor would have obtained this name.[30] The most widely held view is that the

26. According to 1 Macc. 2:1, Mattathias was from the priestly watch of Yehoyariv. Of course, even if he would have been from the watch of Yedayah, the rule of his descendants would have needed legitimization because they were priests and not from the tribe of Judah or the Davidic line.
27. See, e.g., Goldstein, pp. 5-7 and 1 Macc. 2:26 and 2:54. Of course, the parallel to Pinḥas is not perfect. As a result of his zealousness, Pinḥas became a priest; he did not become the high priest.
28. Goldstein, pp. 17-19. Josephus, writing after the destruction of the Temple and not attempting to legitimize the dynasty, would not have had this concern. (I am hesitant to agree with Goldstein on anything, as his editions of 1 & 2 Maccabees are filled with far-reaching speculations. Nevertheless, I am willing to take his suggestion seriously here.)
29. As mentioned earlier, the identification by Josephus of *Ḥashmonai* as the great-grandfather of Mattathias is probably just speculation.
30. It has been suggested that it was the name of an ancestor. See, e.g., H. St. J. Thackeray, ed., *Josephus: Life* (Loeb Classical Library) (Cambridge, Mass. and London: 1926), p. 3, who theorizes that the Hasmoneans were named after "an eponymous hero Hashmon." Julius Wellhausen theorized that, at 1 Macc. 2:1, the original reading was "son of Hashmon," and not

name *Ḥashmonai* derives from a place that some ancestor of Mattathias hailed from a few generations earlier. (Mattathias and his immediate ancestors hailed from Modein.[31]) For example, Josh. 15:27 refers to a place called *Ḥeshmon* in the area of the tribe of Judah.[32] Alternatively, a location *Ḥashmonah* is mentioned at Num. 33:29-30 as one of the places that the Israelites encamped in the desert.[33] In either of these interpretations, the name may have reminded others of the obscure origin of Mattathias' ancestors and hence the author of 1 Maccabees might have refrained from using it.

It has also been observed that the word חשמנים (*Ḥashmannim*) occurs at Psalms 68:32:

יאתיו חַשְׁמַנִּים מני מצרים כוש תריץ ידיו לא-להים.

> *Ḥashmannim* will come out of Egypt; Kush shall hasten her hands to God.

The context is that the nations of the world are bringing gifts and singing to God.[34]

"son of Simon." See Emil Schürer, *The History of the Jewish People in the Age of Jesus Christ*, revised and edited by Geza Vermes, Fergus Millar, and Matthew Black, vol. 1 (Edinburgh: 1973), p. 194, n. 14.

31. See 1 Macc. 2:70, 9:19, and 13:25.

32. See, e.g., Isaac Baer, *Avodat Yisrael* (Rödelheim: 1868), p. 101, *Encyclopaedia Judaica* 7:1455, and *Chanukah* (ArtScroll Mesorah Series, Brooklyn, 1981), p. 68.

33. See, e.g., *Encyclopaedia Judaica* 7:1455.

Based on the names of the individuals Ḥushim mentioned at 1 Chron. 7:12 and 8:11, Binyamin Mazar has suggested that there was a place at the time in the tribe of Benjamin with the name *Ḥashom* or *Ḥashim*. (I am not aware of any other evidence for the existence of such a place.) Someone who hailed from there could have been called a חשמני. As Mazar points out, individuals from the family of Shelah are called Shelani or Shiloni. See Num. 26:20, Neh. 11:5, and 1 Chron. 9:5. Mazar theorizes that the ancestors of Mattathias eventually moved from *Ḥashom/Ḥashim* to Modein. See B. Maisler (Mazar), "*Meḥkarim Topographiyyim*," *Yediyot ha-Ḥevrah ha-Ivrit la-Ḥakirat Eretz Yisrael ve-Attikoteha* 8 (1941), pp. 105-107.

34. The probable implication of the second part of verse 32 is that the people of Kush will hasten to spread their hands in prayer, or hasten to bring gifts with their hands. See Amos Ḥakham, *Sefer Tehillim* (*Daat Mikra*) (Jerusalem:1979), comm. to 68:32.

It has been suggested that the name *Ḥashmonai* is related to חשמנים here.[35] Unfortunately, this is the only time the word חשמנים appears in *Tanakh*, so its meaning is unclear.[36] The Septuagint translates it as πρέσβεις (ambassadors).[37] The Talmud seems to imply that it means "gifts."[38] Based on a similar word in Egyptian, the meanings "bronze," "natron" (a mixture used for many purposes including as a dye), and "amethyst" (a quartz of blue or purplish color) can be suggested.[39] Ugaritic and Akkadian have a similar word with the meaning of a color, or colored stone, or a coloring of dyed wool or leather; the color being perhaps red-purple, blue, or green.[40] Based on this, meanings

35. This is raised as a possibility by many scholars. Some of the rabbinic commentaries that suggest this include R. Abraham Ibn Ezra and Radak. See their commentaries on Ps. 68:32. See also Radak, *Sefer ha-Shoreshim*, חשמן, and R. Yosef Caro, *Beit Yosef, OH* 682. The unknown author of *Maoz Tzur* also seems to adopt this approach (perhaps only because he was trying to rhyme with השמנים).

36. Some scholars are willing to emend the text. See, for example, the suggested emendations at *Encyclopedia Mikrait* 3:317 (Jerusalem: 1965), entry חשמנים (such as משמנים, "from the oil.") *The Brown-Driver-Briggs Hebrew and English Lexicon* (Boston: 1906) writes that there is "doubtless" a textual error here.

37. So too, Origen (third century).

Some Rishonim interpret the term חשמנים here as rulers or people of importance. See, e.g., the commentaries on Ps. 68:32 of Ibn Ezra (סגנים) and Radak. See also Radak, *Sefer ha-Shoreshim*, חשמן, and R. Yosef Caro, *Beit Yosef, OH* 682. What motivates this interpretation is the use of the term in connection with Mattathias. But we do not know the meaning of the term in connection with Mattathias.

38. See *Pesaḥim* 118b (דורון). Perhaps supporting this is verse 68:30 (*lekha yovilu melakhim shai*). See Rashbam to *Pesaḥim* 118b. Also, the interpretation דורונות מנות is found at *Midrash Tehillim* 68:15 (ed. Buber, p. 320). It also seems to be the view of Rashi.

39. On the Egyptian word *ḥsmn* as "bronze" or "natron," and reading one of these into this verse, see William F. Albright, "A Catalogue of Early Hebrew Lyric Poems," *HUCA* 23 (1950-51), pp. 1-39 (33-34). Jeremy Black, "Amethysts," *Iraq* 63 (2001), pp. 183-186, explains that *ḥsmn* also has the meaning amethyst in Egyptian. But he does not read this into Ps. 68:32. (He reads it into the Biblical חשמל.)

40. See, e.g., Black, ibid., and Itamar Singer, "Purple-Dyers in Lazpa," kubaba.univ-paris1.fr/recherche/antiquite/atlanta.pdf.

such as red cloth or blue cloth have been suggested.[41] Based on similar words in Arabic, "oil" and "horses and chariots" have been proposed.[42] A connection to another *hapax legomenon*,[43] אשמנים, has also been suggested. אשמנים perhaps means "darkness,"[44] in which case חשמנים, if related, may mean dark-skinned people.[45] Finally, it has been suggested that חשמנים derives from the word שמן (oil), and that it refers to important people, i.e., nobles, because the original meaning is "one who gives off light." (This is akin to "illustrious" in English.)[46]

But the simplest interpretation is that it refers to a people by the name חשמנים.[47] An argument in favor of this is that חשמנים seems to be

41. Ludwig Koehler and Walter Baumgartner, *The Hebrew and Aramaic Lexicon of the Old Testament* (Leiden, New York, and Köln: 1994), vol. 1, p. 362, interpret "bronze articles or red cloths." Mitchell Dahood, *Psalms II:51-100* (Garden City: 1968) interprets "blue cloth."

Based on the Akkadian, George Wolf suggests that חשמנים refers to nobles and high officials because they wore purple clothing. See his *Studies in the Hebrew Bible and Early Rabbinic Judaism* (New York: 1994), p. 94

42. For "oil," see *Encyclopedia Mikrait* 3:317, entry חשמנים (one of the many possible interpretations mentioned there). For "horses and chariots," see Ḥakham, comm. to 68:32 (citing the scholar Arnold Ehrlich and the reference to the coming of horses and chariots at Is. 66:20).

43. See Is. 59:10 באשמנים (in the *ashmanim*).

44. Ernest Klein, *A Comprehensive Etymological Dictionary of the Hebrew Language for Readers of English* (New York: 1987), p. 58, writes that it usually translated as "darkness." Some Rishonim who adopt this interpretation are Menaḥem ben Saruk (quoted in Rashi) and Ibn Janaḥ. Note also the parallel to Ps. 143:3. On the other hand, the parallel to בצהרים at Is. 59:10 suggests that the meaning of באשמנים is "in the light," as argued by Solomon Mandelkern in his concordance *Heikhal ha-Kodesh* (Lipsiae: 1896), p. 158.

45. See *Midrash Tehillim* 68:15 (ed. Buber, p. 320): אנשים שחורים. This is the fourth interpretation suggested there. Buber puts the second, third, and fourth interpretations in parenthesis, as he believes they were not in the original text. The first interpretation is דורונות מנות. The second and third interpretations are farfetched plays on words.

Also, the original reading in the Targum Pseudo-Jonathan translation of חשמנים seems to be אוכמנא or אוכמנאי, meaning "dark people." See David M. Stec, *The Targum of Psalms* (Collegeville, Minn.: 2004) p. 133. The standard printed editions have a different reading (based on an early printed edition) and imply that חשמנים was the name of a particular Egyptian tribe.

46. See Mandelkern, p. 433, who cites this view even though he disagrees with it.

47. A modern scholar who takes this approach is Menaḥem Tzvi Kadari.

parallel to Kush, another people, in this verse. Also, יאתיו is an active form; it means "will come," and not "will be brought."[48]

Whatever the meaning of the word חשמנים, I would like to raise the possibility that an ancestor of Mattathias lived in Egypt for a period and that people began to call him something like *Ḥashmonai* upon his return, based on this verse. If this is the origin of the term *Ḥashmonai*, this also would explain why the author of 1 Maccabees would have refrained from using it.

Conclusions

Even though Josephus identifies *Ḥashmonai* as the great-grandfather of Mattathias, this was probably just speculation. It is too coincidental that he places *Ḥashmonai* as the father of Simon, precisely where there is room for him.

The most reasonable approach, based on the earliest rabbinic sources, is to interpret *Ḥashmonai* as another way of referring to Mattathias, either because it was his additional name or for some other reason. A main purpose of 1 Maccabees was the glorification of Mattathias in order to legitimize the rule of his descendants. This may have led the author of 1 Maccabees to leave the name out; the author would not have wanted to remind readers of the obscure origin of the dynasty.

See his *Millon ha-Ivrit ha-Mikrait* (Ramat Gan: 2006). This also seems to be the approach taken in the standard printed edition of the Targum Pseudo-Jonathan, even though this does not seem to be the original reading. See also Rashi to Ps. 68:32, citing Menaḥem ben Saruk who claims that they are the residents of *Ḥashmonah*. See also Radak, *Sefer ha-Shoreshim*, חשמן (second suggestion) and Mandelkern, p. 433.

Gen. 10:14 mentions כסלחים as one of the sons of *Mitzrayim*. Interestingly, one of the three early texts of the Septuagint (codex Alexandrinus, 5th cent.) reads Χασμωνιειμ (=Chasmonieim) here. If this were the original reading, this would suggest that there were a people called *Ḥashmanim* (or something similar) in second century B.C.E. Egypt. But the Sinaiticus and Vaticanus codices (which are earlier than the Alexandrinus codex) do not have this reading; they have something closer to the Hebrew. Most likely, the reading in the Alexandrinus codex is just a later textual corruption. See John William Wevers, *Notes on the Greek Text of Genesis* (Atlanta: 1993), p. 136.

48. See similarly Deut. 33:21, Prov. 1:27, Is. 41:5 and 41:25, and Job 3:25, 16:22, 30:14, and 37:22.

Most probably, the name *Ḥashmonai* derives from a place that some ancestor of the family hailed from.

◆ ◆ ◆

A few other points:

- Most probably, the name חשמונאי did not originally include an *aleph*. The two earliest Mishnah manuscripts, Kaufmann and Parma (De Rossi 138), spell the name חשמוניי.[49] This is also how the name is spelled in the two passages in the Jerusalem Talmud.[50] As is the case with many other names that end with אי (such as שמאי), the *aleph* is probably a later addition that reflects the spelling practice in Babylonia.[51]
- The plural חשמונאים is not found in the rabbinic literature of the

---

49. The Kaufmann manuscript dates to the tenth or eleventh century. The Parma (De Rossi 138) manuscript dates to the eleventh century. The vocalization in both was inserted later. In the Kaufmann manuscript, there is a *pataḥ* under the *nun* and a *ḥirik* under the first *yod*. Also, the *vav* is dotted with a *shuruk*. (The Parma manuscript does not have vocalization in tractate *Middot*; the manuscript is not vocalized throughout.).

The Leiden manuscript of the Jerusalem Talmud includes a *ḥirik* under the *nun* in the passage in *Taanit* (66a). See Zusman, *Talmud Yerushalmi*, p. 717. There is no vocalization under the *nun* in the passage in *Megillah* (70c).

50. חשמונאי is the spelling in all but one of the manuscripts and early printed editions of *Seder Olam*. One manuscript spells the name חשמוני. See Chaim Joseph Milikowsky, *Seder Olam: Mahadurah Maddait, Peirush u-Mavo* (Jerusalem: 2013), vol. 1, p. 323.

Also, חשמוניי is the spelling in the text of *Pesikta de-Rav Kahana* in the critical edition edited by Dov Mandelbaum (New York: 1962), p. 107. (But see the notes for the variant readings.) Also, חשמוניי is the spelling in the text of the critical edition of *Bereshit Rabbah* edited by Yehudah Theodor and Ḥanokh Albeck (Jerusalem: 1965), at section 97, p. 1225. (But see the notes for the variant readings.). See also ibid., p. 1274, note to line 6 (חשמניי).

Also, Lieberman-institute.com cites one manuscript of *Menaḥot* 64b with the spelling חשמוניי. This is also the spelling used by R. Eleazar ha-Kallir (early 7th century). See his *piyyut* for Hanukkah איד נכון לצלעי (to be published by Ophir Münz-Manor).

51. I would like to thank Prof. Richard Steiner for pointing this out to me.

Tannaitic or Amoraic periods,[52] and seems to be a later development.[53] (An alternative plural that also arose is חשמונים; this plural probably arose earlier than the former.[54]) This raises the issue of whether the name was ever used in the plural in the Second Temple period.

52. Jastrow, entry חשמונאי, cites the plural as appearing in some editions of *Bava Kamma* 82b (but not in the Vilna edition). Lieberman-institute.com presently records five manuscripts of *Bava Kamma* 82b. All have the word in the singular here.

The *Encyclopaedia Judaica* (7:1454) has an entry "Hasmonean Bet Din." The entry has a Hebrew title as well: בית דין של השמונאים. The entry cites to *Sanhedrin* 82a and *Avodah Zarah* 36b, and refers to "the court of the Hasmoneans." (In the new edition of the *Encyclopaedia Judaica*, the same entry is republished.) Yet none of the manuscripts presently recorded at Lieberman-institute.com on these two passages have the plural. (Lieberman-institute.com presently records two manuscripts of *Sanhedrin* 82a and three manuscripts of *Avodah Zarah* 36b. According to Zusman, *Otzar Kivei ha-Yad ha-Talmudiyyim*, vol. 3, p. 233 and 235, there are three more manuscripts of *Sanhedrin* 82a extant. I have not checked these.)

Probably, the reason *Encyclopaedia Judaica* uses a plural is that scholars began to use the plural for this mysterious *beit din*, despite the two references in Talmud being in the singular. See, e.g., Zacharias Frankel, *Darkhei ha-Mishnah* (Leipzig: 1859), p. 43. Other erroneous citations to a supposed word חשמונאים are found at *Chanukah* (ArtScroll Mesorah Series), p. 68, n. 6.

53. The earliest references to this plural that I am are aware of are at *Midrash Tehillim* 5:11 (חשמונאים ובניו), and 93:1 (בני חשמונאים). But it is possible that חשמונאים may not be the original reading in either of these passages. The reference at 5:11 is obviously problematic. Also, the line may be a later addition to the work. See *Midrash Tehillim*, ed. Buber, p. 56, n. 66. (This work also refers to בית חשמונאי and חשמונאי ובניו. See 22:9, 30:6, and 36:6.) The next earliest use of this plural that I am aware of is at *Bereshit Rabbati*, section *Vayeḥi*, p. 253 (ed. Albeck): בני חשמונאים. This work is generally viewed as an adaptation of an earlier (lost) work by R. Moshe ha-Darshan (11th cent.)

54. חשמונים is found in the *piyyut* אעדיף כל שמנה by R. Eleazar ha-Kallir (early 7th century) and in the works of several 8th-century *paytannim* as well. Perhaps even earlier are the references a *Seder Olam Zuta*. See, e.g., the text of this work published by Adolf Neubauer in his *Seder ha-Ḥakhamim ve-Korot ha-Yamim*, vol. 2 (Oxford: 1895), pp. 71, 74 and 75. See also the Theodor-Albeck edition of *Bereshit Rabbah*, section 97, p. 1225, notes to line 2, recording a variant with the reading חשמונים. Also, *Yosippon* always refers to the חשמונים when referring to the group in the plural. (In the singular, his references are to חשמונאי and חשמוניי.) Also, Lieberman-institute.com cites one manuscript of *Megillah* 6a (Columbia X 893 T 141) with the reading חשמונים.

The first recorded use of the name in the plural is by Josephus, writing in Greek in the decades after the destruction of the Temple.[55] It is possible that the name was never used as a group name or family name in Temple times and that we have been misled by the use of the plural by Josephus.[56] On the other hand, it is possible that by the time of Josephus the plural had already come into use and Josephus was merely following prevailing usage. In this approach, how early the plural came into use remains a question.

Since there is no evidence that the name was used as a family or group name at the time of Mattathias himself, the common translation in *Al ha-Nissim:* "the Hasmonean" (see, e.g., *The Complete ArtScroll Siddur*, p. 115) is misleading. It implies that he was one of a group or family using this name at this time.

DATING *AL HA-NISSIM*

According to most scholars, the daily *Amidah* was not instituted until the time of R. Gamliel, and even then the precise text was not fixed.[57] Probably, there was no *Amidah* at all for most of the Second Temple

---

55. See his *Jewish War*, II, 344, and V, 139, and *Antiquities* XV, 403 (Loeb Classical Library edition, p. 194, but see n. 1).
56. It is interesting that a similar development occurred in connection with the name "Maccabee." The name was originally an additional name of Judah only. Centuries later, all of the brothers came to be referred to by the early church fathers as "Maccabees." See Goldstein, pp. 3-4.
57. See, e.g., Allen Friedman, "The *Amida*'s Biblical and Historical Roots: Some New Perspectives," *Tradition* 45:3 (2012), pp. 21-34, and the many references there. Friedman writes (pp. 26-27):

> The first two points to be noted concerning the *Amida*'s history are that: (1) R. Gamliel and his colleagues in late first-century CE Yavneh created the institution of the *Amida*, its nineteen particular subjects, and the order of those subjects, though not their fully-fixed text, and (2) this creation was a critical part of the Rabbinic response to the great theological challenge posed by the Second Temple's destruction and the ensuing exile....

See also *Berakhot* 28b.

period.[58] The only *Amidot* that perhaps came into existence in some form in the late Second Temple period were those for the Sabbath and Biblical festivals.[59] Based on all of the above, it is extremely unlikely that any part of our text of *Al ha-Nissim* dates to the Hasmonean period.

The concept of an insertion in the *Amidah* for Hanukkah is found already at Tosefta *Berakhot* 3:14. See also, JT *Berakhot* 4:1 (7c) and 7:4 (11c), and BT *Shabbat* 24a, and perhaps *Shabbat* 21b.[60] But exactly what was being recited in the Tannaitic and Amoraic periods remains unknown. The version recited today largely parallels what is found in the sources from Geonic Babylonia. The version recited in Palestine in the parallel period was much shorter. See *Soferim* 20:8 (20:6, ed. Higger).[61] The fact that the Babylonian and Palestinian versions differ so greatly suggests that the main text that we recite today for *Al ha-Nissim* is not Tannaitic in origin. On the other hand, both versions do include a line that begins *biymei Matityah(u)*, so perhaps this line is a core line and could date as early as the late first century or the second century C.E.[62]

---

58. Admittedly, this view disagrees with *Megillah* 17b which attributes the *Shemoneh Esreh* of eighteen blessings to an ancient group of 120 elders that included some prophets (probably an equivalent term for the Men of the Great Assembly). But according to *Megillah* 18a, the eighteen blessings were initially instituted by the 120 elders, but were forgotten and later restored in the time of R. Gamliel and Yavneh. See also *Berakhot* 33a, which attributes the enactment of תפילות to the Men of the Great Assembly.
59. See, e.g., the discussion by Joseph Tabory in "Prayers and *Berakhot*," in *The Literature of the Sages*, vol. 2, pp. 295-96 and 315-316. Tabory points to disagreements recorded between the House of Hillel and the House of Shammai regarding the number of blessings in the *Amidot* for *Yom Tov* and Rosh Hashanah when these fall on the Sabbath. See Tosefta *Rosh Hashanah* 2:16 and Tosefta *Berakhot* 3:13. Disagreements between the House of Hillel and the House of Shammai typically (but not exclusively) date to the last decades of the Temple period. See *Encyclopaedia Judaica* 4:738. The reference to Ḥoni ha-Katan in the story at Tosefta *Rosh Hashanah* also perhaps supports the antiquity of the disagreement. (This individual is not mentioned elsewhere in Tannaitic or Amoraic literature.)
60. With regard to *Birkat ha-Mazon*, the practice of reciting *Al ha-Nissim* here seems to only have commenced in the Amoraic period. See *Shabbat* 24a.
61. The first two words of the Palestinian version, וכניסי פלאיך, are also referred to in אעדיך כל שמנה, a Hanukkah *piyyut* by R. Eleazar ha-Kallir (early 7th century).
62. Early authorship of *Al ha-Nissim* is suggested by the fact that some of its language resembles language in 1 & 2 Maccabees. See particularly

In any event, the prevalent version of *Al ha-Nissim* today, *Matityahu ... kohen gadol Ḥashmonai u-vanav*, can easily be understood as utilizing *Ḥashmonai* as an additional name for Mattathias. But this may just be coincidence. It is possible that the author knew of both names, did not understand the difference between them, and merely placed them next to one another.[63]

On the other hand, we have seen the reading *ve-Ḥashmonai* in both *Al ha-Nissim* and *Soferim*. Perhaps this was the original reading, similar to the reading in many manuscripts of *Megillah* 11a. Perhaps all of these texts were originally composed with the assumption that Mattathias and *Ḥashmonai* were separate individuals. But there is also a strong possibility that these *vavs* arose later based on a failure to understand that the reference to *Ḥashmonai* was also a reference to Mattathias.

◆ ◆ ◆

Postscript: Anyone who is not satisfied with my explanations for *Ḥashmonai* can adopt the explanation intuited by my friend David Gertler when he was a child. His teacher was talking to the class about *Mattityahu-Ḥashmonai* and his five sons, without providing any explanation of the name *Ḥashmonai*. David reasoned: it must be that he is called חשמני because he had five sons (i.e., חמשי metathesized into חשמי/חשמני)![64]

---

1 Macc. 1:49, 3:17-20, 4:24, 4:43, 4:55, and 2 Macc. 1:17 and 10:7. See also perhaps 1 Macc. 4:59. The original Hebrew version of 1 Maccabees was still in existence at the time of Jerome (4th century). See Goldstein, p. 16.

63. It has already been pointed out that Josephus, having 1 Macc. 2:1 in front of him (=Mattathias was the son of John who was the son of Simon), was faced with a similar problem. The solution of Josephus was to conjecture that *Ḥashmonai* was the father of Simon.

64. 1 Macc. 2:2-4 states explicitly that Mattathias had five sons: John, Simon, Judah, Eleazar and Jonathan. Interestingly, another brother, Ιωσηπον (Joseph), is mentioned as a commander of a regiment at 2 Macc. 8:22. But it has been suggested that the original reading here was Ιωαννης (John), or that Joseph was only a half-brother, or that the author of 2 Maccabees erred, having been led astray by the knowledge that most of the commanders were Judah's brothers. For the last suggestion, see Schwartz, p. 340.

6

WHAT MOTIVATED ANTIOCHUS TO ISSUE HIS DECREES AGAINST THE JEWS? [1]

INTRODUCTION

One of the major questions that historians confront is understanding what motivated Antiochus IV (hereinafter, "Antiochus") to issue his decrees against the Jews in 167 B.C.E.[2] There are three main approaches that historians have taken. One approach views the decrees as motivated primarily by a desire of Antiochus to spread Hellenism or to culturally unify what was perhaps a crumbling empire. Another approach views the leading Hellenistic Jews as the main force behind the issuance of the decrees. A third approach views the decrees as primarily a response by Antiochus to what he perceived as a revolt by the Jews. The purpose of this article is to evaluate these varying approaches.

Before we do this, we will provide some background to our main sources for the period, 1 and 2 Maccabees.[3] We will also briefly summarize the events of the Hanukkah story.

1. An earlier version of this article was published in *Ḥakirah*, vol. 16 (2013).
2. Antiochus III, his father, had a good relationship with the Jews. See Josephus, *Antiquities*, XII, 133-153.
3. Of course, Josephus is an available source as well, but he is largely dependent on 1 Maccabees.

Some of Antiochus' actions in Egypt and Jerusalem in the years 170-168 B.C.E. (just before his persecution of the Jews) seem to be alluded to in a Dead Sea text. See Magen Broshi and Ester Eshel, "The Greek King is Antiochus IV (4Q Historical Text=4Q248)," *Journal of Jewish Studies* 48 (1997), pp. 120-129. Antiochus is not mentioned by name in this text.

Part I: 1 & 2 Maccabees

1 Maccabees spans the period from the beginning of the reign of Antiochus IV until the death of Simon son of Mattathias. These are the years 175-134 B.C.E. The author of the work is unknown, but it is evident that he was a Jew who was an admirer of Mattathias and his sons.[4] The work was originally composed in Hebrew, but what has survived is only a Greek translation (and ancient translations made from this Greek translation).[5] Probably, the book was composed sometime

4. Close reading of the book points to it being a dynastic work, i.e., a work whose main purpose was the glorification of Mattathias and the legitimization of the rule of his descendants. See, e.g., Daniel R. Schwartz, *2 Maccabees* (Berlin: 2008), pp. 54-55, Isaiah M. Gafni, "Josephus and I Maccabees," in *Josephus, the bible, and history*, eds. Louis H. Feldman and Gohei Hata (Detroit: 1989), pp. 119 and 127, and 131 n. 49, and Jonathan A. Goldstein, *I Maccabees* (Garden City: 1976), pp. 7 and 12. See particularly 1 Macc. 5:62. One way the author achieves his purpose is by setting up parallels between Mattathias and Pinḥas, who was rewarded in the Bible for his zealousness. See, e.g., Goldstein, *I Maccabees*, pp. 5-7, and 1 Macc. 2:26 and 2:54.

5. That the Greek is only a translation from a Hebrew original is evident from the character of the Greek translation. See, e.g., *Encyclopaedia Judaica* (Jerusalem: 1972) 11:657, and Goldstein, *I Maccabees*, p. 14. The original Hebrew was seen by the church father Jerome (4th cent.), "I have found the First Book of Maccabees in Hebrew; the Second is a Greek book as can also be proved from considerations of style alone."

The third-century church father Origen, quoted in Eusebius, refers to 1 Maccabees as *sarbêthsabanaiel*. See Goldstein, *I Maccabees*, p. 15. Probably, this title is connected to the nickname for the priestly order of Yehoyariv, the order that Mattathias came from. The nickname for this order was מסרבי. See Goldstein, *I Maccabees*, pp. 16-21, and JT *Taanit* 4:5 (4:7, 68d). Probably, Eusebius or the manuscripts of his work have not accurately recorded the title, and the original title was something like *sefer beit sarbanei el*, "the book of the dynasty of God's resisters." See Goldstein, *I Maccabees*, p. 16.

Unfortunately, no Hebrew text of 1 Maccabees was found among the Dead Sea Scrolls, perhaps due to the strong anti-Hasmonean stance of the Qumran sectarians. See Lawrence H. Schiffman, *Qumran and Jerusalem* (Grand Rapids and Cambridge: 2010), p. 62.

after the death of John Hyrcanus in 104 B.C.E., or at least when his reign was well advanced.[6]

2 Maccabees is an entirely different work, also by an unknown author. The author tells us that his work is an abridgement of the work of Jason of Cyrene.[7] Unfortunately, this Jason is also unknown.[8]

---

6. After describing the murder of Simon and the attempted murder of his son John, the book ends (16:23-24):

> As for the remainder of the history of John, his wars and his valorous deeds and his wall building and his other accomplishments, all these are recorded in the chronicle of his high priesthood, from the time he succeeded his father as high priest.

(All my translations of verses from 1 & 2 Maccabees are taken from Jonathan Goldstein's edition.)

The positive attitude towards the Roman Empire in 1 Maccabees strongly suggests that the book was composed before 63 B.C.E. See, e.g., 1 Macc. 8:1. Some scholars take the position that 1 Maccabees may have been composed closer to the beginning of the reign of John Hyrcanus. Both views are briefly summarized at Schwartz, p. 15, n. 32.

The Biblical canon may have been considered closed by Jewry even before 1 Maccabees was composed. See Sid Z. Leiman, *The Canonization of Hebrew Scripture* (New Haven: 1976), pp. 29-30 and 131-32. According to Leiman, the second-century C.E. Sages in M. *Yadayim* 3:5 and M. *Eduyyot* 5:3 were merely debating the inspired status of books in a canon that was already closed in the middle of the second century B.C.E. Even if the canon was still open when 1 Maccabees was composed (see, e.g., Lawrence H. Schiffman, *Reclaiming the Dead Sea Scrolls* [Philadelphia: 1994], pp. 162-169), 1 Maccabees was perhaps never a candidate for canonization since it did not claim to be a book composed before the period of prophecy ended. 2 Maccabees would never have been a candidate for canonization since it was composed in Greek.

7. Cyrene is a city on the northern coast of Libya. The reference can also be not to the city but to the whole region.

8. It is widely agreed that Jason wrote very close in time to the events he described. See Schwartz, p. 15. For example, Victor Tcherikover, *Hellenistic Civilization and the Jews* (Philadelphia: 1959), p. 385, writes:

> [I]t may be concluded—if not with absolute assurance, at least with a very high degree of certainty—that Jason of Cyrene was a contemporary of Judah the Maccabee and saw most of the events which he described with his own eyes.

2 Maccabees covers a shorter time period than 1 Maccabees. It begins in the years before the reign of Antiochus IV and ends with Judah's victory over the general Nicanor in 161 B.C.E.[9] 2 Maccabees was composed in Greek.[10] We do not know exactly how long after 161 B.C.E. it was composed, but it seems to have been composed at least before 63 B.C.E.[11]

Both 1 & 2 Maccabees were preserved because they were incorporated into the canon of the early church.[12] Neither of these works is referred to in the Babylonian or Jerusalem Talmud.

Perhaps Jason was born and raised in Cyrene but spent the rest of his adult life in Jerusalem. Perhaps he was a lifetime resident of Cyrene who spent some intervening years in Jerusalem. Finally, perhaps he was a lifetime resident of Jerusalem who retired to Cyrene to write his work. No one knows. See further Schwartz, p. 175 and Tcherikover, pp. 386-87. It has been suggested that he is to be identified with Jason son of Eleazar, mentioned at 1 Macc. 8:17 as having been sent by Judah on a mission to Rome. But this identification is only conjecture.

2 Maccabees is not simply an abridgement of Jason's work. The author of 2 Maccabees seems to have incorporated material from other sources as well and to have added his own reflections and guidance. See Schwartz, pp. 24-25 and 36-37.

9. The work is preceded by two epistles that may or may not have been part of the original epitome. For a recent discussion of this issue, see Schwartz, pp. 519-529.

10. The work of Jason was almost certainly composed in Greek as well. 2 Maccabees was likely composed in a location in the Hellenistic Diaspora, perhaps Alexandria. See Schwartz, pp. 45-56 (particularly p. 45, n. 100 and p. 52, n. 120).

11. This is so because the last few lines of the work include the following remark (15:37), "Such was the outcome of the affair of Nicanor. From that time on, the city has been held by the Hebrews." Pompey captured Jerusalem in 63 B.C.E.

12. Probably, the books were canonized by the early church because they modeled steadfastness in the defense of God, and because the persecuted Jews were seen as forerunners of Christian martyrs. Centuries later, the Protestant church denied the sanctity of 1 & 2 Maccabees and all the other books known today as the Apocrypha. But the books of the Apocrypha are still part of the canon of the Roman Catholic and Greek Orthodox churches.

Part II: Brief Historical Overview and Background to Hanukkah

The Temple was rebuilt in the late sixth century B.C.E., but the Jews of Judea did not enjoy independence. They lived under the rule of the Persians for about 200 years, until the Persian empire fell to Alexander in 332 B.C.E. Alexander died shortly thereafter, and for over a century Judea came under the rule of the Ptolemaic Greek dynasty centered in Egypt. Around 198 B.C.E., Antiochus III of the Syrian Seleucid dynasty wrested Judea away from Ptolemy V. Antiochus III was succeeded by his son Seleucus in 187 B.C.E. The latter ruled until his assassination and the accession of his younger brother Antiochus IV in 175 B.C.E.

In the beginning of the reign of Antiochus IV, a priest named Jason purchased the high priesthood with a bribe, usurping the position from his brother Onias. At Jason's initiative, a gymnasium[13] was built in Jerusalem and many Jews in Jerusalem began to follow a Hellenistic way of life. According to 2 Macc. 4:14, priests were no longer eager to perform their duties at the altar and preferred the activities in the gymnasium. A few years later, Menelaus usurped the high priesthood from Jason with his own bribe to Antiochus IV.

In 167 B.C.E., Antiochus IV issued his decrees against the Jews. 1 Macc. 1:44-50 describes the decrees as follows:

> The king sent letters by messengers to Jerusalem and the towns of Judah containing orders to follow customs foreign to the land, to put a stop to burnt offerings and meal offering and libation in the temple, to violate Sabbaths and festivals, to defile temple and holy things, to build illicit altars and illicit temples and idolatrous shrines, to sacrifice swine and ritually unfit animals, to leave their sons uncircumcised and to draw abomination upon themselves by means of all kinds of uncleanness and profanation, so as to forget the Torah and violate all the commandments. Whoever disobeyed the word of the king was to be put to death.[14]

13. A gymnasium was the center for not only physical education and recreation but also for Hellenistic civic and literary education. Goldstein, *I Maccabees*, p. 200.

14. 1 Macc. 1:44-50. Nowhere in classical rabbinic literature are the decrees of Antiochus listed or a reason for their enactment given. (I am not

Antiochus also ordered the burning of Torah scrolls and the death of anyone found with such scrolls in his possession. He also ordered the temple converted into one dedicated to Zeus Olympios.[15]

Some Jews chose death as martyrs, but many complied with the king's orders, willingly or out of fear of punishment.[16]

The persecution reached Modein, where Mattathias, a priest from the order of Yehoyariv, had settled with his five sons after fleeing Jerusalem.[17] In Modein, Mattathias slew a Jew who had publicly

---

considering *Megillat Antiochus* to be within classical rabbinic literature. On this work, see the additional note at the end of this article. Nor am I considering the late *midrashim* on Hanukkah first published by Adolf Jellinek in the 19th century and republished by Judah David Eisenstein in his *Otzar Midrashim* [New York: 1915]. It has been estimated that these *midrashim* date to the 10th century. See *Encyclopaedia Judaica* 11:1511.)

Admittedly, *Al ha-Nissim* includes a vague reference to the decrees of Antiochus (*ke-she-amedah malkhut yavan... le-hashkiḥam toratekha u-le-haaviram mei-ḥukkei retzonekha*). (The concept of an insertion for Hanukkah is found already at Tosefta *Berakhot* 3:14. See also JT *Berakhot* 4:1 (7c) and 7:4 (7:5, 11c), and BT *Shabbat* 24a, and perhaps *Shabbat* 21b. But exactly what was being recited in the Tannaitic and Amoraic periods remains unknown. The version recited today largely parallels what is found in the sources from Geonic Babylonia. The version recited in Palestine in the parallel period was much shorter. See *Soferim* 20:8 [20:6, ed. Higger]. The first two words of the Palestinian version, וכניסי פלאיך, are also referred to in a Hanukkah *piyyut* by R. Eleazar ha-Kallir (early 7th cent.). The fact that the Babylonian and Palestinian versions differ so greatly suggests that the version recited today is not Tannaitic in origin. On the other hand, early authorship of *Al ha-Nissim* is suggested by the fact that some of its language resembles language in 1 and 2 Macc. See particularly 1 Macc. 1:49, 3:17-20, 4:24, 4:43, 4:55, and 2 Macc. 1:17 and 10:7. See also perhaps 1 Macc. 4:59. As mentioned earlier, the original Hebrew version of 1 Macc. was still in existence at the time of Jerome, 4th century.)

15. 2 Macc. 6:2.

16. See 1 Macc. 1:43, 1:52, and 2:16, and Josephus, *Antiquities*, XII, 255.

17. Modein was where the family of Mattathias originally hailed from. See 1 Macc. 2:70, 9:19, and 13:25. It is possible that Mattathias and his family had been in Jerusalem only temporarily. See 1 Macc. 2:17. Josephus (*Antiquities*, XII, 265) writes that Mattathias was a native of Jerusalem, but this was probably just a guess. Earlier, in his *Jewish War* (I, 36), Josephus had said that Mattathias was from Modein.

sacrificed upon a pagan altar. He also slew the king's official who had ordered the sacrifice. Mattathias then fled with his sons to the mountains. Other Jews joined them, so that they too could avoid the persecution and observe the commandments.

Eventually, the Jewish fighters gained in numbers and the Jews began to strike back at the royal government and the apostate Jews. They demolished some of the pagan altars that had been erected. Mattathias died early in the revolt, but the revolt and the effort to liberate territories continued, led by his son Judah. Eventually, the Temple area was liberated, and on 25 Kislev in 164 B.C.E. the Temple was rededicated, and the sacrificial service restored.[18]

The fight for independence continued after the liberation of the Temple, as parts of Jerusalem and most of the country were still under Syrian control. Judah died in battle in 160 B.C.E. But in 142 B.C.E. Judea finally achieved independence. In 140 B.C.E. the Jews officially accepted Simon as their leader. He was the only son of Mattathias still surviving.

Part III: Explanations for the Decrees of Antiochus

There are three main approaches that historians have taken to explain the decrees of Antiochus IV:[19]

Despite the language in *Al ha-Nissim*, it is clear from 1 & 2 Maccabees that neither Mattathias nor his father Yoḥanan ever held the position of high priest in the Temple. Traditionally, the high priest came from the priestly watch of Yedayah, not from the watch of Yehoyariv. (It is possible that *Al ha-Nissim* initially referred to Mattathias only as a *kohen*, and that the title *gadol* erroneously made its way into the prayer later. There is at least one reference to Mattathias elsewhere in rabbinic literature as a *kohen*, without the title *gadol*. See *Shemot Rabbah* 15:6. But Mattathias is referred to as כהנא רבא in the Targum to Song of Songs 6:7. See also *Pesikta Rabbati*, section 2, *Piska de-Ḥanukkah*: חשמונאי הכהן הגדול.)

18. Antiochus IV died towards the end of 164 B.C.E in connection with an expedition to Persia. See Schwartz, pp. 148 and 352, and Goldstein, *I Maccabees*, p. 307.

19. For an overview of the various approaches, see Tcherikover, pp. 175-203. More recently, see Fergus Millar, "The Background to the Maccabean Revolution: Reflections on Martin Hengel's 'Judaism and Hellenism,' "

- One approach views the decrees as motivated primarily by the desire of Antiochus to spread Hellenism or to culturally unify what was perhaps a crumbling empire.[20] In this approach, Antiochus presumably would have desired to interfere with other religions in his empire as well.
- Another approach views Menelaus and his Hellenistic followers as the main force behind the enactment of the decrees.[21] In this

---

Journal of Jewish Studies 29 (1978), pp. 1-21; Erich S. Gruen, "Hellenism and Persecution: Antiochus IV and the Jews,' in Hellenistic History and Culture, ed. Peter Green (Berkeley: 1993), pp. 238-274; Steven Weitzman, "Plotting Antiochus's Persecution," *JBL* 123 (2004), pp. 219-234; and Robert Doran, "The Persecution of Judeans by Antiochus IV," in *The "Other" in Second Temple Judaism: Essays in Honor of John J. Collins*, eds. Daniel C. Harlow, Karina Martin Hogan, Matthew Goff, and Joel S. Kaminsky (Grand Rapids: 2011), pp. 423-433.

20. These are really two different approaches. In the first, Antiochus is an enthusiastic Hellenist. In the second, he is not.

21. The scholar who first suggested this approach was Elias Bickerman. See his *Der Gott der Makkabäer* (Berlin: 1937). This work was translated into English by Horst R. Moehring under the title: *The God of the Maccabees* (Leiden: 1979). The fifth chapter of *Der Gott der Makkabäer*, the most important one for our purposes, was translated into English by Krishna Winston in Judah Goldin, ed., *The Jewish Expression* (New Haven: 1976), pp. 66-86. When I cite to Bickerman, I cite to Winston's translation.

Bickerman has also written (p. 80) that while posterity remembers the Maccabean movement as a war against the Seleucids, the movement "was primarily a civil war, a religious battle between the orthodox and the reformers." This statement has been oft-quoted, and is extremely misleading, since we do not know the percentage of Jews that sided with the reformers. As M. Gwyn Morgan has written (describing the period before Antiochus' decrees):

> As for the Jews themselves, there were, to be sure, priests in Jerusalem eager to ape Hellenistic custom, but that tells us little about the views of the priesthood as a whole, less about the feelings of the common people in the city, and nothing at all about the attitudes of the Jews out in the countryside.

See Gruen, p. 268. Also, after Antiochus issued his decrees, we do not know the percentage of Jews that sided with the Seleucids. Admittedly, according to 1 Macc. 1:43, many Jews accepted the king's religion, sacrificed to idols, and violated the Sabbath. (See similarly 1 Macc. 1:52.) But this may still have been only a very small percentage.

approach, it is thought that Antiochus himself was indifferent about whether the Jews observed the Sabbath and holidays, the rite of circumcision, and the dietary laws. But in the minds of the Hellenistic Jews who found these rituals barbaric, it was important to reform Judaism to eliminate them.

- A third approach views the decrees as primarily a response by Antiochus to what he perceived as a revolt by the Jews.[22]

Language that supports the first approach is found at 1 Macc. 1:41-43:

41. The king wrote to all his kingdom, for all to become one people and for each to abandon his own customs.[23]
42. All the gentiles agreed to the terms of the king's proclamation.
43. Many Israelites, too, accepted his religion and sacrificed to idols....

The first approach is also supported by language in a letter from Antiochus V revoking his father's decrees. In this letter, quoted at 1 Macc. 11:23-26, Antiochus V is recorded to have written. "We have heard that the Jews do not accept our father's decree for a changeover to Greek ways...."[24]

22. The scholar primarily associated with this approach is Tcherikover. See Tcherikover, pp. 186-203.

23. See also 1 Macc. 3:29: "the tribute from his territories was small because of the dissension and disorder which he had caused in his land by abrogating the laws which had been in force from the earliest times."

24. Another support for this approach is 2 Macc. 6:8-9:

> A decree was published in the neighboring Greek cities, on the proposal of Ptolemy that they proceed against the Jews in the same manner and compel them to partake of the meat of pagan sacrifices and that they butcher those Jews who refused to go over to the Greek way of life.

(There is a major issue with regard to the text and meaning of this passage. This will be discussed further below.)

This approach is also supported by the following passage in Josephus: "And [Antiochus] compelled them to give up the worship of their own God, and to do reverence to the gods in whom he believed." *Antiquities*, XII, 253. See also the following statement of the first-century Roman historian

But a weakness with the first approach is that we have very little evidence of attempts by Antiochus to interfere with the religious practices of other peoples in his kingdom.[25] One scholar has observed:

> Nor have we any information that other oriental cults were forbidden or in any way restricted.... Neither Antiochus' work as a founder of new settlements nor his religious policy entitle us to conclude that the king was an ardent protagonist of Hellenistic culture who concentrated all his efforts on the attempt to provide his kingdom with a common cultural basis....[26]

Tacitus (*Histories*, V, 8): "King Antiochus endeavoured to abolish Jewish superstition and to introduce Greek civilization." Finally, see the letter of Antiochus to the Samaritans reported by Josephus (discussed below).

25. According to Bickerman (p. 61), four famous sanctuaries were secularized under Antiochus, aside from the sanctuary at Jerusalem. But Bickerman observes that in none of these other cases were measures involving force employed in order to bring about a change of faith or were the sacred writings of the native population burnt.

There is a cuneiform tablet from the year 169 B.C.E. that perhaps evidences an interference at the instruction of Antiochus with Babylonian religious practice. See Samuel K. Eddy, *The King is Dead* (Lincoln, Nebraska: 1961), pp. 135-36, and Goldstein, *I Maccabees*, p. 128. But the text of this tablet is mutilated and its meaning obscure. See Otto Mørkholm, *Antiochus IV of Syria* (København: 1966), p. 132, n. 53, and Goldstein, ibid.

Gruen writes (p. 251):

> Eastern cities and territories under the suzerainty of the Seleucid kingdom continued to mint coinage with local symbols and types; the great temples at Uruk and Babylon betray no trace of Hellenization; and the priests and officialdom of the ancient sites retained native titles and responsibilities.

26. Mørkholm, pp. 131-33. Tcherikover writes (p. 180):

> [T]he Seleucids were never "bearers of culture" and never intended to Hellenize the populations of the Orient on profound spiritual matters, Hellenization expressing itself in a purely external political form, that of the transformation of oriental towns into Greek poleis. There are no grounds for supposing that the "philhellenism" of Antiochus was expressed in any other form....

Accordingly, many scholars believe that the scenario described in 1 Macc. 1:41-42 is just an invention by the author.[27]

In our second approach, Menelaus and his Hellenistic followers are the main force behind the enactment of the decrees. There is a support for such an approach in a statement by Josephus. At *Antiquities* XII, 384-85, Josephus writes:

> For Lysias had advised the king [Antiochus V] to slay Menelaus, if he wished the Jews to remain quiet and not give him any trouble;[28] *it was this man, he said, who had been the cause of the mischief by persuading the king's father to compel the Jews to abandon their fathers' religion.* Accordingly, the king sent Menelaus to Beroea in Syria, and there had him put to death; he had served as high priest for ten years, and had been a wicked and impious man, who in order to have sole authority for himself had *compelled his nation to violate their own laws*... (emphasis added).

(According to Millar, p. 14, two innovations by Antiochus IV are undeniable. He was the first Seleucid king to use the title 'God manifest' and he moved away from his dynasty's traditional devotion to Apollo to a reverence for Olympian Zeus.)

Of course, we do not have complete information on Antiochus' dealings with the peoples in his empire. Moreover, his interference with the religion of the Jews may have been the only time he embarked on a policy of forced religious interference only because the policy failed here and this convinced him not to pursue it elsewhere.

Earlier, Antiochus had lived in Rome for about twelve years. Goldstein conjectures that Antiochus was influenced by the fierce measures the Roman government took against a subversive sect there, and that, in the eyes of Antiochus, the Jews resembled this sect. See Goldstein, *I Maccabees*, pp. 104-60 and *II Maccabees* (Garden City: 1983), pp. 103-12. (These two volumes by Goldstein are filled with wild conjectures. This is one of them.)

27. With regard to the language in the letter of Antiochus V, it can be consistent with the second and third approaches. The "decree for a changeover to Greek ways" may have come at the instigation of Menelaus and his Hellenistic followers (second approach) or may have been the decision of Antiochus IV and his Seleucid advisors as a means of punishing the Jew for the perceived revolt (third approach).

28. Lysias was the chief minister to Antiochus V, who was nine years old when he began to reign.

But where Josephus would have obtained this information about Menelaus persuading Antiochus IV is unknown. Very likely, it was merely his own speculation.[29] None of the other narrative sources connect the decrees with Menelaus or his followers.[30] Even Josephus

29. 2 Macc. 13:4 records, "When Lysias argued [to Antiochus V] to show that Menelaus was to blame for all the troubles, the king ordered that he be taken to Beroia and executed...." But there is nothing here about Menelaus persuading the king's father to enact decrees. Menelaus sufficiently earned the blame referred to by supplanting Jason, robbing the Temple, and committing other misdeeds. (Goldstein, *I Maccabees*, p. 159.)

It might be argued that Josephus has simply expanded on 2 Macc. 13:4, based on his own speculation. But the widely accepted view is that Josephus did not have 2 Macc. or the work of Jason of Cyrene. See, e.g., Schwartz, pp. 86-87, Gafni, p. 130, n. 39, and Menaḥem Stern, "*Moto Shel Ḥonyo ha-Shelishi*," *Tziyyon* 25 (1960), pp. 1-16 (11).

It has been observed that Josephus and the author of 2 Maccabees seem to have had a common source for the material found at 2 Macc. 13:3-8. See Schwartz, pp. 35-37. Most likely, the common source stated something similar to what was recorded at 2 Macc. 13:4 ("Menelaus was to blame for all the troubles") and Josephus merely expanded on what he found in this source.

Even though the author of 2 Maccabees hated Menelaus, he never blames the anti-Jewish decrees on him. (Menelaus is not mentioned at all in 1 Maccabees.) At 2 Macc. 13:8, upon the death of Menelaus, the following observation is made: "he who had perpetrated many sins against the altar (the fire and ashes of which are holy) met his death in ashes." But the sins referred to are probably his robbing of the Temple. See Schwartz, p. 451. At 2 Macc. 4:50, Menelaus is called a "plotter against fellow Jews," and at 2 Macc. 5:15, he is called "the man who betrayed the laws and his country." But these criticisms refer to earlier misdeeds by Menelaus. Antiochus does not enact his decrees until chapter 6. (The criticism at 5:15 refers to Menelaus' robbing of the Temple. See Schwartz, p. 259. Perhaps the criticism at 4:50 refers to this as well or to his arranging of the murder of the former high priest Onias III, or perhaps it refers to both together.)

30. Bickerman claims support for his suggestion in the words ויבן על עזבי ברית קדש, at Dan. 11:30. Assuming the context is the reign of Antiochus IV (a common assumption), the words imply his looking favorably at the Hellenizers. Moreover, in the 3rd century C.E., Porphyry interpreted this passage to indicate that the king was "impelled... by those who had deserted the sacred law and adopted the rites of the pagans." See Bickerman, p. 73. But Porphyry was probably just giving his own interpretation of the

himself does not do so when he discusses the motivation for the decrees elsewhere.[31] Moreover, the decrees of Antiochus were not limited to particular rituals that Hellenistic Jews might have viewed as barbaric. The decrees essentially compelled the Jews to reject their entire religion. It seems unlikely that this was the vision of Menelaus and his followers, even assuming that Menelaus was an ardently Hellenistic Jew.[32] Finally, it seems from 2 Macc. 4:16 that the Jews who followed a Hellenistic way of life were punished just like everyone else.[33]

---

passage, not reporting a tradition. Moreover, verse 11:30 implies only that the king looked favorably at the Hellenizers, and perhaps worked with them, but not that the idea for the decrees came from them. It is clear from 2 Maccabees that Antiochus worked with Menelaus. (Porphyry was the first to theorize that parts of the book of Daniel were composed in the time of Antiochus IV.)

31. In his *Jewish War* (I, 34), his earlier work, Josephus had explained the decrees by stating that Antiochus "was carried away by his ungovernable passions" and had "the rankling memory of what he had suffered in the siege [of Jerusalem]." At *Antiquities*, XII, 253, Josephus explained the decrees with the following remark: "he compelled them to give up the worship of their own God, and to do reverence to the gods in whom he believed."

32. Menelaus is never explicitly referred to in 2 Maccabees as a Jew who advocated Hellenistic practices. This allows Gruen to claim that Menelaus may have had little sympathy with the Hellenistic practices sponsored by his rival Jason. See Gruen, p. 259.

33. "[T]he Greeks, whose way of life they admired and whom they wished to ape in every way, became their enemies and the executers of their punishment."

According to 2 Macc. 11:27-33, Menelaus was used as an emissary by Antiochus V to put the minds of the Jews at ease when the decrees were cancelled. As Goldstein comments (*II Maccabees*, p. 422): "Could even the most obtuse regime have so used Menelaus if he had been one of the instigators of the imposed cult?"

For these and other reasons, Bickerman's approach has been rejected by many scholars. See Albert I. Baumgarten, "Elias Bickerman on the Hellenizing Reformers: A Case Study of an Unconvincing Case," *JQR* 97 (2007), pp. 149-79 (152-53). The other main criticism of Bickerman's approach is that, in the era of Antiochus IV, the Hellenism of the Hellenized Jews of Jerusalem was probably superficial. It is unlikely that they had the philosophic attitudes towards Jewish rituals that Bickerman attributes to them.

The third approach seems to be closest to the truth. It relies in large part on the fifth chapter of 2 Maccabees, which describes the events of 168 B.C.E. The chapter begins with mention of Antiochus' second incursion into Egypt. According to the author of 2 Maccabees, the deposed high priest Jason heard a false report that Antiochus had passed away while in Egypt. Jason then took 1000 men and mounted a surprise attack on Jerusalem (presumably to recapture his office from Menelaus). Some sketchy details about the fighting are provided, and it is also mentioned that Menelaus had to take refuge in the citadel. This is followed by a digression about Jason's tragic fate. The narrative concludes, "[w]hen the king received news of the events, he concluded that Judaea was in revolt" (2 Macc. 5:11).

The author of 2 Maccabees continues (5:11-16):

> [H]e broke camp and set out from Egypt. With the fury of a wild beast, he took the city, treating it as enemy territory captured in war. He ordered the soldiers to slay mercilessly whomever they met and to butcher those who withdrew into their houses.... [Forty thousand fell by the sword and an equal number were sold as slaves. Unsatisfied with these atrocities, Antiochus had the audacity to enter the holiest temple in the whole world.... With polluted hands he seized the sacred vessels and swept up the gifts deposited by many other kings....

An argument that the decrees were the idea of Menelaus himself, without any goal of reforming Judaism to conform to a Hellenistic vision, can be based on the fact that Menelaus seems to be very influential at the end of the fifth chapter of 2 Maccabees. (The decrees are enacted in chapter six of this work.) At 2 Macc. 5:15, Antiochus loots the temple with Menelaus as his guide. At 2 Macc. 5:23, Antiochus gives Menelaus an important position. (Also, according to this last verse, Menelaus is described as "being of hostile disposition" towards his fellow Jewish citizens. See the translation of Schwartz, pp. 249 and 264-65. In Goldstein's translation, these words refer to someone else.) Perhaps the decrees of chapter six were the idea of Menelaus, and there is no mention of this in 2 Maccabees because it was not known to Jason of Cyrene. But in this approach, we are lacking a motive for Menelaus. There is no reason for him to have advised Antiochus to enact decrees that would result in instability and rebellion, and endanger Menelaus' own position.

The author of 2 Maccabees clearly implies that Antiochus misunderstood the situation before him.[34] In this view, there was no Jewish revolt in Jerusalem against Seleucid rule at this time, just a misunderstanding by Antiochus.[35] But several scholars have taken a further step and speculated that Antiochus was correct and that there was a Jewish revolt in Jerusalem against Seleucid rule at this time. The scholar who first took such an approach was Victor Tcherikover.[36]

34. See Schwartz, p. 257.
35. See, e.g., Goldstein, *II Maccabees*, pp. 250-51:

> When Antiochus arrived at Jerusalem, he assumed that the Jews besieging Menelaus were rebels.... [O]nly a careful student of the intricacies of Jewish belief could have discerned the difference between rebellion and the pious Jews' conduct toward... the high priest appointed by the king. Hence, the king assumed that the Jews' religious beliefs had turned them into rebels, and he proceeded to punish the city....

36. See Tcherikover, pp. 186-92 and his revolutionary statement there that "it was not the revolt which came as a response to the persecution, but the persecution which came as a response to the revolt." Schwartz agrees and concludes that there was an attempt by traditionalist or nationalist Jews in Jerusalem to rebel against Seleucid rule at this time, and that it was this rebellion that Antiochus put down. See, e.g., Schwartz, pp. 54, 55, 251, 254, and 255.

Both Tcherikover and Schwartz claim that there are hints to a rebellion by traditionalist or nationalist Jews in the narrative at 2 Macc. 5. Schwartz writes (pp. 54-55):

> Must we really believe that no Judaeans rebelled against Antiochus IV Epiphanes upon hearing of his troubles in Egypt? Must we really believe that the rumors of Judaean rebellion that reached Antiochus had been false but the Jews of Jerusalem were for some reason incapable of making that clear to the king upon his arrival at the city? On the contrary, it seems—as Tcherikover argued...—that in fact a rebellion was underway, and that hints of this may be discovered in 2 Maccabees 5 despite our author's attempt to cover it up.

Admittedly, the narrative at 2 Macc. 5:5-7 is vague and many questions are left unanswered (e.g., who defeated Jason and his followers, and why was Menelaus taking refuge in the citadel). But Tcherikover and Schwartz

Whether or not Antiochus was correct in his understanding, it is clear that Antiochus now regarded Jerusalem as a hostile city and behaved toward it accordingly.[37] Tcherikover theorized that Antiochus viewed the scribes and the interpreters of Jewish Law as leaders in the revolt and its aftermath, and as the ones who had the support of the masses. This Jewish Law had to be extirpated, Antiochus reasoned, if the city was to be controlled.[38]

Interestingly, a story has come down to us in various sources about the humiliating manner in which Antiochus' attempt to invade Egypt was rebuffed in 168 B.C.E. It has been suggested that this humiliation also influenced him and led him to overcompensate in the manner in which he responded to the rebellion he perceived in Judea.[39]

---

are taking a big leap when they postulate a rebellion by a group that is not mentioned in the narrative. To defend their theory, Schwartz makes the interesting argument that 2 Maccabees was likely authored by a Diasporan Jew and a Diasporan Jew would want to cover up a rebellion by Jews against their rulers.

37. Tcherikover, p. 188.

38. Tcherikover, pp. 196-198.

39. See Gruen, pp. 262-264. The story is brought down in Polybius (2nd century B.C.E.) and in other ancient writers (see Gruen, p. 262, n. 82 for the references). When Antiochus was with his forces in Egypt in 168 B.C.E., Roman forces caught up with him in the suburb of Eleusis and ordered him to withdraw. When Antiochus said he needed time to consult with his advisors, the leader of the Roman forces took out a stick that he was carrying, drew a circle in the sand around Antiochus, and insisted that he make his decision before he took another step. Humiliated, Antiochus yielded and agreed to withdraw his army from Egypt. This event occurred about eighteen months before the persecution of Judea was launched late in 167 B.C.E.

Gruen writes:

> The explanation has both psychological and political plausibility.... The rage of Antiochus IV is readily intelligible. It could not, of course, be vented against Rome. But the upheaval in Judea came at a convenient time and offered a suitable target. The introduction of a garrison and the intimidation of the populace by state terrorism had a larger design than simply to punish the Jews. It would announce Antiochus Epiphanes' resumption of control to the diverse peoples and nations nominally under the Seleucid regime.... Antiochus would answer any potential questions about his withdrawal from Egypt by taking the offensive

The issue of precisely which Jewish communities were subjected to the decrees of Antiochus IV is also a matter that needs to be addressed to answer our question. If we could determine precisely which Jewish communities were originally targeted, this would help shed light on the motivation behind the prosecution.[40]

I will comment on the key passages:

- At 1 Macc. 1:51, we are told that copies of the decrees were sent to the entire kingdom. This could imply that the decrees were ordered for the entire kingdom. But alternatively, the implication could be only that officials outside Judea were invited to extend the persecution at their option,[41] or that the decrees were sent as a warning to the Jewish communities elsewhere.

- At 2 Macc. 6:8-9, we are told:

  A decree was published in the neighboring Greek cities, on the proposal of Ptolemy that they proceed against the Jews in the same manner and compel them to partake of the meat of pagan sacrifices and that they butcher those Jews who refused to go

in Palestine.

Of course, the eighteen-month gap between the humiliation in Egypt and the persecution of Judea militates against the psychological component of this explanation. (But there is an alternative view that the persecution of Judea was launched in 168 B.C.E., much closer in time to Antiochus' humiliation in Egypt. See Schwartz, p. 274.) As to the political component, actions taken against Judea could have been undertaken to send a message if other areas of the regime would have learned of these actions. But this seems a questionable assumption in ancient times.

Gruen observes that a connection between Antiochus' withdrawal from Egypt and his subsequent persecution of the Jews is perhaps implied at Dan. 11:30: ובאו בו ציים כתים ונכאה ושב וזעם על ברית קודש ... .

40. Some possibilities for the targets of the original decrees: (1) The decrees were limited to Jerusalem; (2) The decrees were limited to Jerusalem and Judea (and perhaps the capital Antioch); (3) The decrees were enforced on Jews in the entire province of Coele-Syria and Phoenicia. (This is suggested by Mørkholm, p. 147, n. 41.) This would include parts of Babylonia, but not Persia; (4) The decrees were enforced on Jews throughout the empire of Antiochus.

41. Goldstein, *I Maccabees*, p. 223.

over to the Greek way of life.

One way to understand this passage is that the persecution referred to is outside of Judea (but still in the area of Palestine). But this persecution is not stated to be at the order of Antiochus. It seems to have begun on the initiative of someone named Ptolemy.[42]

- At 2 Macc. 7:1-42, we are told of the king's involvement in the torturing and murder of a Jewish mother and her seven sons. The location of this story is not specified. The fact that the king is involved might suggest that it took place in Antioch, Syria. But the story seems legendary, not historical.[43]

- At 2 Macc. 11:27-33, we are told that the letter from Antiochus V canceling his father's decrees is addressed to "the Council of Elders of the Jews and to the rest of the Jews." The reference to this Council implies that this notice was addressed to the Jews of Jerusalem. This seems to imply that the decrees themselves had been in effect only in Jerusalem and its province Judea.[44]

- Josephus writes:

> The Jewish race... is particularly numerous in Syria.... But it was at Antioch that they specially congregated, partly owing to

42. There is a major issue regarding the text of this passage. In one reading, the text refers to a proposal by the citizens of the city of Ptolemais (=Acre). In the alternative reading that I adopted, it refers to a proposal by an individual named Ptolemy. This may be the same Ptolemy mentioned at 2 Macc. 4:45-46, who may or may not be the Ptolemy mentioned at 2 Macc. 8:8 as the governor of Coele-Syria and Phoenicia.

Schwartz (pp. 279-80) takes the position that this was an order by Antiochus, based on a suggestion by Ptolemy. He argues that the Ptolemy mentioned here (who he believes is not identical with the one at 2 Macc. 8:8) may not have had the authority to issue such an order himself. Schwartz suggests that this order was a later expansion by Antiochus of his original order, which had covered only Jerusalem, and that "neighboring Greek cities" refers to cities outside of Jerusalem (but not to cities outside of Judea).

43. This story is discussed extensively by Goldstein. See his *II Maccabees*, pp. 296-98. See also Schwartz, p. 299.

44. Bickerman, p. 69.

> the greatness of that city, but mainly because the successors of King Antiochus had enabled them to live there in security. For, although Antiochus surnamed Epiphanes sacked Jerusalem and plundered the temple, his successors on the throne restored to the Jews of Antioch all such votive offerings as were made of brass, to be laid up in their synagogue, and, moreover, granted them citizen rights on an equality with the Greeks (*Jewish War*, VII, 43-44).

Josephus first implies that Antiochus IV did not let the Jews of Antioch live in security, but the only anti-Jewish actions that he points to are the sack of Jerusalem and the plundering of the Temple.

- Finally, we must mention the various sources documenting the persecution of the Samaritans by Antiochus. The Samaritans were centered at Mount Gerizim, outside Judea. According to 2 Macc. 5:22-23 and 6:1-2:

> [Antiochus] went so far as to leave officials in charge of maltreating our race; at Jerusalem, Philip...and at Mount Gerizim, Andronikos...[45]

> [T]he king sent Geron the Athenian...to defile both the temple in Jerusalem and the temple on Mount Gerizim..."

Moreover, Josephus (*Antiquities,* XII, 258-263) presents us with two documents regarding the persecution of the Samaritans by Antiochus. The first is a petition from the Samaritans asking that the persecution of their people be canceled, and the second is a reply of Antiochus consenting to their request. The following is the relevant language in the petition:

> Now you have dealt with the Jews as their wickedness deserves, but the king's officers, in the belief that we follow the same practices as they through kinship with them, are involving us

45. Verses 5:22-23 describe events that take place in an intermediate period before the decrees are enacted in chapter 6, but after the perceived revolt.

> in similar charges, whereas we are Sidonians by origin, as is evident from our state documents. We therefore petition you... not to molest us in any way by attaching to us the charges of which the Jews are guilty, since we are distinct from them, both in race and in customs...

The following is the reply of Antiochus:

> The Sidonians in Shechem have submitted a memorial which has been filed. Now since the men sent by them have represented to us sitting in council with our friends that they are in no way concerned in the complaints brought against the Jews, but choose to live in accordance with Greek customs, we acquit them of these charges and permit their temple to be known as that of Zeus Hellenios, as they have petitioned.

But most scholars believe that these documents are fabrications, either by Josephus or by some other anti-Samaritan Jewish polemicist.[46]

In all the above material, there is no clear source documenting that Antiochus IV ordered his decrees on the Jews of the Diaspora. The source that would be the strongest support for this proposition, 1 Macc. 1:51 ("letters to the same effect he wrote to all his kingdom"), does not have to be interpreted this way. Even if it is, the passage is found in a section that does not sound credible.[47]

---

46. See Schwartz, p. 539. With regard to Josephus, he tells us of his distrust of the Samaritans at *Antiquities* IX, 291:

> [B]ut they alter their attitude according to circumstance and, when they see the Jews prospering, call them their kinsmen... but, when they see the Jews in trouble, they say that they have nothing whatever in common with them...and they declare themselves to be aliens of another race.

He repeats his allegation again at XII, 257, in our context.

47. See 1 Macc. 1:41-42: "The king wrote to all his kingdom, for all to become one people and for each to abandon his own customs. All the gentiles agreed to the terms of the king's proclamation."

This idea of an empire-wide attempt at unification is repeated later at 1 Macc. 3:29: "the tribute from his territories was small because of the

Some form of persecution of the Samaritans is clearly documented, but the Samaritans may have been viewed as kin to the Jews of Judea and deserving of punishment even in the second and third approaches.[48]

Conclusion

The most reasonable reading of all the material points to punishment of a rebellious city as being the primary motivation for the decrees. Although some of the documents (assuming their legitimacy) include language about an attempt by Antiochus IV to convert the Jews to Greek ways,[49] this may have been only the external form in which Antiochus IV formulated his actions. The underlying motivation may still have been punishment of a rebellious city.[50] The author of 2 Maccabees sets forth clearly that "the king…concluded that Judaea was in revolt" (5:11).

The author of 2 Maccabees clearly implies that Antiochus misunderstood the situation before him and that there was no Jewish

---

dissension and disorder which he had caused in his land by abrogating the laws which had been in force from the earliest times." Here, the implication is that there was resistance to the supposed unification program. Since the author is inconsistent and describes two different reactions to the program, it can be argued that the whole notion of such a program was just a conjecture. It better served the author to blame the persecution on some grand plan by Antiochus than to blame it in some way on the Jews themselves, as the second and third approaches do.

Despite 2 Macc. 6:9, neither 1 or 2 Maccabees reports any specific persecution of Jews outside of Judea in the years 167-164 B.C.E. (This is consistent with Schwartz's interpretation of "neighboring Greek cities.") There is a view that Modein, a site of persecution, was outside of Judea in this period. But one does not have to adopt this view. See Goldstein, *I Maccabees*, p. 231.

48. Schwartz (p. 264) writes that Antiochus saw Jews and Samaritans as part of the same people. Bickerman (p. 71) theorizes that there was some kind of administrative linkage between Judea and the Gerizim area.

49. See the response of Antiochus IV to the Samaritans (*Antiquities*, XII, 263) and the letter of Antiochus V (2 Macc. 11:24).

50. See, e.g., Goldstein, *II Maccabees*, p. 270: "By forcing the Jews to observe the imposed cult, Antiochus IV intended to punish and correct a turbulent subject-people… He was not imposing Greek patterns upon the Jews."

revolt in Jerusalem against Seleucid rule prior to the enactment of the decrees. But some scholars have argued that perhaps Antiochus was correct and that there was a Jewish revolt in Jerusalem against Seleucid rule prior to the enactment of the decrees. Although fascinating and provocative, this still remains only speculation.

The author of 2 Maccabees tells us that undertaking an abridgment "exacts a price of sweat and sleepless nights."[51] At first glance, this seems like an exaggeration. But whatever material he chose to omit has indeed been relegated to oblivion. We are fortunate that he took his task so seriously and that verse 5:11 made it into his abridgement.[52]

NOTE ON *MEGILLAT ANTIOCHUS*

I have not considered passages from *Megillat Antiochus* (herein, MA) anywhere in this study.[53] There are several important contradictions between this work and 1 & 2 Maccabees[54] and the work is generally

---

51. 2 Macc. 2:26.

52. Of course, Bickerman could argue that the author of 2 Maccabees fundamentally failed us. Perhaps Jason of Cyrene, like Josephus, had included a statement that Menelaus had persuaded the king to compel the Jews to abandon their religion, and the author of 2 Maccabees left this out. But the author of 2 Maccabees hated Menelaus (see above, n. 29). If Jason of Cyrene had included a statement that Menelaus was the one who persuaded Antiochus to act against the Jewish religion, the author of 2 Maccabees would certainly not have left this out.

53. This work is familiar to many in modern times because a Hebrew text of this work was included in the *Siddur Otzar ha-Tefillot* and in the Birnbaum Siddur. The work was originally composed in Aramaic.

54. For example, MA reports that Antiochus decided to persecute the Jews in the 23rd year of his reign. But Antiochus reigned only 11 years. MA associates the name מקבי with Yoḥanan, son of Matityahu. But according to 1 & 2 Maccabees, this name is associated only with Judah. MA describes Yoḥanan, son of Matityahu, as serving as high priest at the time of the persecution. But the high priest at the time of the persecution was Menelaus. MA describes Yoḥanan as killing the general Nicanor in a private encounter in the area of the Temple. But according to 1 & 2 Maccabees, Nicanor was killed by Judah and his forces in a battle that took place outside of Jerusalem. MA describes Judah as being killed before the Temple was retaken and describes Mattathias as stepping in to fight with the other brothers. But according to 1 Maccabees, Mattathias died before the Temple

viewed as very unreliable.[55] It is not referred to in either the Babylonian or Jerusalem Talmud, and most likely was composed in the Geonic period.[56] In MA, Antiochus announces to his ministers, without any particular provocation, that the Jews need to be eliminated, and that the rituals of *Shabbat*, *rosh ḥodesh* and *milah* must be abolished. The king's complaint was that the Jews do not sacrifice to his gods or follow his laws, and someday hope to rule the world.

---

was retaken and Judah led the brothers in battle thereafter. (2 Maccabees does not even mention Mattathias and describes Judah as leading the brothers in battle.) Finally, in its dating of the story of Hanukkah, MA assumes that the retaking of the Temple coincided with the beginning of Hasmonean rule in Palestine. But over two decades separated these events.

55. See, e.g., *Encyclopaedia Judaica* 14:1046-47 ("Scroll of Antiochus").

56. See Aryeh Kasher, "The Historical Background of *Megillath Antiochus*," *Proceedings of the American Academy for Jewish Research* 48 (1981), pp. 207-30, and Ze'ev Safrai, "The Scroll of Antiochus and the Scroll of Fasts," in *The Literature of the Sages*, vol. 2, eds. Shmuel Safrai, Ze'ev Safrai, Joshua Schwartz, and Peter J. Tomson (Assen, The Netherlands: 2006), pp. 238-241. According to Safrai, linguistic analysis of the Aramaic indicates that the scroll dates from sometime between the 6th and 8th centuries, and the Aramaic is Babylonian for the most part.

The Palestinian *paytannim* of the 6th through 8th centuries do not seem to have had MA. See Shulamit Elitzur, "*Piyyutei ha-Ḥanukkah: Semel Mul Realiyah*," in David Amit and Ḥanan Eshel, eds., *Yemei Beit Ḥashmonai* (Jerusalem: 1995), p. 309.

Mishnat R. Eliezer (ed. Hillel Gershom Enelow, New York, 1934, p. 103) refers to four sons of *Ḥashmonai* after Judah, the eldest, was killed. These details match the scenario depicted in MA. But this does not prove that MA was known to the author or final editor of *Mishnat R. Eliezer*. (*Mishnat R. Eliezer* perhaps dates to 8th century Palestine. *Encyclopaedia Judaica* 16:1515.) *Mishnat R. Eliezer* may merely have been recording a tradition similar to one that made its way into MA. (*Mishnat R. Eliezer* is also known as *Midrash Agur* and *Midrash Sheloshim u-Shetayim Middot*.)

The first printed edition of the *Halakhot Gedolot* (Venice, 1548), a work authored in the early or middle 9th century, includes a statement that *Megillat Beit Ḥashmonai* was composed by the elders of Beit Shammai and Beit Hillel. Many have argued that the reference here is to MA. But most likely, the correct reading in the passage is not *Megillat Beit Ḥashmonai* but *Megillat Taanit*. See Vered Noam, *Megillat Taanit* (Jerusalem: 2003), pp. 383-85 and *Shabbat* 13b.

For references to the practice of reading *MA* on Hanukkah, see Natan Fried, "*Al Minhag Kriyat Megillat Antiochus be-Hanukkah,*" in Daniel Sperber, *Minhagei Yisrael,* vol. 5, pp. 102-113, and Nosson David Rabinowich, *Binu Shenot Dor va-Dor*, pp. 138-146.[57]

---

57. An early reference to the practice of reading MA on Hanukkah is perhaps found in a statement by R. Saadiah Gaon (10th century). In his introduction to MA, R. Saadiah writes that "most of the nation read it." See the translation of S. Atlas and M. Perlmann, "Saadia on the Scroll of the Hasmonaeans," *Proceedings of the American Academy for Jewish Research* 14 (1944), pp. 1-23 (7). R. Saadiah does not state that it was read on Hanukkah as part of the ritual, but this is a reasonable interpretation of the passage.

R. Yosef Kafaḥ translates R. Saadiah's Arabic differently: *rabbim min ha-umah modim bah*, "many of the nation admit to it." See his *Daniyyel u-Megillat Antiochus im Targum u-Peirush RSG* (Jerusalem: 1981), p. 221. The translation of Atlas and Perlmann seems more consistent with the context.

7

THE ORIGIN OF *TAANIT ESTHER*[1]

The origin of this fast has always been a mystery. A fast on the 13th of Adar is not mentioned in the Megillah. Nor is such a fast mentioned in Tannaitic or Amoraic literature. *Megillat Taanit*, compiled in the 1st century C.E., includes the 13th of Adar (*Yom Nikanor*) as a day upon which Jews were prohibited from fasting.[2]

A widespread view today is that the fast arose as a post-Talmudic custom intended to commemorate the three days of fasting initiated by Esther in Nisan. There are Rishonim who take this approach.[3] But

1. This article is a summary of my much longer article "The Origin of Ta'anit Esther," in *AJS Review*, Vol. 34, No. 2 (November 2010), pp. 309-351. Copyright © 2010 Association for Jewish Studies. Summarized here with the permission of Cambridge University Press. A summary of my original article also appeared on Mar. 3, 2011 at seforim.blogspot.com; that summary is very similar to this one.

I would like to again thank Prof. Robert Brody, Prof. Daniel R. Schwartz, Dr. Roni Shweka, Rabbi Moshe Yasgur, Rabbi Mordy Friedman, Rabbi Ezra Frazer, Sam Borodach, Yitzchok Stern, Allen Friedman, and my sons Shaya First and Daniel First for their thoughts and assistance in composing the original article. My article would not have been possible without Prof. Brody's works, including *Le-Toledot Nusaḥ ha-She'iltot* (New York and Jerusalem: 1991), *Teshuvot Rav Natronai bar Hilai Gaon* (Jerusalem: 1994), and *The Geonim of Babylonia and the Shaping of Medieval Jewish Culture* (New Haven: 1998).

2. On the 13th of Adar in 161 B.C.E., Judah Maccabee defeated the Syrian military commander Nicanor. See 1 Macc. 7:47-49 and 2 Macc. 15:35-36. See also Josephus, *Antiquities*, XII, 412.

3. An early example is probably Rambam. An erroneous period and *vav* (the *vav* of ובי"ג) made their way into the standard printed text of his *Hilkhot Taaniyyot* 5:5, after the sixth word. (The necessary corrections have already been made in the Frankel edition.) The corrected text reads:

Geonic Babylonia is where the fast first arose and this approach is not expressed in any of the sources from Geonic Babylonia. Moreover, the statements in these sources are inconsistent with this approach. I am going to suggest an approach to the origin of the fast that is consistent with the material in the Babylonian Geonic sources.

I. The Earliest Sources that Refer to a Practice of Fasting on 13 Adar

The earliest sources that refer to a practice of fasting on the 13th of Adar are the following:

- One of the four *she'iltot* for Purim included in the *She'iltot* of R. Aḥai Gaon, a work composed in eighth-century Babylonia. The relevant *she'ilta* is #79.[4]
- An anonymous Babylonian Geonic responsum that made its way into *Midrash Tanḥuma* (*Bereshit*, section 3). (The discussion in this responsum and in *she'ilta* #79 is very similar.)
- A responsum of R. Natronai, head of the academy at Sura from 857-865. This responsum refers to the fast as תענית פורים.[5]

ונהגו כל ישראל בזמנים אלו להתענות בי"ג באדר לזכר לתענית שהתענו בימי המן שנאמר דברי הצומות וזעקתם... (Esth. 9:31).

Rambam clearly states that the custom of fasting on the 13th is only of recent origin, and that it is a commemoration of a fast that took place in the time of Haman, i.e., in Nisan. Rambam is forced to cite to Est. 9:31 because chapter 4 does not expressly state that the Jews of Shushan fasted in response to Esther's request.

4. I am following the numbering in Samuel Kalman Mirsky's edition of the *She'iltot* (Jerusalem: 1960-77). This numbering is followed by Brody. These numbers are artificial, as the *she'iltot* can be broken up in different ways. In Mirsky's edition, *she'iltot* 76-79 are located where the *she'iltot* for *Parashat Va-Yakhel* would be, and are called *she'iltot* for Purim. In some of the other printed editions, these *she'iltot* are called *she'iltot* for *Va-Yakhel* (and have a different numbering).

5. Brody, *Teshuvot Rav Natronai Bar Hilai Gaon*, pp. 303-04, responsum # 177.

- The *Siddur* of R. Saadiah (882-942).[6] Here, the fast is referred to as צום אלמגלה (the fast of the Megillah).[7] The *Siddur* of R. Saadiah was composed in Babylonia.[8]
- An index to a collection of Babylonian Geonic responsa.[9] The compiler of the index recorded the first few words of each responsum. In our case, the compiler recorded: ובתענית יוש[10] יג באדר רגילין אנו לנפול. The responsum itself is no longer extant.
- A responsum addressed to R. Hai (d. 1038).[11] This responsum inquires whether, in the case of a *hakhnasat kallah* that occurs on a fast day such as the 13th of Adar, the one who makes the blessing on the *kos* of *berakhah* is permitted to drink.
- An anonymous Babylonian Geonic responsum that includes the following statement: וי"ג של אדר הראשון נמי מתענין כי"ג של אדר השני.[12]

II. Analysis

According to the most recent scholarship, the four *she'iltot* for Purim were probably not in the original *She'iltot* when it left the hands of R. Aḥai in the 8th century; they were authored in a later stage.[13] *She'ilta* #79 is even more problematic than the other three. After the first few lines in Aramaic, the balance of this *she'ilta* is almost entirely in Hebrew, unlike the rest of the *She'iltot*.

---

6. *Siddur Rav Saadiah Gaon*, eds. Israel Davidson, Simḥah Assaf, and Yissakhar Joel (Jerusalem: 1941), pp. 258 and 319-338.
7. Ibid., p. 319.
8. It was not composed in Palestine, where R. Saadiah lived earlier. Ibid., intro., pp. 22-23.
9. Louis Ginzberg, *Geonica* (New York: 1909), vol. 2, pp. 67-68.
10. Ginzberg suggests that the correct reading is *shel* or *yom*.
11. Shelomoh Wertheimer, *Sefer Kohelet Shelomoh* (Jerusalem: 1899), p. 14.
12. Louis Ginzberg, *Ginzei Schechter*, vol. 2 (New York: 1929), p. 136.
13. Brody, *Le-Toledot Nusaḥ ha-She'iltot*, p. 186 n. 5, and *The Geonim of Babylonia and the Shaping of Medieval Jewish Culture*, p. 209 n. 29. Structurally, they are deficient as *she'iltot*. Also, there is some variation in the manuscripts with regard to their location in the work. This suggests that they were later additions, attempted to be integrated into an already fixed work.

Careful comparison of *she'ilta* #79 with the Geonic responsum that made its way into *Midrash Tanḥuma* suggests that the Geonic responsum is the earlier source.[14] It is reasonable to work with the assumption that this responsum dates from the 8th or 9th centuries.

This responsum adopts a very unusual interpretation of the sections of the Mishnah at the beginning of Tractate *Megillah*. These sections permit villagers to fulfill their Megillah obligation on the 11th, 12th, or 13th of Adar, on *yom ha-kenisah*, under certain conditions. In the plain sense of these sections, *yom ha-kenisah* refers to Mondays and Thursdays, and the teaching is that the reading for the villagers is allowed to be advanced to these days when the villagers enter, or gather in, the cities.

But in the interpretation adopted by the Geonic responsum, *yom ha-kenisah* means the fast of the 13th of Adar (= the day on which the Jews gather to fast). The reading for the villagers is allowed to be advanced because the date of the observance of the fast day is being advanced due to a prohibition to fast on *Shabbat* and *erev Shabbat* that is being read into the Mishnah. In this interpretation, the advanced fast day is a day upon which the reading for the villagers is allowed.

The Geonic responsum included in *Midrash Tanḥuma* (at *Bereshit*, section 3) reads as follows:

> שאלו הא דתנן מגילה נקראת באחד עשר בשנים עשר בשלשה עשר בארבעה עשר בחמשה עשר לא פחות ולא יותר, וא"ר יהודה אימתי בזמן שהשנים כתקנן וישראל שרוין על אדמתן, אבל בזמן הזה הואיל ומסתמא בקיאין הן אין קורין אותה אלא בזמנה והלכה כת"ק או הלכה כרבי יהודה, השיבו בין לרבי יהודה בין לת"ק מגילה אינה נקראת אלא בזמנה הכי קאמר ת"ק כרכין המוקפין חומה מימות יהושע בן נון קורין אותה בחמשה עשר כפרים ועירות גדולות קורין בי"ד אלא שהכפרים מקדימין ליום הכניסה והא דתנן מגלה נקראת בי"א בי"ב בי"ג וכו' ליושב בתענית שכבר פי' בסוף המשנה אלא שהכפרים מקדימין ליום הכניסה, ומאי יום הכניסה יום הקהל', דאמר מר שלשה עשר יום[15] קהלה לכל היא דכתיב ובשנים עשר חדש הוא חדש אדר בשלשה עשר יום בו וגו' נקהלו היהודים בעריהם וגו' נקהלו וגזרו תענית

14. It is organized and concise, and seems to reflect an attempt to record an official interpretation of M. *Megillah* 1:1-2. *She'ilta* #79, on the other hand, seems to be taking for granted an already established explanation of M. *Megillah* 1:1-2 that it is reiterating and commenting upon.

15. This source has *yom*, while *Megillah* 2a and *she'ilta* #79 have *zeman*.

בשלשה עשר באדר אבל ארבעה עשר יו"ט הוא דכתיב ונוח בארבעה עשר בו ועשה אותו יום משתה ושמחה, ובשושן הבירה לא נחו אלא בחמשה עשר לפיכך שושן וכל המוקפין קורין בט"ו ועושין יום טוב. זה ששנינו מגילה נקראת וכו', ליושב בתענית שאסור לישב בתענית בשבת שאם חל י"ד להיות באחד בשבת אסור להתענות בשבת ובערב שבת נמי אסור מפני טורח שבת אלא מקדימין ומתענין בחמישי שהוא אחד עשר באדר. ואם חל ארבעה עשר בשבת אסור להתענות בע"ש מפני טורח שבת שעיקר תענית סליחות ורחמים הוא, ואתי לאימנועי מכבוד שבת, וכבוד שבת עדיף מאלף תעניות, דכבוד שבת דאורייתא ותענית דרבנן ואתי כבוד שבת דאורייתא ודחי תענית דרבנן, אלא מקדימין ומתענין בחמישי בשבת שהוא י"ב, ואם חל י"ד בע"ש מתענין בחמישי שהוא שלשה עשר וכן פי' במשנה[16] כיצד חל להיות בשני כפרים ועירות גדולות קורין בו ביום ומוקפין חומה למחר, חל להיות בשבת או באחד בשבת כפרים מקדימים ליום הכניסה וכו', אבל ט' באב שחל להיות בשבת מאחרין לאחר שבת מפנ' שהוא פורעניות לכך מאחרין ולא מקדימין.

They asked: It was taught that the Megillah may be read on the 11th, 12th, 13th, 14th and 15th, but not earlier or later. R. Judah said that this rule is only in effect when the calendar is established by the testimony of witnesses and Israel dwells on its own land, but in our times…[17] the Megillah can only be read on the proper date (=the 14th or 15th). Does the *halakhah* follow the first opinion or does it follow R. Judah?

They responded: According to both R. Judah and the first opinion, the Megillah can only be read on the proper date. The following is what the first opinion meant. Towns that were surrounded by walls at the time of Joshua son of Nun read on the 15th. Villages and cities read on the 14th, but villages may advance their reading to *yom ha-kenisah*. When the Mishnah

16. In the next few lines, the responsum is quoting selectively from the Mishnah and paraphrasing.

17. I did not translate the phrase הואיל ומסתמא בקיאין הן, as it seems to be an erroneous reading. (*Etz Yosef* takes this position as well.) The phrase makes little sense coming from a Tanna. The statement of R. Judah is found at both *Megillah* 2a and Tosefta *Megillah* 1:3. In these sources, the words immediately following *ba-zeman ha-zeh* are either הואיל ומסתכלין בה (because they anticipate it) or הואיל ומסתכנין בה (because they endanger themselves through it). See Saul Lieberman, *Tosefta ki-Feshutah*, on Tosefta *Megillah* 1:3.

taught that the Megillah may be read on the 11th, 12th, 13th, etc., that applied to one who is engaged in fasting, as it was taught at the end of the Mishnah: "but villages may advance their reading to *yom ha-kenisah*." What is *yom ha-kenisah*? The day of gathering, as it is stated (*Meg*. 2a): The thirteenth was a day of gathering for all, as it is written (Est. 9:1-2): "in the 12th month, the month of Adar, on its thirteenth day... the Jews gathered themselves in their cities." They gathered themselves and decreed a fast on the 13th of Adar. But the 14th was a holiday, as it is written (Est. 9:17) "and they rested on its 14th and made it a day of feasting and gladness." In Shushan *ha-birah*, they only rested on the 15th. Therefore, Shushan and all walled towns read on the 15th and make that a festive day. When the Mishnah taught that "the Megillah may be read (on the 11th, 12th, 13th ...)" that concerned one who is engaged in fasting, because it is forbidden to engage in fasting on *Shabbat*. If the 14th falls on the first day of the week, it is forbidden to fast on *Shabbat*. It is also forbidden to fast on *erev Shabbat*, because of the necessity of preparing for *Shabbat*. Rather, the fast is advanced to Thursday, which is the 11th of Adar. If the 14th falls on *Shabbat*, it is forbidden to fast on *erev Shabbat* because of the necessity of preparing for *Shabbat*. The primary reason for a fast day is the recital of *seliḥot* and *raḥamim*, and reciting these (instead of preparing for *Shabbat*) will detract from honoring the *Shabbat*. <u>Honoring the *Shabbat* is more important than a thousand fasts,</u> for honoring the *Shabbat* is a commandment from the Torah, while the fast is a rabbinic decree. The Torah commandment of honoring the *Shabbat* takes precedence over the fast, a rabbinic decree. Hence the fast is advanced to Thursday, the 12th. If the 14th falls on *erev Shabbat*, the fast is observed on Thursday, which is the 13th. This is set forth in the Mishnah. How does this occur? If it falls on a Monday, villages and cities read that day and walled towns read the next day. If it falls on *Shabbat* or the first day of the week, villages advance the reading to *yom ha-kenisah*, etc. But when the 9th of Av falls on *Shabbat*, the fast is postponed until after *Shabbat*, since this fast was instituted as a punishment. Therefore, the fast is postponed and not advanced.

One of the cases discussed in the above responsum is the case of the 14th falling on *Shabbat*. Almost certainly, this was not something still occuring at the time this responsum was composed.[18] This suggests, as does a close reading of the responsum, that the responsum is not describing a practice of fasting on the 13th that was occurring in its time. It is only interpreting M. *Megillah* 1:1-2, the ninth chapter of the book of Esther, and a statement in the Talmud (*Megillah* 2a: *yod-gimmel zeman kehillah la-kol hi*), and describing a practice of fasting on the 13th that theoretically occurred in ancient times, according to the interpretations it was offering.

The interpretation of *yom ha-kenisah* expressed in the Geonic responsum is far from its plain sense. If M. *Megillah* 1:1-2 was referring to the advancement of the reading to a fast day, the term we would expect it to use would be *yom ha-taanit*. Moreover, M. *Megillah* 1:3 includes the following statement by R. Judah: "When [may the reading be advanced]? In a place where they enter [*makom she-nikhnasin*] on Monday and Thursday."

This strongly suggests that the term *yom ha-kenisah* at M. *Megillah* 1:1-2 refers to Mondays and Thursdays. Finally, an anonymous Talmudic discussion at *Megillah* 4a-b understands *yom ha-kenisah* as a reference to Mondays and Thursdays.[19]

18. When the 14th of Adar falls on *Shabbat*, the upcoming Yom Kippur would fall on Friday. Already in the time of R. Yose b. Bun (c. 300), the 14th of Adar was not being allowed to fall on *Shabbat* or Monday, so that Yom Kippur would not fall on Friday or Sunday. See JT *Megillah* 1:2 (70b), *Encyclopaedia Judaica* (Jerusalem: 1972) 5:49, and Yosef Tabory, *Moadei Yisrael bi-Tekufat ha-Mishnah ve-ha-Talmud* (Jerusalem: 1995), p. 28. See also *Rosh Hashanah* 20a. *She'ilta* #79 stated explicitly that the 14th of Adar no longer fell on *Shabbat* in its time.

19. The severe difficulties with interpreting *yom ha-kenisah* as the 13th of Adar are noted by many authorities. Interestingly, there exists a manuscript of *Megillah* 2a (NY-Columbia X 893 T141) in which this interpretation (taken from the *She'iltot*) is included on the Talmudic page. The statement included is:

פיר' רב אחא שלשה עשר זמן קהילה לכל היא שנ' נקהלו היהודים בעריהם ולא צריך
למכתב דהוא יום תענית שמתכנסין בו ישראל לתענית

It is therefore incorrect to state that the fast of the 13th of Adar is nowhere mentioned in the Talmud!

The interpretations expressed of Esther 9:1-2 and of the Talmudic statement *yod-gimmel zeman kehillah la-kol hi* are far from plain sense interpretations as well.

The critical question in determining the origin of the fast of the 13th of Adar is what motivated these unusual interpretations. Obviously, one possible motivation was an attempt to justify an existing practice to fast on the 13th. But I am going to suggest something entirely different that motivated these interpretations. Then we can understand the practice of fasting on the 13th as having originated as a consequence of the interpretations.

The responsum included in *Midrash Tanḥuma* was from Babylonian Geonim. As stated earlier, it is reasonable to work with the assumption that it dates from the 8th or 9th centuries. A major issue of *halakhah* in this period was the permissibility of fasting on *Shabbat*.[20]

The unusual interpretations can be explained under the assumption that the authors were responding to, and opposing contemporary practices of, fasting on *Shabbat* and *erev Shabbat*. Interpreting *yom ha-kenisah* the way they did enabled them to cite M. *Megillah* 1:1-2 as a source which prohibited fasting on *Shabbat* and *erev Shabbat*. In their interpretation, the reading for the villagers is allowed to be advanced because the date of the observance of the fast day is being advanced, due to a prohibition to fast on *Shabbat* and *erev Shabbat* that they were reading into the Mishnah.

The practices that the authors of the unusual interpretations could have been responding to could have been: (1) the practice in Babylonia of fasting on the *Shabbat* before Yom Kippur; (2) practices in Babylonia of fasting on *Shabbat* as a form of repentance or piety, or by those whose ideal *Shabbat* consisted of studying or praying all day, or by those who enjoyed fasting; or (3) practices of fasting on *Shabbat* in Palestine in the above contexts. It is also possible that the main motivation of the authors of the unusual interpretations was opposition to a practice of fasting on *erev Shabbat*.

I suggest that the unusual interpretations expressed in the Geonic responsum arose as a result of one or more of these polemical motivations. This led M. *Megillah* 1:1-2 to be interpreted to imply a prohibition to fast on *Shabbat* and *erev Shabbat*. A new "tradition" about an ancient fast on the 13th of Adar was the result.

---

20. See my article, pp. 335-339. Much of the relevant material is found at *Otzar ha-Geonim, Yom Tov*, secs. 41-49.

One clue that the authors were responding to contemporary practices of fasting on *Shabbat* and *erev Shabbat* is that the responsum includes a polemical line stressing the importance of honoring the *Shabbat*: וכבוד שבת עדיף מאלף תעניות.[21] The early ninth-century polemical letter of Pirkoi ben Baboi uses almost the same language:

וגדול עינוג שבת אחד יותר ממקריב אלף קרבנות ומאלף תענית.[22]

A difficulty with my approach to the origin of the fast is the argument that it is not likely that a Mishnah would be polemically interpreted to such an extent that the interpretation would result in the observance of a new fast day. My response is that those who authored the interpretation did not foresee that a new fast day would come to be observed as a result of their interpretation.

That the fast of the 13th of Adar did not arise as commemoration of the three days of fasting initiated by Esther is seen from the name for the fast day in the earliest sources. The responsum of R. Natronai is the earliest source that refers to the fast by a name, and it refers to the fast as *Taanit Purim*. Of the four sources in the Geonic period from Babylonia and its environs that refer to the fast by a name, most likely none of them calls it *Taanit Esther*.[23]

21. The material in the Geonic responsum and in *she'ilta* #79 is very similar. But the above line is found only in the Geonic responsum.

The fact that the responsum does not illustrate seven scenarios, but only illustrates the scenarios of the 14th falling on Friday, Saturday, Sunday, and Monday, also suggests that the main motivation for its interpretations was related to *Shabbat* and *erev Shabbat*.

22. *Otzar ha-Geonim, Yom Tov*, p. 20, sec. 41. This was a polemical letter written to the Jews of North Africa and Spain, instructing them that Palestinian customs should not be followed. Pirkoi, a Babylonian Jew, tells us that he was a disciple of someone named Rava who was a disciple of R. Yehudai. (R. Yehudai was head of the academy at Sura, approximately 757-761 C.E.) Pirkoi writes that many of the Palestinian customs originated as emergency measures during times of persecution, or were customs resulting from ignorance. It was only in Babylonia that accurate traditions were preserved. Among the Palestinian practices that Pirkoi criticizes was their practice of fasting on *Shabbat*.

23. The four are: R. Natronai, R. Saadiah, Al-Biruni, and the expanded version of *Seder Parashiyyot shel Yamim Tovim ve-Haftarot Shellahen*. R. Natronai refers to the fast as *Taanit Purim*. R. Saadiah refers to the fast as צום אלמגלה. Al-Biruni, a Muslim scholar of Persian origin (writing in 1000

When the Babylonian Geonic sources express or imply something about the origin of the fast, what is consistently expressed or implied is that the fast is a rabbinic obligation, and not merely a post-Talmudic custom. For example, the Geonic responsum included in *Midrash Tanḥuma* refers to the fast as a דרבנן (*de-rabbanan*). Moreover, it was mentioned earlier that an anonymous Babylonian Geonic responsum takes the position that, in a leap year, one fasts even on the 13th of the first Adar. Most likely, it takes this position because it views fasting on the 13th of Adar as an obligation, based on the interpretation of Esther 9 expressed in the Geonic responsum included in *Midrash Tanḥuma*. If it viewed the fast as a post-Talmudic custom meant to commemorate fasting that took place in Nisan, a fast on the 13th of the second Adar would almost certainly have been viewed as sufficient.

There are four sources that refer to a Palestinian practice of fasting three days (on a Monday-Thursday-Monday cycle) in Adar. These sources are: *Soferim* (chapters 17 and 21), and three other sources that have come to light from the Genizah.[24] The Palestinian practice almost certainly was a commemoration of the three days of fasting initiated by Esther in Nisan.[25]

C.E.), calls the day "the fasting of Alburi" (Purim). *Seder Parashiyyot* probably dates from the late 9th or early 10th century. It includes a shortened version of the responsum of R. Natronai that had referred to the fast. There are only three manuscripts of the expanded version of *Seder Parashiyyot*, none of which was actually copied in Geonic Babylonia. Two of the manuscripts read *Taanit Esther*, while one reads *Taanit Purim*. Since R. Natronai's original responsum read *Taanit Purim*, it seems likely that the manuscript of *Seder Parashiyyot* that reflects this reading has preserved the original reading and that the other reading originated with a copyist altering the name to fit the name for the fast prevailing in his locale.

Soferim refers to *sheloshet yemei tzom Mordekhai ve-Esther*. But the reference is to the Palestinian practice of fasting three days on a Monday-Thursday-Monday cycle. *Soferim* was most likely composed in the 9th or 10th century, in a community under Palestinian influence, such as Italy or Byzantium. See Debra Reed Blank, "It's Time to Take Another Look at 'Our Little Sister' Soferim: A Bibliographical Essay," *JQR* 90 (1999), pp. 1-26 (4, n. 10), and M. B. Lerner, "The External Tractates," in *The Literature of the Sages*, vol. 1, ed. Shmuel Safrai (Assen, The Netherlands, and Philadelphia: 1987), pp. 399-400.

24. See my article, pp. 324-327.

25. This Palestinian practice may even have preceded the Babylonian practice of fasting on the 13th, although this cannot be proven. See my article, pp. 326-27.

Summary and Conclusions

The practice of fasting on the 13th of Adar originated in Geonic Babylonia. The approach most consistent with the Geonic sources is that the fast arose as a consequence of an interpretation of M. *Megillah* 1:1-2. The authors of the interpretation were responding to, and opposing, contemporary practices of fasting on *Shabbat* and *erev Shabbat*. This led them to interpret M. *Megillah* 1:1-2 to imply a prohibition to fast on *Shabbat* and *erev Shabbat*. The result was a new "tradition" about an ancient fast on the 13th of Adar. There had not been a practice of fasting on the 13th at the time the Geonic interpretation of M. *Megillah* 1:1-2 originated. The origin of this fast in Babylonia had nothing to do with the three days of fasting initiated by Esther (in Nisan), even though today the fast bears her name.[26] *Soferim* (chapters 17 and 21), and three other sources that have come to light from the Genizah refer to a Palestinian practice of fasting three days in Adar. This practice almost certainly was a commemoration of the three days of fasting initiated by Esther.

We are fortunate that it is the Babylonian practice of fasting one day (the practice not based on Esther's actions) that prevailed, and not the more difficult Palestinian practice!

---

26. That the Palestinian practice was a commemoration of the three days of fasting initiated by Esther probably contributed to the name for the Babylonian fast of the 13th evolving into *Taanit Esther*. See my article, p. 333, n. 98. The fast of the 13th was already known in some areas as *Taanit Esther* by the 11th century. Ibid., pp. 332-333.

8

Achashverosh and Esther in Secular Sources: Their Identities Finally Unmasked!

Introduction[1]

This article has two purposes. The first is to explain how Achashverosh was able to be identified in secular sources. The second is to show that Esther can almost certainly be identified as well. A growing number of Orthodox Jewish sources identify Achashverosh with Xerxes,[2] but these

---

1. I am grateful to Dr. Jan P. Stronk for his valuable assistance. This article is the result of many years of thought and research.

An earlier version of this article will be published as "Achashverosh and Esther: Their Identities Unmasked," in *Essays for a Jewish Lifetime: The Burton D. Morris Jubilee Volume* (forthcoming). I have made only a few minor additions here. A much shorter version of the article appeared on Feb. 20, 2013 at seforim.blogspot.com ("Identifying Achashverosh and Esther in Secular Sources").

Although I have transliterated ח as *ḥ* in the balance of this book, I have transliterated ח with *ch* in this article to be consistent with the transliteration used in the original article. (I have transliterated כ with *kh* throughout this book, except when appearing in the names of Biblical figures.)

2. See, e.g., the *Daat Mikra* edition of *Tanakh* (published by Mosad HaRav Kook): *Chamesh Megillot* (1973), introduction to Esther, pp. 5-6, *Trei Asar*, vol. 2 (1976), appendix, p. 3, and *Ezra ve-Nechemiah* (1980), appendix, pp. 12-13. See also the edition of the *Talmud of R. Adin Steinsaltz, Megillah* (Jerusalem: 1983, Hebrew edition), p. 47, *ha-Chayyim*, and p. 50, *ha-Chayyim*. Additionally, figures such as R. Yoel Bin-Nun, R. Menachem Liebtag, and R. Yaakov Medan accept the identification of Achashverosh with Xerxes in their writings. Even ArtScroll's *History of the Jewish*

sources tend to avoid the subject of the wife of Xerxes altogether.[3] The only wife of Xerxes mentioned in secular sources is named Amestris, and stories are told by ancient Greek historians about her cruelty. The issue of the identification of Esther in secular sources is one that cries out for a solution, and one will be proposed here.

PART I. IDENTIFYING ACHASHVEROSH

Before we get to the secular sources regarding Achashverosh, it must be stressed that an important clue in identifying Achashverosh is found in the book of Ezra. In the Megillah, the king who preceded Achashverosh

---

People: The Second Temple Era (Brooklyn: 1982) includes the following line (p. 45): "according to some historians, King Xerxes was Ahasuerus, the husband of Queen Esther."

For references to sources in Orthodoxy from earlier periods that adopt the identification of Achashverosh with Xerxes, see my *Jewish History in Conflict* (Northvale, N.J.: 1997), pp. 178-79.

That the name Achashverosh is a linguistic match to Xerxes' name in Persian, Khshayarsha, is accepted by legions of scholars today, even if they dispute the historicity of the story.

3. For example:

- R. Avigdor Miller, in his *Torah Nation* (New York: 1971), clearly takes the position that Achashverosh is Xerxes (pp. 40 and 42), but avoids the issue of the wife of Xerxes altogether.
- R. Shelomoh Eliezer Danziger, in his "Who Was the Real Akhashverosh?," *Jewish Observer*, Feb. 1973, pp. 12-15, provides detailed arguments in support of the identification of Achashverosh with Xerxes. But he avoids the issue of the wife of Xerxes altogether.
- The *Daat Mikra* edition of *Trei Asar* avoids the issue altogether in its paragraph about Achashverosh-Xerxes. In its next paragraph, about Artachshasta, a brief remark is made that Artachshasta is the son of Achashverosh and "אמסטריס (אסתר?)." The matter is not discussed further.
- R. Yehuda Landy, in his *Purim and the Persian Empire* (Jerusalem: 2010), follows the approach that Achashverosh is Xerxes. See particularly, pp. 40-42. But he never mentions Amestris. (A very brief and vague allusion to a possible problem is made at p. 57.)

One source in Orthodoxy which does discuss the issue is the *Daat Mikra* edition of *Chamesh Megillot*, introduction to Esther. See Part II.

and the king who followed him are not mentioned. But in the book of Ezra, Achashverosh is mentioned,[4] and the kings who preceded and followed him are mentioned as well. The following is a translation of the relevant verses, Ezra 4:4-7:

> 4. Then the people of the land weakened the hands of the people of Judah, and harried them while they were building. 5. They hired counsellors against them, to frustrate their purpose, all the days of **Koresh**, king of Persia, even until the reign of **Daryavesh**, king of Persia.[5] 6. In the reign of **Achashverosh**, in the beginning of his reign, they wrote an accusation against the inhabitants of Judah and Jerusalem.[6] 7. In the days of

---

4. Both the Tannaitic work *Seder Olam* ("SO"), in chapter 29, and the Talmud, at *Megillah* 11a, identify the Achashverosh of the book of Ezra with the Achashverosh of the Megillah.

Outside the Megillah and Ezra 4:6, the name Achashverosh is found only one other time in the Bible, at Dan. 9:2. The Achashverosh named there is the father of Daryavesh of Madai. According to *SO* (chapter 28), based on Dan. 6:1 and 9:1, Daryavesh of Madai reigned for one year prior to Koresh. (But at *Megillah* 11b, his reign is assumed to have spanned two years. See Chaim Milikowsky, *Seder Olam: Mahadurah Maddait, Peirush u-Mavo* [Jerusalem: 2013], vol. 2, p. 454.)

To date, Daryavesh of Madai has not been identified in conventional chronology. None of the suggestions for identification that have been offered are convincing. See further Rivkah Raviv, "*Daryavesh ha-Madai al pi Sifrut Chazal*," *Sidra* 27-28 (2013), pp. 245-57 (245-47).

5. This verse ("they hired counsellors against them… *kol yemei Koresh melekh Paras ve-ad malkhut Daryavesh melekh Paras*") implies that one or more kings reigned between Koresh and Daryavesh. If there were no kings between Koresh and Daryavesh, the verse would not have used the word *ve-ad* (until); it would have referred to the hiring of counsellors in the reigns of Koresh and Daryavesh. In conventional chronology, a king named Cambyses reigned between Koresh and Daryavesh.

6. Ran Zadok makes the interesting observation that the Jews' eventual victory in the twelfth year of Achashverosh is perhaps circumstantially confirmed in these verses. He notes that, after the letter of verse 4:6 (dated to the beginning of the reign of Achashverosh), no further complaints are recorded as having been sent out in his reign. He suggests that it was not until the reign of the next king that those opposing the Jews saw fit to complain again. See his "On the Historical Background of the Book of Esther," *Biblische Notizen* 24 (1984), pp. 18-23 (22). Achashverosh/Xerxes reigned for twenty-one years.

> **Artachshasta,** wrote Bishlam, Mitredat, Tavel and the rest of his companions…[7]

The simplest understanding of these verses is that Achashverosh reigned between a king named Daryavesh and a king named Artachshasta.[8]

---

7. This section, describing a complaint made in the reign of Artachshasta about the building of the city of Jerusalem and its walls, continues through verse 23.

8. *SO* has a different understanding of these verses, and the view of *SO* is followed in the Talmud. In this view, Achashverosh reigned between Koresh and Daryavesh, and the Persian period spanned the reigns of only three Persian kings: Koresh, Achashverosh, and Daryavesh=Artachshasta. See, e.g., *SO* chapters 29 and 30, *Megillah* 11b, *Avodah Zarah* 9a-10a, *Rosh Hashanah* 3b, and *Arakhin* 13a. For an extensive discussion of the view of *SO*, see Milikowsky, vol. 2, pp. 462-75.

The *SO*/Talmudic chronology disagrees with conventional chronology in two ways. It places Achashverosh between Koresh and Daryavesh, and it omits the many Persian kings who reigned between Daryavesh (=Darius I) and Alexander the Great. See the list of the Persian kings provided in the Appendix. For further background, see my *Jewish History in Conflict*. The present Jewish count from creation is based on the *SO*/ Talmudic chronology.

Since verse 4:5 implies that one or more kings reigned between Koresh and Daryavesh, and since events from the reign of this Daryavesh are narrated from 4:24 through the end of chapter 6, it was a reasonable interpretation of Ezra chapter 4 that Achashverosh reigned before Daryavesh. Almost certainly, the author of the *SO*/Talmudic chronology viewed the Artachshasta of Ezra 4:7-23 as Achashverosh (being referred to by a throne name). See Milikowsky, vol. 2, p. 467, n. 112, and pp. 493 and 505. See also *Esther Rabbah* 1:3. But the *SO*/Talmudic chronology cannot reasonably be reconciled with Ezra 6:14, which clearly indicates that there was a separate king named Artachshasta who reigned at some point after Daryavesh. This has been noted by many Rishonim and Acharonim.

The proper understanding of Ezra chapter 4 only became evident in modern times. The author of the book of Ezra decided to digress, and to supplement the reference to accusations made against the Jews in the reigns of Koresh through Daryavesh with mention of further accusations against them in the reigns of the subsequent kings, Achashverosh (Xerxes) and Artachshasta (Artaxerxes I). Verse 4:24 then returns to the main narrative, the reign of Daryavesh. The role played by verse 4:24 is that of "resumptive repetition." This is the interpretation adopted in the *Ezra*

◆ ◆ ◆

But what about the secular sources? Was there any Persian king known as Achashverosh or something close to that in these sources?

Until the nineteenth century, a search outside the Bible for a Persian king named Achashverosh or something close to that would have been unsuccessful. The information about the Persian kings from the Biblical period came entirely from Greek historians, and none of the names that they recorded were close to Achashverosh. The Greek historians (Herodotus, mid-fifth century B.C.E, and the others who came after him) described the following kings as reigning during the early Persian period (=the Biblical period): Cyrus, Cambyses,[9] Darius, Xerxes, and Artaxerxes.[10]

Historians were thus left to speculate as to the identity of Achashverosh. It did not seem reasonable to identify him with Cyrus or Darius, since these would most reasonably be identified with the כורש and the דריוש of the book of Ezra. But with regard to the remaining kings, was Achashverosh to be equated with Artaxerxes? This was the Septuagint's position in the book of Esther. Was he to be equated with Cambyses? Or was he, as Ezra 4:5-7 implied, the king between Daryavesh and Artachshasta. But why did the Greeks refer to this king

---

ve-Nechemiah commentary in the *Daat Mikra* edition (pp. 27 and 35), and is the interpretation adopted by many modern scholars. See the references at Richard Steiner, "Bishlam's Archival Search Report in Nehemiah's Archive: Multiple Introductions and Reverse Chronological Order as Clues to the Origin of the Aramaic Letters in Ezra 4-6," *JBL* 125 (2006), pp. 641-85 (674, n. 164). This understanding of the fourth chapter only became evident in modern times when it was realized that linguistically Achashverosh was to be identified with Xerxes.

An Old Persian cuneiform foundation inscription records that the palace at Shushan (the one referred to throughout the Megillah) was built by Daryavesh (=Darius I). This also confirms that Achashverosh could not have preceded Daryavesh.

9. For a short period before and after the death of Cambyses, Gaumata (also referred to as Smerdis and Bardiya) pretended to be the brother of Cambyses and reigned for several months. He was assassinated in a conspiracy by Darius and six others. Darius was a distant relative of Cambyses. One can view the reign of Gaumata as implied in verse 4:5 as well.

10. Darius II is also probably mentioned in the Bible, at Neh. 12:22.

as Xerxes, a name that at first glance seems to have no relation to the name Achashverosh?

It was only in the nineteenth century, as a result of the decipherment of Old Persian cuneiform, that these questions could be answered.[11] It was discovered that the name of the king that the Greeks had been referring to as "Xerxes" was in fact "Khshayarsha."[12] This name is very close to אחשורוש. In their consonantal structure, the two names are identical. Both center on the consonantal sounds *kh*, *sh*, *r*, and *sh*. The Hebrew added an initial *aleph* (a frequent occurrence when foreign words with two initial consonants are recorded in Hebrew[13]), and added

11. The main work in the decipherment of Old Persian cuneiform was done by Henry Rawlinson in the 1830's and 1840's. But others had made contributions prior to this. See, e.g., Edwin M. Yamauchi, *Persia and the Bible* (Grand Rapids: 1990), pp. 134-135, and Robert William Rogers, *History of Babylonia and Assyria* (New York and Cincinnati: 1900), vol. 1, pp. 46-83. The main text which enabled the decipherment of Old Persian cuneiform, and subsequently of Elamite and Akkadian cuneiform, was a lengthy trilingual text (with an accompanying relief) composed at the instruction of Darius I. It was inscribed on the rockface at Behistun, overlooking a main road leading to Hamadan.

12. To see what Khshayarsha's name looked like in Old Persian cuneiform, see, e.g., the photo at Landy, p. 41. The name in Old Persian means "ruling over heroes" or "he who rules over men" (Yamauchi, p. 187). This suggests that this was not the name he was born with, but was a throne name. See, e.g., Richard N. Frye, *The History of Ancient Iran* (München: 1983), p. 106. The names Darius and Artachshasta (in their original Persian forms) may have been throne names as well. See Frye, ibid., and Milikowsky, vol. 2, p. 505, n. 6. (Our first attested source of a Persian king taking on a throne name is the case of Darius II. The Greek historians report that his original name was Ochus. Babylonian texts now show that it was Umakush.)

13. Another instance where Hebrew added an initial *aleph* to an Old Persian word beginning with "khsh" is the word אחשדרך (satrap). See Yamauchi, p. 178. The noun אחשדרך appears four times in the Megillah, in various forms, all with an initial *aleph*. Another such instance is the word אחשתרנים, at Est. 8:10 and 8:14. This word is probably derived from the Old Persian word *khshatra*, which means "royal." See, e.g., Zvi Ron, "*Ha'Achashtranim Bnei Ha'Ramachim:* Translating Esther 8:10," *Jewish Bible Quarterly* 36:1 (2008), pp. 33-38 (36), and Yamauchi, p. 241.

Both the Elamite and the Akkadian versions of the king's name also have an initial vowel sound. In Elamite, the name has an initial "i" sound, and in Akkadian, the name usually has an initial "a" sound See, e.g., Yamauchi, p. 187, and George G. Cameron, "Darius and Xerxes in Babylonia," *The*

two *vavs*.[14] Interestingly, the Megillah spells Achashverosh several times with only one *vav*[15] and one time (10:1) with no *vavs*.[16]

Later, at the beginning of the twentieth century, Aramaic documents from Egypt from the fifth century B.C.E. came to light. In these documents, this king's name was spelled חשיארש, חשירש, and אחשירש.[17] The close resemblance to the name אחשורוש is easily seen.

How did Khshayarsha (consonants: *kh*, *sh*, *r*, *sh*) come to be referred to by the Greeks as Xerxes?

- The Greek language does not have a letter to represent the *sh* sound.
- The initial sounds *kh* and *sh* of the Persian name were collapsed into one Greek letter (ξ) that made the *ks* sound. A tendency to parallelism probably led the second *sh* to become *ks*, even though *s* would have been more appropriate.[18] Thus, the consonants became *ks*, *r*, and *ks*.[19]

American Journal of Semitic Languages and Literatures 58 (1941), pp. 314-25 (322). Many of the inscriptions of Khshayarsha were composed in three languages: Old Persian, Elamite and Akkadian.

The name of the king is found in Aramaic in the panels of the Dura-Europos synagogue (third century C.E., Syria) without the initial *aleph*. (The name varies in other ways here as well.)

14. Probably, the first *vav* was an approximation of the "y" in "Khshayarsha," and the second *vav* was added to facilitate the pronunciation of the *resh*, *shin* ending (Danziger, p. 12). At that time, *vav* was pronounced "w."

15. At 2:21, 3:12, 8:7, and 8:10. See R. Shelomoh Ganzfried, *Keset ha-Sofer* to 2:21, and R. Yedidiah Norzi, *Minchat Shai* to 2:21. (The Koren *Tanakh* originally had two *vavs* at 2:21, but this was corrected in later editions.)

16. The spelling with both *vavs* is found twenty-four times.

17. See Bezalel Porten and Jerome A. Lund, *Aramaic Documents from Egypt: A Key-Word-in-Context Concordance* (Winona Lake, Ind.: 2002), p. 356. The name of the king has also been discovered in Egyptian. It is similar. See William H. Shea, "Esther and History," *Andrews University Seminary Studies* 14 (1976), pp. 227-46 (228).

18. The transmission of foreign names is by no means an exact science, as shown by how the name of the successor to Xerxes was transmitted by the Greeks. The Greeks preserved the "Arta" of his Persian name, Artakhshaça, but with regard to the rest of his name, they just tacked on "xerxes," the name of his father.

19. The Greek letter ξ that reflects the *ks* sound is represented by convention in English today as "x." (χ is a different Greek letter.)

- The *-es* at the end was just something added by the Greeks to help turn the foreign name into a conventional Greek form.[20] (It is for this same reason that the Hebrew משה became "Moses" when the Bible was translated into Greek.)

Identifying Khshayarsha/Xerxes with Achashverosh thus makes much sense on linguistic grounds. Critically, it is consistent with Ezra 4:5-7 which places Achashverosh between Daryavesh (=Darius I) and Artachshasta (=Artaxerxes I).[21] This is exactly when Xerxes reigned.

Now that Achashverosh has been identified in secular sources, further background to the Megillah is available. Xerxes reigned from 486-465 B.C.E., when the Temple was already rebuilt. It was rebuilt in the reign of his father Darius I in 516 B.C.E. According to Herodotus (VII, 3), Xerxes was the son of Darius by Atossa, daughter of Cyrus. Xerxes was also the first son born to Darius after Darius became king. These factors distinguished him from his older half-brother Artabazanes, and merited Xerxes being chosen to succeed Darius. At his accession in 486 B.C.E., Xerxes could not have been more than 36 years old.[22]

The party at which Vashti rebelled took place in the third year of the reign of Achashverosh (1:3), and Esther was not chosen until the seventh year (2:16). Why did it take Achashverosh so long to choose a replacement? It has been suggested that Xerxes was distracted by his foreign policy. In the early years of his reign, Xerxes ordered a full-scale invasion of Greece.[23] Xerxes went on the invasion himself, which

---

It is striking that the name of Xerxes was transliterated as שרשן in the book of *Yosippon* (tenth century), i.e., the *ks*, *r*, *ks* was transliterated into שרש. Without realizing it, *Yosippon* essentially solved the problem of the identification of Achashverosh. (Of course, *Yosippon* referred to אחשורוש as well, and clearly viewed him as a different king than שרשן.)

20. Sometimes other endings were used, such as -on, for example, שלמה became "Solomon."

21. Also, we have an inscription from Khshayarsha that lists the countries over which he ruled. Among the countries listed are Hidush and Kushiya. See, e.g., Roland G. Kent, *Old Persian*, p. 151 (New Haven: 1953). These are most likely the Hodu and Kush of the Megillah. (This is a trilingual inscription. Hidush and Kushiya are what these countries were called in the Old Persian version.)

22. Since he was born after the accession of Darius in 522 B.C.E.

23. Many find allusions in the Megillah to the preparation for the invasion and to the invasion. See, e.g., Est. 1:3 and 10:2.

took him out of Persia commencing in the spring or summer of his fifth year[24] and continuing through part of his seventh year. This invasion ended in defeat.

Based on the material in Herodotus, it has been estimated that Xerxes did not arrive back in Susa (=Shushan) until the fall of 479 B.C.E.[25] According to the Megillah (2:16), Esther was taken to the palace in Tevet of the seventh year of Achashverosh, which would have been about Jan. 478 B.C.E.[26] Accordingly, Esther was taken to the palace shortly after Xerxes' return.[27]

Herodotus (VII, 89) mentions the Syrians of Palestine as contributing vessels to Xerxes' fleet. In two other places where Herodotus refers to Syrians, or Syrians of Palestine, the Jews are implied. See Menachem Stern, *Greek and Latin Authors on Jews and Judaism*, vol. 1 (Jerusalem: 1974), pp. 1-5. But the reference at VII, 89 cannot be a reference to the Jews, since the Jews did not live on the coast in this era. (Or if Herodotus did intend a reference to the Jews, he was mistaken.) Josephus, *Against Apion* (I, 172-75), claims that the Jews were one of the groups listed by the fifth-century B.C.E. Greek historian Choerilus as taking part in the invasion of Xerxes. But Josephus' interpretation of Choerilus is mistaken. See Stern, pp. 5-6.

24. Shea, p. 233.

25. See, e.g., Shea, p. 239, and Robert B. Strassler, ed., *The Landmark Herodotus* (New York: 2007), p. 718. We are aided by the allusion in Herodotus (IX, 10) to a partial solar eclipse. This eclipse can be dated to Oct. 2, 480 B.C.E. See Shea, p. 233, Strassler, p. 669 and Yamauchi, p. 214. According to Herodotus (IX, 108), Xerxes first retreated to Sardis and stayed there for a period before he returned to Susa.

The later and unreliable historian Ctesias, after mentioning Sardis, mentions a stop by Xerxes in Babylon, on his way back to Persia. On this possible stop, see Amélie Kuhrt, *The Persian Empire* (London and New York: 2007), pp. 249 and 295.

In the Persian system of regnal reckoning, 485 B.C.E. was year 1 of Xerxes. 486 B.C.E. was only the accession year. I am making the reasonable assumption that the years for Achashverosh mentioned in the Megillah are following the Persian system of reckoning.

26. It has been estimated that on the Babylonian calendar (which was not the same as the calendar used by the Jews and not necessarily the one referred to in the Megillah), Tevet of the seventh year of Xerxes ran from Dec. 22, 479 B.C.E. to Jan. 20, 478 B.C.E. See Shea, p. 234, and Richard A. Parker and Waldo H. Dubberstein, *Babylonian Chronology 626 B.C.-A.D. 75* (Providence: 1956), p. 31.

27. The long preparation time for the maidens before they would see the king is now even more understandable. Xerxes was out of the country

Is there any evidence in secular sources for the main plot of the Purim story, the threat to destroy the Jews in the twelfth year (3:7)? There is not, but this is to be expected. No works from any Persian historians from this period (=the Achaemenid period) have survived. Probably, no such works were ever composed. With regard to the Greek historian Herodotus, his main interest was Xerxes' invasion, and this ended in 479 B.C.E. A leading Achaemenid period scholar has written: "[T]he abrupt end of the *Histories* in 479 leaves the historian of the Achaemenid Empire something of an orphan."[28]

This does not mean that are no references to events after the seventh year of Xerxes in Herodotus. But when these references occur, they are brief and only tangential to the main narrative.[29]

One might expect to find information about subsequent events in the reign of Xerxes in the history of Persia composed by the later Greek historian Ctesias. A little background about Ctesias is necessary.

Ctesias served as one of the physicians for the Persian king Artaxerxes II (404-358 B.C.E.). The circumstances of how he began his service for this king are unclear.[30] But it seems that he left the

---

when the preparations began. (It is somewhat surprising that the Megillah does not mention that Xerxes was now returning after having been at war and out of the country. But the Megillah may have been composed decades later, and the war was perhaps not otherwise relevant to the narrative.)

Interestingly, the Septuagint has Esther being taken "in the twelfth month, which is Adar." Shea, p. 235.

28. Pierre Briant, *From Cyrus to Alexander*, trans. by Peter T. Daniels (Winona Lake, Ind.: 2002), p. 7.

29. For example, he mentions Artaxerxes a few times, and he tells a story about Amestris when she was advanced in years. The last events he refers to are from the first two years of the Peloponnesian War. This war commenced in 431 B.C.E.

Material dating from the reign of Xerxes is found in his royal inscriptions, and in the Persepolis Treasury Tablets, and in other cuneiform and Aramaic texts, but these provide little concrete history. See Shea, pp. 229-230.

30. The first-century B.C.E. historian Diodorus writes (II, 32,4) that Ctesias was captured by Artaxerxes II and spent seventeen years in his service. But this length of time is certainly incorrect. Some scholars disregard this statement by Diodorus altogether and suggest that Ctesias was invited to serve Artaxerxes II.

The various sources that refer to Ctesias only refer to him as a physician for Artaxerxes II and his family. But it seems doubtful that a Persian king would allow a complete Greek newcomer to be a physician to the king and his family. It has been suggested that Ctesias held other positions first.

Persian court in 398/397 B.C.E. at the latest,[31] and wrote his history of Persia thereafter in his home city of Cnidus, in Asia Minor.[32] Practically nothing of this 23-book work has survived. We are forced to rely on references to it and summaries by others. Our source for the material in Ctesias for the part of the Persian period that concerns us (the reigns of Darius, Xerxes and Artaxerxes I) is a summary by Photius, a ninth-century Byzantine scholar.[33]

---

31. See Jan P. Stronk, *Ctesias' Persian History: Part I: Introduction, Text, and Translation* (Düsseldorf: 2010), p. 6, and Briant, p. 265. (Part II of Stronk's work, a commentary on Ctesias, is forthcoming.)

32. We do not know exactly when it was composed. See Stronk, p. 11, n. 27, for some estimates.

Ctesias claims to have had access to royal Persian historical records. See Diodorus II, 32,4. (But a passage in Photius seems to imply otherwise. See Stronk, p. 201.) Whether such records existed and whether Ctesias could have read them (although Persians could have read and translated for him) are matters of debate. Even assuming such records existed, a further issue is whether Ctesias conceived of this work already during his stay in Persia. See Stronk, p. 34. If he did not, he would not have had access to such records upon his return home, and would probably not have had any notes or summaries either. (Stronk believes that Ctesias did conceive of this work while in Persia and was able to make notes.)

33. The summary is included in a long letter by Photius to his brother in which he summarizes 279 different works. Photius' summaries are usually, but not always, reliable. See, e.g., Joan M. Bigwood, "Ctesias' Account of the Revolt of Inarus," *Phoenix* 30 (1976), pp. 1-25 (3-4), and Stronk, pp. 143-148. We can determine the reliability of the summaries because many of the works summarized have been preserved. Almost certainly, Photius had no motive to alter the basic content of the material, even though he left out much. Stronk, pp. 143-148. It is very possible that Photius no longer had access to Ctesias' history of Persia when he was composing his summary, and based his summary only on memory and notes made many years before. Even if he still had access to Ctesias' work, he may not have had time to consult it, as the summaries were composed in a relatively hurried manner. See below, n. 99.

In my references to the summary of Ctesias by Photius, I have not troubled to cite paragraph numbers. All the relevant passages are easily found, whatever edition of Photius/Ctesias is used. In Stronk's edition, the passages referred to are found at pp. 327-45. When I quote a passage from Ctesias, I am following Stronk's translation.

The only events of the reign of Xerxes after 479 B.C.E. that we learn of from this summary is that the daughter of Xerxes was accused of an extramarital affair by her husband, and that Xerxes reprimanded her for it.[34] Thereafter, the summary moves on to the assassination of Xerxes.[35] Later classical writers such as Diodorus (first century B.C.E.) and Justin[36] provide further details about the assassination of Xerxes,[37] but no one fills in the gap and describes other events of the reign of Xerxes after 479 B.C.E.[38]

◆ ◆ ◆

Verses 2:5-6 of the Megillah are sometimes raised as a difficulty with the identification of Achashverosh and Xerxes. They read:

> 5. There was an *ish yehudi* in Shushan the castle, whose name was Mordechai, son of Yair, son of Shimi, son of Kish, *ish yemini.* 6. Who had been exiled from Jerusalem with the captives that had been carried away with Yekhanyah, king of Judah....

---

34. Perhaps this occurred in 479 B.C.E. as well. It is unclear because the events from 479 B.C.E. to the assassination are all condensed into a few lines.
35. The accusation was mentioned because it related to the accession of Artaxerxes. We are told that the son-in-law of Xerxes was bitterly aggrieved because of the suspected adultery. This led him to take part in a conspiracy to kill Artaxerxes shortly after Artaxerxes was enthroned.
36. Justin III, 1 (*Marcus Junianus Justinus*, ed. Rev. John Selby Watson, London: 1853). The exact period Justin's work was composed is unknown; it was sometime between the second and fourth centuries. His work was an abridgement of an earlier work (now lost) by the Roman historian Pompeius Trogus, composed in the late first century B.C.E.
37. There are contradictions between these sources on various details about the assassination. See Briant, pp. 563-64. The assassination of Xerxes and some of these contradictions will be discussed further below.
38. Briant, p. 516. Thucydides (c. 460 to 400 B.C.E.) mentions Xerxes a few times. All but one of the references are very brief. The one reference that is not brief (I, 128-29) covers an event that occurred not long after 479 B.C.E. The references to Xerxes in Xenophon (c. 430 to 350 B.C.E.) are very brief.

If Mordechai was exiled with Yekhanyah in 597 B.C.E., he would have been over 120 years old when appointed to a high position in the twelfth year of Xerxes. Moreover, his first cousin Esther would surely not have been young enough to have been the one chosen by Xerxes a few years earlier.

A solution is to interpret the teaching of verse 6 to be that Mordechai's great-grandfather Kish was the one who was exiled.[39] This would be consistent with youthful ages for Mordechai and Esther during the reign of Xerxes. In this interpretation, the phrase *ish yemini* refers to Kish and switches the subject away from Mordechai, the *ish yehudi. Ish yehudi* was a general term for a Jew by the time the Megillah was authored[40] (probably the fifth cent. B.C.E.), so an *ish yehudi* could have been described as descending from an *ish yemini*. If the name Mordechai derives from the name of the Babylonian deity Marduk, as many have suggested, it would be much more likely that it was given to one born in exile than to one born in Israel.[41]

---

39. See Aaron J. Koller, "The Exile of Kish: Syntax and History in Esther 2.5-6," *JSOT* 37:1 (2012), pp. 45-56. See also *Chamesh Megillot* (*Daat Mikra*), commentary to Est. 2:6.

It is worth noting that the Greek translation of Esther has a few additional sections and in one such section ("the first addition"), it is stated explicitly that Mordechai was exiled with Yekhanyah. Also, the implication of the Greek translation of Est. 2:6 is that Mordechai was the one who was exiled with Yekhanyah. See Koller, p. 48.

40. See *The Five Megilloth* (London: 1946, Soncino edition), commentary to Est. 2:5, and Adele Berlin, *The JPS Bible Commentary: Esther* (Philadelphia: 2001), p. 24.

41. Some might argue that the Kish referred to at 2:5 is not the great-grandfather of Mordechai, but the father of Saul, and that the genealogy specified was a greatly abbreviated one. (At 1 Sam. 9:1, Kish, the father of Saul, is referred to as descending from an *ish yemini*.) In this view, the subject of verse 6 is Mordechai. If the subject of verse 6 is Mordechai, the teaching of the verse can be merely that Mordechai came from a family that had been exiled. See, e.g., *The Five Megilloth* (Soncino edition), commentary to Est. 2:6, and *Chamesh Megillot* (*Daat Mikra*), commentary to Est. 2:6 (second interpretation).

PART II. IDENTIFYING ESTHER

In Part I, it was shown that Achashverosh is to identified with the king the Greeks had called "Xerxes." This was determined when it was discovered that the name of the king that the Greeks had been calling "Xerxes" was in fact "Khshayarsha" in Old Persian. Now it is time to identify Esther.

The only wife of Xerxes referred to by Herodotus is named Amestris. He mentions her in three contexts:

- At VII, 61, in the context of a detailed account of Xerxes' invasion force, he writes that the Persian contingent of the army was commanded by Otanes,[42] who was the father of Xerxes' wife Amestris.[43]

42. According to Ctesias, the name of the father of Amestris was Onophas. (Ctesias also mentions an Onophas as one of the six who conspired with Darius, and as a naval commander in Xerxes' invasion. Perhaps he viewed some or all of these as the same individual.) But it is widely accepted that Herodotus recorded the names of the Persians much more accurately than Ctesias did. For example, as can be determined from the inscription of Darius I at Behistun, Herodotus correctly named five of the six individuals who conspired with Darius. See Briant, p. 108. Ctesias only recorded the names of two of these individuals correctly, although in two instances (his recording of the names Onophas and Mardonius), his mistake may be only that he named the son instead of the father. See, e.g., Kuhrt, p. 170, and Herodotus' reference at VII, 62 to "Anaphes son of Otanes."
43. A translation of the Greek here is: "they were commanded by Otanes, the father of Xerxes' wife Amestris." This is the translation followed in most editions. But the structure of the Greek sentence is ambiguous and there is another possible translation: "[t]heir commander was Otanes, father of Xerxes' wife and son of Amestris." In this alternate translation, Xerxes' wife is unnamed, and Amestris is a man. This alternate translation is followed in the Loeb Classical Library edition (ed. A.D. Godley, Cambridge, Mass. and London, 1920-25), and in a few other editions. But the only wife of Xerxes that Herodotus ever mentions is Amestris, and it would be too coincidental for the commander to have been the son of someone named Amestris as well. This makes the alternate translation very unlikely. Briant, who is perhaps the foremost modern scholar of the Achaemenid period, follows the first translation, as does Kuhrt. See Briant, p. 135 and Kuhrt, p. 520. This passage does not necessarily imply that Amestris was already the wife of Xerxes at the time of the invasion.

- At VII, 114, after mentioning that Xerxes' invasion force entered a town called Nine Ways, he writes:

> There, learning that Nine Ways was the name of the place, they [=the Persians] buried alive that number of boys and maidens, children of the people of the country. To bury alive is a Persian custom; I have heard that when Xerxes' wife Amestris attained to old age she buried fourteen sons of notable Persians, as a thanks-offering on her own behalf to the fabled god of the nether world.[44]

- At IX, 108-113, he tells a story depicting the cruelty of Amestris. The following is a brief outline of the story:

> While at Sardis, Xerxes fell in love with the wife of his brother Masistes. (Sardis was where Xerxes resided temporarily after he began his retreat from the invasion, but before he returned to Susa.) The wife of Masistes rejects his advances. Xerxes then arranges a marriage between his son Darius and the daughter of Masistes, thinking that this would eventually help him seduce the mother. The story continues at Susa, with the exact time of the continuation unspecified.[45] In the continuation, Amestris gives Xerxes a beautiful robe which she had woven with her own hand. By this time, Xerxes had transferred his affections to the daughter, now married to his son Darius, and Xerxes was successful in having an affair with her. Xerxes ends up giving the daughter the robe. When Amestris finds out, she takes revenge on the mother.[46] She sends for the soldiers of the royal bodyguard and has the mother mutilated. Many of her body parts are ordered cut off and are thrown to the dogs. When

44. Loeb edition.
45. "But as time went on the truth came to light..." (IX, 109, Loeb edition).
46. Herodotus writes (IX, 110, Loeb edition):

> [W]hen she learnt the truth, her anger was not with the girl; **she supposed rather that the girl's mother was guilty and that this was her doing,** and so it was Masistes' wife that she plotted to destroy.

Exactly what Herodotus means in the passage I have bolded is unclear.

Masistes sees what was done to his wife, he decides to stir up a revolt against Xerxes. In the end, Xerxes' forces kill Masistes, his sons, and all the men under his command.

Ctesias refers to only one wife of Xerxes, and that is Amestris. The following is a summary of what Ctesias reports about her:[47]

- Amestris outlived Xerxes and died at an advanced age.
- After years of pestering, Amestris is finally able to convince her son[48] Artaxerxes to let her avenge the death of another son Achaemenides. She is able to have fifty Greeks decapitated and their leader Inarus impaled, in revenge for Inarus and his men having slain Achaemenides five years earlier, when Inarus had led a revolt.
- She orders the murderer of her grandchild impaled.
- She is given the authority by Artaxerxes to punish a physician who deceived her daughter Amytis into having sexual relations with

47. From this point on, I will refer to the material from Ctesias as if it is coming directly from him, even though it is really coming from the ninth-century summary by Photius.

Interestingly, all the events involving Amestris that are described occur in the reign of Artaxerxes. The only reference to Amestris in the reign of Xerxes is a brief statement at the beginning which states that Xerxes married Amestris, who was the daughter of Onophas, and provides the names of the children they had together. I will discuss this passage below.

48. Ctesias refers to Amestris and Artaxerxes as mother and son several times. It would be very surprising if he was wrong about this relationship. Artaxerxes reigned over 40 years, until 424 B.C.E. This was not long before the time Ctesias served in the Persian court. If we believe Ctesias, Amestris was alive and influential for a large part of the reign of Artaxerxes. Plato (fourth century B.C.E.) also refers to Amestris and Artaxerxes as mother and son. See his *Alcibiades*, I, para. 123C (Loeb Classical Library edition). (But perhaps he only learned this from Ctesias.)

If Amestris was the mother of Artaxerxes I, this means that he was technically a Jew. (Although I am not suggesting that he knew the *aleph-bet* or had *bar-mitzvah* lessons!) Perhaps it is more than coincidence that he empowered Ezra and later Nehemiah. On the other hand, he also issued a decree ordering the cessation of work (see Ezra 4:7-23). Presumably, this was before his later authorization of this work to Nehemiah (see Yamauchi, p. 251).

him; she orders him kept in chains and tortured for two months, and eventually buried alive.

- She was frequently intimate with men.[49]
- She is able to convince Artaxerxes to forgive Amytis' husband Megabyzus on various occasions.

Neither Herodotus nor Ctesias uses a term like "queen" for Amestris,[50] but neither gives any indication that Xerxes had any other wife.[51]

◆ ◆ ◆

One approach to reconciling this material with the material in the Megillah is to identify Amestris with Vashti.[52] But this identification is extremely unlikely. According to the Megillah (1:19), the punishment of Vashti was that "she would come no more before king Achashverosh,

---

49. The passage reads: "Amytis, like her mother Amestris before her, was frequently intimate with men." The implication is licentiousness or perhaps even nymphomania.
50. It seems that the Persians did not have a concept of a queen, i.e., a wife of the king with special rights solely because she was the wife of the king. Nevertheless, being the mother of the designated heir to the throne gave such a wife some special status. See Briant, pp. 520 and 920, Maria Brosius, *Women in Ancient Persia* (Oxford and New York: 1996), p. 69, and Robert L. Hubbard, Jr., "Vashti, Amestris and Esther 1,9," *Zeitschrift Fur Die Alttestamentliche Wissenschaft* 119/2 (2007), pp. 259-71 (267). It is likely that the female who held the most important position at the Persian court was the mother of the king, not the wife of the king. Brosius, p. 17.
51. Briant, p. 565. There is no indication that Xerxes had any other wife, unless we adopt the unlikely alternate translation of VII, 61 mentioned above, in which case an unnamed wife of Xerxes is referred to, who could be other than Amestris. There are references to illegitimate children of Xerxes. See Herodotus VIII, 103, and Diodorus, XI, 60. But this only means that he had children through concubines. Also, Ctesias mentions an Artarios who he describes as the satrap at Babylon and as a brother of Artarxerxes. Since Ctesias does not list Artarios among the children of Xerxes and Amestris, Artarios also seems to have been an illegitimate child of Xerxes (unless he was perhaps a son of Vashti).
52. A main advocate of this approach in the modern period is Shea, pp. 235-242. For references to some others who take this approach, see Yamauchi, pp. 230-232.

and *malkhutah* would be given by the king to another...." The severe demotion implied here, commencing from the third year of Achashverosh, does not match the depictions of Amestris in Herodotus and Ctesias. In Herodotus, she gives Xerxes a beautiful robe and still has authority over soldiers from the royal bodyguard years after any supposed severe demotion. In Ctesias, she is still influential and powerful at court in the reign of Artaxerxes.

Another approach is to postulate that Esther was never the main wife of Xerxes, but one of other wives of lesser status.[53] Support for this might be found in verse 2:19, which refers to a second gathering of maidens after Esther was chosen. Also, verse 4:11 records that Esther had not been called to the king for 30 days. Gavriel Chaim Cohen, in his introduction to the book of Esther in the *Daat Mikra* edition of the *Chamesh Megillot*, relies on these verses and takes such an approach.[54]

The problem with this approach is that the clear impression that one receives from the Megillah is that Esther *was* the Persian wife of the highest status from the time she was chosen in the seventh year of the reign of Achashverosh through the balance of the years described in the book. Verse 2:17 states: *va-yasem keter malkhut be-roshah va-yamlikheha tachat Vashti*. Thereafter, in chapters 2 through 9, she is called *ha-malkah* 17 times.[55]

---

53. Even though no such other wives of Xerxes of other status are ever mentioned.

54. *Chamesh Megillot* (*Daat Mikra*), introduction to Esther, p. 6. See also, P. Korngrin, "*Megillat Esther le-Or ha-Papyrusim mi-Yeiv ve-Sippurei Herodut*," in Eliezer Eliner, et al, eds., *Sefer Zeidel* (Jerusalem: 1962), pp. 214-28. Such an approach was suggested long ago by J.A. M'Clymont in the *Dictionary of the Bible*, ed. James Hastings (New York: 1899), vol. 1, p. 773: "The most tenable hypothesis seems to be that E. (as well as Vashti) was merely the chief favourite of the seraglio." (I am sure that this approach was suggested prior to this source as well.)

Stephen Gabriel Rosenberg, *Esther Ruth Jonah Deciphered* (Jerusalem and New York: 2004), p. 71, suggests that Amestris was the chief wife in Persepolis, the main palace, while Esther was the chief wife in the palace of Shushan.

55. At 2:22, 4:4, 5:2, 5:3, 5:12, 7:1, 7:2, 7:3, 7:5, 7:6, 7:7, 7:8, 8:1, 8:7, 9:12, 9:29, and 9:31. Her elevated status is also implied in other ways. See, e.g., 4:14, 5:3, 5:6, and 7:2.

The approach that has the least difficulties is to identify Amestris with Esther.[56]

First, let us begin with an analysis of the name.[57] Close examination

---

56. This identification was suggested long ago by Joseph Justus Scaliger (1540-1609), and by others in the centuries after him (see, e.g., M'Clymont, p. 773). It is rarely suggested by scholars today, since most do not believe in the historicity of the story or the existence of Esther at all. The idea that a Persian king could have had a Jewish queen is usually considered too implausible. Moreover, Herodotus reports an agreement between Darius I and his six co-conspirators that the Persian king would not marry outside their families. But see my discussion below.

One modern scholar who seriously considers the identification of Esther with Amestris is Robert Gordis. See his "Religion, Wisdom and History in the Book of Esther—A New Solution to an Ancient Crux," *JBL* 100 (1981), pp. 359-88 (384-85). Also, in an article published in 2007 (see above, n. 50), Robert Hubbard Jr. carefully reviewed all the evidence from Herodotus and came to the conclusion that, while the identification of Amestris with Vashti is unlikely, the identification with Esther remains a possibility. (Hubbard wrote that he was not considering any statement by Ctesias, due to Ctesias' unreliablity.)

In the Orthodox world, I have found the following:

- *Trei Asar* (*Daat Mikra*), vol. 2 (1976) includes a brief suggestion that Esther may be Amestris, without any discussion. See above, n. 3. The appendix section of the work, where this suggestion is found, was authored by Mordechai Zer Kavod.
- I raised the identification as a possibility in my *Jewish History in Conflict* (Northvale, N.J.: 1997), pp. 176-78.
- R. Yigal Ariel, *Mor ve-Hadas* (Chispin: 2000), p. 291, n. 32, briefly makes the suggestion, commenting on the resemblance of the names.
- *Ezra ve-Nechemiah* (*Daat Mikra*) (1980), appendix p. 14, authored by Mordechai Zer-Kavod, includes a line that the mother of Artachshtata was named אמסתר. This probably reflects an identification of her with Esther. This author realized that the *-is* in Amestris was just a Greek addition, and he wrote the name with a ת, not a ט, thereby making it closer to אסתר. See also Zer-Kavod, *Sifrei Ezra ve-Nechemiah* (Jerusalem: 1949), p. 173.

57. There are no cuneiform sources (Persian, Akkadian or Elamite) that refer to the wife of Khshayarsha. A landowning Persian woman named Am-mi-is-ri-' or A-mi-si-ri-' is mentioned in Babylonian texts from Nippur from 431/30 and 423/22 B.C.E. See Brosius, p. 128 (texts BE 9 39 and 10 45). Also, a text from the 34th year of Artaxerxes I records that the Murašu

of the name "Amestris"[58] supports its identification with Esther. The *-is* at the end was surely just a suffix added to turn the foreign name into a conventional Greek form,[59] just as *-es* was added at the end of "Xerxes." When comparing the remaining consonants, the name of the wife of Xerxes as recorded in Herodotus and Ctesias is based around the consonants *m*, *s*, *t*, and *r*, and the name as recorded in the Megillah is based around the consonants *s*, *t*, and *r*. **Out of the numerous possible consonants in these languages, three consonants are the same and in the same order.** Mathematically, this is overwhelmingly a match.[60] It is extremely unlikely to attribute this to coincidence. Probably, her original name was based on the consonants *m*, *s*, *t*, and *r*, and the *m* did not get preserved in the Hebrew.[61]

---

firm requested rights to draw off water that belonged to the king and to *A-mi-si-ri-'* in order to irrigate land that the firm had leased. See Matthew W. Stolper, *Enterpreneurs and Empire: The Murašû Archive, The Murašû Firm, and Persian Rule in Babylonia* (Leiden and Istanbul: 1985), p. 231 (text CBS 5199). It has been suggested that *Am-mi-is-ri-'/A-mi-si-ri-'* is Amestris. But others believe that this identification is too speculative. See, e.g., Stolper, p. 64 and Hubbard, p. 262, n. 18. One who leans towards the identification is Ran Zadok. He suggests that, over time, *str* became *sr*. See his "Old Iranian Anthroponyms and Related Material in Late Babylonian Sources," *Revue d'assyriologie et d'archéologie orientale* 98 (2004), pp. 109-120 (109-110). (The description of CBS 5199 in Brosius is misleading. *A-mi-si-ri-'* is only mentioned once in CBS 5199, at line 5. Stolper's inclusion of her name in line 4 seems to be only a conjecture. Brosius described only line 4 of CBS 5199, when she should have described line 5.)

58. In Greek: Αμηστρις.

59. Many who attempt to locate Esther in secular sources do not realize this. For example, it is evident to me that neither Gavriel Chaim Cohen (the author of the introduction to Esther in the *Chamesh Megillot, Daat Mikra* edition) nor Korngrin realized this.

60. It is ironic that many scholars reject the identification of Esther and Amestris based on the superficial dissimilarity of the names, when close analysis of the names reveals that they are essentially a match!

61. This is not unusual. Letters often drop when names go from one language to another.

It is of course possible that the omission of the initial *m* in the Hebrew was intentional. To cite another example, Judges chapter 3 refers to a foreign king named כושן רשעתים. It is hardly likely that the second word here reflects an exact transliteration of his original name. Much more likely, his name was transformed slightly so as to give the impression of one who

There is a contradiction, since the Megillah describes Esther as the daughter of Avichayil[62] while Herodotus states that her father was the military commander Otanes. But it is easy to postulate that Herodotus simply erred regarding her ancestry. Herodotus traveled widely in the 450's, but he never set foot in Persia.[63] He had to rely only on what he heard. Every scholar knows that he could not possibly be correct on a large percentage of the details he records (whether about the history of Persia or any matter). Also, the impression that one receives from the Megillah is that Esther did not disclose her true ancestry from the seventh year until the twelfth year. Whatever rumors first arose about her ancestry may have been what made their way to Herodotus.[64]

---

was "doubly wicked." In the case of *mstr*, it is at least possible that there was a desire to transform her name into one that more clearly alluded to the hidden (סתר) Divine involvement reflected in the book of Esther. I would like to thank Rachel Friedman for this suggestion.

62. 2:15 and 9:29.

63. Yamauchi, p. 77. See also Strassler, pp. x and xxvii-xxviii. Herodotus was born in Halicarnassus (now western Turkey). Halicarnassus was a part of the Persian empire for the early part of his life.

64. Also, it may have been in the interest of the Persian government to maintain a false ancestry for her and not to publicize that she was a Jewess.

It has often been argued that Esther could not have been the wife of Xerxes because Herodotus tells of an agreement between Darius I and his six co-conspirators that the Persian king would not marry outside these seven families (Herodotus III, 84). Herodotus names co-conspirator Otanes son of Pharnaspes as the head of one of these families. (Herodotus errs here on the father's name. In the Behistun inscription, the father's name is Thukra.) Of course, even if we believe Herodotus that there was such an agreement, and interpret the agreement as intended to bind all future Persian kings (an interpretation that is not mandatory, see Brosius, p. 63), this is the kind of agreement that would surely be violated when a king was attracted to a woman who was not from one of these families. More importantly, Herodotus nowhere states that the Otanes who was the father of Amestris was Otanes son of Pharnaspes. According to Briant (p. 135), it would have been unlikely that Darius would have consented to a marriage between Xerxes and a daughter of co-conspirator Otanes, due to its political ramifications, and if Amestris had been the daughter of co-conspirator Otanes, Herodotus would certainly have mentioned it. (Co-conspirator Otanes would also probably have been too old to lead a division at the time of the invasion.) Therefore, implicit in Herodotus is that Xerxes married outside the seven families. See also Kuhrt, pp. 247 and

The above contradiction with regard to her father's name should not at all be viewed as troublesome. Contradictions between ancient sources on details like this are to be expected. But it is striking that the name Avichayil means "military commander," and Otanes (the name Herodotus gives for Esther's father) was by profession a military commander.[65] Perhaps Avichayil had another name which included the consonants *T* and *N*. The Megillah tells us that Esther seems to have had both a Hebrew name and a Persian name.[66]

---

527. Herodotus refers to other Persians named Otanes. It seems to have been a common name.

It is noteworthy that Ctesias records the name of the father of Amestris as Onophas, and lists an Onophas as one of the conspirators, and also as one of Xerxes' naval commanders. Perhaps he identifies the father of Amestris with a conspirator. But Ctesias is extremely unreliable as a historian of the reigns of Darius and Xerxes. See below, nn. 78 and 108.

The many wives of Darius I also merit discussion. According to Herodotus, before his accession, Darius married a daughter of conspirator Gobryas. After his accession, he married two daughters of Cyrus (Atossa and Artystone), the daughter of Cyrus' son Smerdis (Parmys), a daughter of conspirator Otanes (Phaedyme), and the daughter of his brother Artanes (Phratagune). But archaeology has provided us with more information. Three Babylonian documents record a wife of Darius named Ap-pa-mu-ú (or Pa-am-mu-ú). Also, a woman named Irdabama (with a high position during the reign of Darius) is mentioned in several Elamite texts (see Brosius, pp. 127 and 129-44), and it is possible that she was a wife. It is possible that Ap-pa-mu-ú and Irdabama were not from the family of Cyrus or the families of the conspirators. But it has also been suggested that Ap-pa-mu-ú and Irdabama are the same individual. Moreover, one of these (or both, if they are the same individual) may be identical with the first wife of Darius, the daughter of Gobryas, whose name was not given by Herodotus. See Kuhrt, pp. 173 and 596-97, and Ran Zadok, "An Achaemenid queen," *Nouvelles Assyriologiques Brèves et Utilitaires* 2002/65, pp. 63-66 and "Updating the Appamu Dossier," *Nouvelles Assyriologiques Brèves et Utilitaires* 2003/33, pp. 30-33 (30-31).

65. I would like to thank Rabbi Richard Wolpoe who first made this observation to me.

66. 2:7 (Hadassah). For a discussion of the practice of Jews using both a Jewish and a Gentile name in this period, see Aaron Demsky, "Double Names in the Babylonian Exile and the Identity of Sheshbazzar," pp. 23-39, in Aaron Demsky, ed., *These are the Names: Studies in Jewish Onomastics*, vol. 2 (Ramat Gan:1999).

◆ ◆ ◆

Of course, we still need an approach to the unflattering stories told about Amestris by Herodotus and Ctesias.

In a fictional and satirical work, the ancient writer Lucian (second century C.E.) described visiting an island where dead people remain in perpetual punishment for crimes committed during their lives. He wrote:

> [A] terrible odour greeted us... a vile, insufferable stench as of roasting human flesh.... [W]e heard the noise of scourges and the wailing of many men...[W]e saw many kings undergoing punishment and many commoners too.... [T]he severest punishment of all fell to those who told lies while in life and those who had written what was not true, among them were Ctesias of Cnidos, Herodotus, and many more.[67]

I will try to take a more nuanced approach.

In Herodotus, the concern is mainly with one story,[68] that of the vengeance of Amestris on Masistes' wife. A few observations can be made:

1. There is no question that Herodotus had no hesitation in relaying stories of doubtful origin. He tells us (VII, 152): "my business [is] to set down that which is told me, to believe it is none at all of my business." Moreover, many ancient writers believed that he invented many of the stories he tells, and many modern scholars take the same position.[69]
2. In this particular story, it is clear that Herodotus was not an eyewitness to any of the events described.

---

67. *A True Story*, II, 29-31 (Loeb Classical Library edition). Lucian's comments may have been motivated more by Ctesias' history of India than by his history of Persia. See Stronk, p. 33, n. 65 and *A True Story*, I, 3.
68. The story about Amestris' burying fourteen children can easily be dismissed as mere folklore.
69. Herodotus, called the "Father of History" by Cicero in the first century B.C.E., has also been called the "Father of Lies." Josephus wrote that "everyone" attacks Herodotus. See his *Against Apion* (I, 3).

3. Herodotus, who identified himself as a Greek, was here writing about a royal woman of the Persians, the enemies of the Greeks. His depiction of Amestris should be considered polemical, and evaluated in this light.[70]
4. The story includes sensational and hard-to-believe elements; many different events are weaved together into one long tale.[71]
5. The stories that Herodotus tells about Atossa and Phaedyme, two of the wives of Darius, are highly unusual as well.[72]

---

70. Briant writes (p. 516) that Herodotus inserted the tale to foster "the image of a king subject to the nefarious influences of the women of the palace and more interested in slaking his guilty passions than in defending the territorial inheritance of Darius."

71. The story is much longer than I summarized it above. The notion that Amestris would take revenge on the mother for an affair by the daughter is one of the aspects that is particularly hard to believe. The notion that Xerxes would arrange a marriage for his son as a part of a scheme to seduce the bride's mother also strains credulity. Brosius raises some other difficulties, and calls it a "cryptic story" with "many problems." See Brosius, p. 113, n. 68, and the references there.

72. Herodotus writes (III, 133-35) that Atossa had a breast illness and was cured by a Greek physician whom Darius had previously captured and forced to work in the Persian court. The physician cured her on the condition that she give Darius the idea to invade Greece; this would give the physician a chance to return home and escape. Atossa did as told (and the physician eventually was able to escape as well). Thus, Herodotus has blamed Atossa for Darius' invasion of Greece.

With regard to Phaedyme, Herodotus (III, 68-69) tells the following story. For a short period before and after the death of Cambyses, Smerdis pretended to be the brother of Cambyses and reigned for several months. He took over all of Cambyses' wives, one of whom was Phaedyme. Smerdis bore a close resemblance to the brother of Cambyses, except that Smerdis' ears had previously been cut off. Phaedyme is asked by her father, a Persian noble, to feel for Smerdis' ears when he is asleep. Phaedyme determines that Smerdis has no ears, confirming that he was only a pretender.

Brosius writes (p. 69):

> [T]he women of the Achaemenid court were used by fifth- and fourth-century [Greek] writers to fill the gaps in the narratives and to add a bit of sensationalism.... We ought to be very cautious in accepting the image in which women of the Persian court are depicted.

For reasons such as this, serious doubts have been cast on the reliability of the story of Amestris and Masistes' wife.[73] A leading modern scholar on the Achaemenid period has written that "the story is a romance, characterized by a whole series of repetitive motifs on which it is extremely imprudent to base any historical extrapolation."[74]

With regard to the unflattering material about Amestris found in Ctesias, our ability to discredit this is even easier:

1. It has been argued that Ctesias was not writing a historical work but a novel based on a historical nucleus. In this approach, Ctesias is viewed as freely mixing fact and fiction.[75]
2. Even if we adopt the more likely approach that Ctesias was largely writing an historical work, a widespread view is that he

---

73. See, e.g., Hubbard, pp. 269-71 and the references there, particularly p. 269, n. 46.

74. Briant, p. 516. See also Heleen Sancisi-Weerdenburg, "Exit Atossa: Images of Women in Greek Historiography on Persia, in Averil Cameron and Amélie Kuhrt, eds., *Images of Women in Antiquity* (Detroit: 1983), p. 30:

> It is, of course, impossible to extract historical evidence from this story.... The few generally known data may have served as the backbone for a tale which was elaborated in the oral tradition using age-old motifs.... [This story] should be treated as literature and not as historiography.

It is noteworthy that some had used this story about the cruelty of Amestris to support the identification of Esther with Amestris. They usually based their argument on Est. 9:13, where Esther asks for an additional day of fighting in Shushan and for Haman's ten sons to be hanged. See, e.g., *Encyclopaedia Biblica*, eds. T.K. Cheyne, and J.S. Black (New York: 1901), vol. II, 1401: "It is true that the coarseness and cruelty of [Amestris] answer in some measure to the vindictive character of Esther." See also *The International Standard Bible Encyclopaedia*, ed. James Orr (Grand Rapids: 1952, revised edition), vol. 2, p. 1008. (There had been a tendency among early historians to accept this story about Amestris. It was the main story that Herodotus told about her. Disregarding it leaves one with little information about her from Herodotus.)

75. See, e.g., the discussion at Stronk, pp. 36-54, and at Lloyd Llewellyn-Jones and James Robson, eds., *Ctesias' History of Persia: Tales of the Orient* (London and New York: 2010), pp. 3-7, and 68-80.

freely interspersed his work (more than Herodotus did) with fictional and sensational elements to entertain his readers.[76]

3. Ctesias has traditionally been viewed as a very poor historian.[77] It has long been recognized that he makes numerous significant errors about events prior to his time.[78]

4. Ctesias was not an eyewitness to any event regarding Amestris. His service as a physician to Artaxerxes II was in the years around 400 B.C.E., probably around thirty years after the death of Amestris.[79]

5. Ctesias thought of himself as a Greek and was here writing about a royal woman of the Persians. As in the case of Herodotus, his depiction of Amestris should be evaluated as a polemical one. As one modern scholar has written:[80]

---

76. In the first century, Plutarch commented that Ctesias "put into his work a perfect farrago of extravagant and incredible tales," and "often his story turns aside from the truth into fable and romance." See Plutarch's *Lives* (Artaxerxes, paras. I and VI, Loeb Classical Library edition). Criticisms of Ctesias are found even earlier than this, in Aristotle (fourth cent. B.C.E., criticizing Ctesias' history of India) and Strabo (first cent B.C.E). See Llewellyn-Jones and Robson, pp. 100-102.

77. See, e.g., Yamauchi, p. 79, Bigwood, p. 1, and Stolper, p. 15 ("the common opinion of his veracity—both ancient and modern—is one of contempt"). A good summary of the attitudes towards Ctesias throughout the ages is found at Llewellyn-Jones and Robson, pp. 22-35.

78. Some of his most noteworthy errors are: 1) he did not realize that the monumental inscription at Behistun depicted Darius I; 2) he only recorded the names of two of the six co-conspirators of Darius correctly (while Herodotus was correct on five out of six); and 3) in his description of the invasion of Xerxes, he placed the battle of Plataea before the battle of Salamis. See also Bigwood's general evaluation of Ctesias' depiction of the wars of Darius and Xerxes, quoted below, n. 108. Nowadays, some scholars have made a limited attempt to rehabilitate Ctesias by suggesting that he may sometimes have been accurately reporting (incorrect) Persian oral traditions. See, e.g., Kuhrt, p. 8, Stronk, p. 25, and Llewellyn-Jones and Robson, pp. 61-63 and 82. Also, in some instances, one can argue that the errors may only be the result of Photius' faulty summary.

79. Ctesias does not provide an exact date of death for Amestris but implies that she died before Artaxerxes I, who died in 424 B.C.E.

80. Berlin, p. xxix.

> The main question posed to those [Greek historiographical texts] has changed. No longer is it: What can we learn about Persian history from the Greeks? Now it is: What was the Greek view of the Persians and why did they hold that view?[81]

Let us now focus on the main story that Ctesias tells about Amestris. According to Ctesias, after years of pestering her son Artaxerxes, Amestris is able to have fifty Greeks decapitated and their leader Inarus impaled, in revenge for Inarus and his men having slain her son Achaemenides five years earlier.

But no other source records that Artaxerxes had a brother named Achaemenides.[82] In Herodotus, the individual that Inarus slays is recorded as Achaemenes, a brother of Xerxes.[83] More importantly, in Thucydides, who was writing closer in time to the events, there is no mention of any involvement by Amestris in impaling Inarus, and Inarus seems to have met this fate without the five-year delay portrayed by Ctesias.[84] Thus, the main story that Ctesias tells about Amestris seems to be unhistorical.[85] Indeed, a leading scholar on Ctesias has suggested

81. See similarly, Sancisi-Weerdenburg, p. 32: "It is time, I think, to liberate ourselves from the Greek view on Persian history. The notorious women in this history should be confined to their real place, that is in literature."
82. Even in Ctesias, there is no mention elsewhere of such a brother. Ctesias lists the son of Xerxes and Amestris, and the only sons listed are Darius, Hystaspes and Artaxerxes. It seems unlikely that Achaemenides would have been a son of Amestris from a marriage prior to Xerxes, or a son of Xerxes who was not from Amestris.
83. Bigwood, p. 7.
84. Thucycides writes (I, 110): "Inaros, the king of the Libyans, who had been the person responsible for the Egyptian revolt, was betrayed to the Persians and crucified." The implication is that the death came shortly after the revolt was put down (Bigwood, p. 18). Moreover, there is no mention in Thucydides of Greeks being deported to Persia.
85. See Bigwood, p. 21. Bigwood also does not seem to believe Ctesias' story that Amestris punished her grandchild's murderer. See p. 19, n. 70. About the revolt of Inarus, Briant has written (p. 578):

> But taken as a whole, despite the veracity of some details, Ctesias's tale is far from believable.... The entire narrative is built on a series of literary motifs (cruel Persian princesses seeking vengeance for their child...).

that Ctesias was simply reshaping events from his own time, or from an earlier time, and projecting them into the time of Artaxerxes I. [86]

For all of the above reasons, there is every reason to be highly suspicious about every single item in Ctesias' portrayal of Amestris.[87]

◆ ◆ ◆

A difficulty that arises in equating Esther and Amestris is that one gets the impression from Herodotus that Amestris was the wife of Xerxes even in his early years of reign, since he never says that Amestris was a new wife. Also, perhaps implicit in the story about Amestris taking revenge on Masistes' wife is that Amestris was the wife of Xerxes when Xerxes initially became attracted to her.[88] (This initial attraction occurred at Sardis, before Xerxes returned to Susa to choose Esther.)

But as discussed above, one should be very skeptical about Herodotus' entire tale about the wife of Masistes. To raise a question based on the timing of this tale is a further leap. More importantly, it would be understandable if Herodotus believed that Amestris was the wife of Xerxes even for his entire reign. According to the Megillah, Vashti was gone by his third year. Xerxes reigned 18 years after that. To Herodotus and his informants, Vashti may have been long forgotten.[89]

Kuhrt as well (p. 325) does not believe Ctesias' version of the death of Inarus.

86. Bigwood writes (p. 21):

> The whole episode is a tangled web of items which are intrusions from the events which surround Cunaxa (or from Cambyses' reign) or are perhaps even stock themes of the raconteur. To base on it any historical conclusions would be an absurdity.

The reference to Cunaxa is a reference to the time of Artaxerxes II.

87. There is no reason to give any credence to Ctesias' depiction of Amestris (and her daughter!) as licentious. This can easily be viewed as mere polemics against Persian royal women and part of an effort to entertain his readers. Also, it has been suggested that part of the polemical Greek effort to weaken the Persian kings was to portray them as being manipulated by the women of the court. Brosius, p. 105. Ctesias has created such a picture here.

88. Part of the issue here is what motivated Amestris to take revenge on the mother and not the daughter. The explanation provided by Herodotus for Amestris' decision is not clear.

89. On the one hand, the narrative story that Herodotus tells about Xerxes

Given that is clear that Achashverosh is to be identified with Xerxes, there should be a presumption that the one queen-like wife described in the Greek sources (composed at a time when Vashti would have been long forgotten) and the *malkah* described in the Megillah are one and the same. As shown above, in their consonantal structure, the names essentially match (*str* vs. *mstr*). The issue is not whether there is enough evidence to equate Esther with Amestris, but **whether there is sufficient evidence to rebut the presumption that they are the one and the same**. When the issue is phrased this way, the correct conclusion is reached. The contradiction on the detail of the name of the father is woefully insufficient to rebut such a presumption. That Herodotus seems to have believed that Amestris was the wife of Xerxes even in the early years of his reign is also not a contradiction to Amestris being Esther. It is understandable that Herodotus might have had such a belief. It would be throwing out the baby with the bathwater to reject the identification of Esther with Amestris based on "contradictions" such as these.

◆ ◆ ◆

There is one remaining issue that needs to be discussed in connection with the identification of Esther with Amestris. The issue relates to the age of Artaxerxes. According to Ctesias:

> Xerxes married Amestris, the daughter of Onophas,[90] who bore him a son, Darius, two years later a second one, Hystaspes, and then Artaxerxes, and two daughters, one named Amytis after her grandmother and another called Rhodogune.

If Ctesias is to be believed, Artaxerxes had two older full brothers, and Darius, the eldest, was about three years older than he.[91]

---

covers only Xerxes' first seven years (aside from some digressions, including regarding Amestris). On the other hand, Herodotus is writing many decades later, when Vashti could easily have been forgotten.

90. This probable error by Ctesias was discussed earlier.

91. But note that the passage does not definitively state that the two daughters were born last.

A cuneiform text mentions a daughter of Xerxes named Ratahšhah, who was an infant in 486 B.C.E (see Brosius, pp. 29 and 73). It is at least remotely possible that this is Rhodogune by another name.

The Megillah records that Esther was first taken to the palace in Tevet of the seventh year of Xerxes. It was mentioned earlier that this can be estimated as Jan. 478 B.C.E. A tradition that the reign of Xerxes ended with his assassination has been preserved in many sources.[92] This assassination perhaps occurred as early as August 465 B.C.E., but it certainly occurred by January 464 B.C.E.[93] If Esther/Amestris was first brought to the palace in January 478 B.C.E., and there was a three-year age difference between Darius and Artaxerxes, **Artaxerxes could not have been more than around ten years old in January 464 B.C.E.**

Such an age for Artaxerxes at this time, although surprising, is not so inconsistent with what is found in the narrative sources. The main narrative sources for the assassination of Xerxes and the accession of Artaxerxes are Ctesias, Diodorus, and Justin. The first two do not discuss the age of Artaxerxes at his accession, perhaps implying that there was nothing extraordinary about it. But Justin, an abridgment of a late first-century B.C.E. source,[94] writes that Artaxerxes was just a boy (Latin: *puer*) at the time of the assassination.[95] Justin compares the age of Artaxerxes with that of Darius, whom he calls an *adolescens.*[96]

---

92. See, e.g., Julia Neuffer, "The Accession of Artaxerxes I," *Andrews University Seminary Studies* 6 (1968), pp. 60-87 (64-67), Briant, pp. 563-567, and Kuhrt, pp. 306-309.
93. In this month, a document exists which is dated to the beginning of the reign of Artaxerxes. See Arthur E. Cowley, *Aramaic Papyri of the Fifth Century B.C.* (Oxford: 1923), no. 6. This interesting document is analyzed in detail by Neuffer at pp. 72-87.
94. See above, n. 36.
95. Justin, III, 1. Albert T. Olmstead writes, in his *History of the Persian Empire* (Chicago and London: 1948), p. 289, that Artaxerxes was eighteen at the time of the assassination. I have not found any source for this, and Neuffer writes (p. 71) that this was just a guess by Olmstead, based on Justin. Unfortunately, Olmstead's guess is often adopted by others.
96. This was just prior to the murder of Darius; Darius was murdered shortly after Xerxes. According to Ctesias, an Artapanus (an influential advisor to Xerxes) and another conspirator murdered Xerxes and then misled Artaxerxes into thinking that Darius was the murderer. Artaxerxes then had Darius killed. Diodorus and Justin report essentially the same story. (They call the conspirator Artabanus, but I will use the name Artapanus throughout.) See also the brief remarks of Aristotle, in his *Politica* 5, 10, about the assassination.

Justin does call Artaxerxes an *adolescens* a few lines after he calls him a *puer*. But this is after he described how Artaxerxes tricked Artapanus and stabbed him to death. This probably motivated the change in term, even though there was no change in age.

Arguments can be made based on the narrative sources for an older age for Darius, Hystaspes, and Artaxerxes in 464 B.C.E. But all these arguments can be responded to.[97] Moreover, in light of the poor

97. The following are the main arguments and some responses:

1) In the story about the cruelty of Amestris, Herodotus had Xerxes arranging Darius' marriage in 479 B.C.E. (as part of a plan to seduce the mother of the bride). This would imply that Darius was significantly older than 13 in 464 B.C.E. But, to quote Briant (p. 516), this story "is a romance... on which it is extremely imprudent to base any historical extrapolation."
2) According to Diodorus (XI, 69), Hystaspes was not living in the palace at the time of the deaths of Xerxes and Darius. He was serving as the satrap at Bactria. If we would accept this detail, this would suggest an older age for Hystaspes, and the age of Darius, the eldest, would have to be increased accordingly. But according to Ctesias, the satrap at Bactria at the time was named Artapanus (a different Artapanus). (In the version of Ctesias, we do not have an explanation of where Hystaspes was at the time of the assassination and why he did not seek the throne.)

   Two Persepolis Fortification Tablets (PF 1287 and PF 1555) perhaps imply that Irdabanuš was the name of the satrap at Bactria in the 22nd year of Darius I, but this was long before 465 B.C.E.

   Diodorus can be read as implying that Artaxerxes was the second son and Hystaspes, the third. But one does not have to read Diodorus this way, and even if we did, there would be no reason to prefer Diodorus' order over that of Ctesias.
3) According to Diodorus, Artaxerxes was able to kill Artapanus in a physical battle (and Artapanus had his sons by his side as well). This suggests that Artaxerxes could not have been so young. But Ctesias does not state that this was how Artapanus died, and Justin's version of the killing of Artapanus differs from that of Diodorus. Briant, p. 565, writes that the version of Diodorus is "scarcely credible."
4) According to Diodorus (XI, 71), there seems to have been a period of perhaps two years before Artaxerxes was able to establish himself on the throne. (There is also an ancient source that records that Artapanus reigned for seven months.) One can ask how likely it would have been that Artaxerxes' rule would have survived any initial period of instability if he was only ten years old at its inception.

A Babylonian tablet from c. 300 B.C.E. records that Xerxes was killed by his son. See Kuhrt, p. 306. It has been suggested that this tablet reflects a

reputation of Ctesias as a historian, we should seriously consider the possibilities that Darius and perhaps even Hystaspes were not sons of Amestris but sons of Vashti, and that the three sons were not close in age.[98] It is also possible that errors and unwarranted assumptions were made by Photius in his summary of Ctesias.[99] If Artaxerxes was the first

Babylonian tradition that Artaxerxes murdered his father and that this is what actually occurred, and that all the other versions of Xerxes' death originate with post-accession propaganda by Artaxerxes! See Kuhrt, pp. 242-43, and Briant, pp. 566-67. (A third-century C.E. Roman historian also reports that Xerxes was killed by his son. See Briant, p. 516.)

98. Vashti was gone by the third year of Xerxes. Perhaps she was unknown to Herodotus, or perhaps he knew about her but never mentioned her. Almost certainly, she would have been unknown to the later Greek historians.

Ctesias certainly has credibility with regard to his depiction of Amestris and Artaxerxes as mother and son. Artaxerxes reigned over 40 years until 424 B.C.E., not long before the time Ctesias served in the Persian court, and Amestris (according to Ctesias) was alive and influential for a large part of the reign of Artaxerxes. But Darius was killed in 465 B.C.E. Ctesias certainly knew very little about him.

Ctesias may have known very little about Hystaspes as well. Perhaps Hystaspes was the satrap at Bactria in 465 B.C.E. or was appointed to this position later, and perhaps he remained there, a great distance away, until his death. (Bactria is approximately the present Afghanistan, Tajikistan and Uzbekistan.) Other than the fact that Diodorus claims that Hystaspes was the satrap at Bactria in 465 B.C.E., Hystaspes is not mentioned in the sources. Ctesias claims that Bactria and its satrap revolted from Artaxerxes, and were defeated. But in Ctesias, the satrap is named Artapanus (a different Artapanus than the conspirator).

99. As mentioned earlier, Photius' summary of Ctesias' work was prepared at the same time as 278 other summaries. All of these summaries must have been prepared relatively hastily, and were probably not reviewed after they were prepared (Stronk, pp. 141-42, and Llewellyn-Jones and Robson, p. 43). Moreover, it is very possible that Photius no longer had access to Ctesias' work when he was composing his summary, and based his summary on memory and notes made many years before. Even if he still had access to Ctesias' work, he may not have had time to consult it. Also, some of the summaries, perhaps even the summary of Ctesias' work, were composed by someone working with Photius. This individual was composing his summaries based on Photius' notes and probably never read the original works he was summarizing. Stronk, p. 131.

It is instructive to quote from Photius' preface to the 279 summaries sent to his brother:

son that Xerxes had with Amestris, this would allow him to have been around 13 at the time of his accession.

◆ ◆ ◆

Finally, it must be pointed out that Ctesias perhaps refers to Mordechai.[100] In an introductory statement about the reign of Xerxes, after mentioning two of Xerxes' influential advisors, Ctesias writes that "among the eunuchs,[101] Natacas exercised the greatest influence."[102] A few lines

> Late perhaps in relation to your lively desire and warm request, yet sooner than anyone else might have expected, we found a secretary, and... put together all that our memory preserved....
>
> If, on any occasion when you come to the texts themselves and work through them, some of the contents appear to be incompletely or inaccurately recorded, do not be in the least surprised. To read any single book, understand its contents and record them in the memory and in writing, is no great task for anyone who wishes; but when there are many texts, particularly if time has elapsed in the meanwhile, I do not think it is easy to achieve accurate recollection.

Photius, *The Bibliotheca*, ed. N.G. Wilson (London: 1994), p. 25. (Regarding the phrase "all that our memory preserved," see Stronk, p. 142.)

100. More than thirty Elamite texts from Persepolis (some of which date from the reign of Xerxes) include officials with the name Marduka or Marduku. Up to four different individuals are referred to in these texts (see Yamauchi, p. 235). Also, an Akkadian text from the last years of Darius I or the early years of Xerxes mentions a government official named Marduka (but not in Susa). It is complete conjecture to connect any of these texts to the Biblical Mordechai.

101. In many instances, this seems to have been merely a term used to indicate a holder of a high position in the king's entourage. See Briant, pp. 274-77, who concludes that it is "highly doubtful that all of the counselors and intimates of the Great Kings whom Ctesias and others call eunuchs were castrated men." His doubts are even greater in the case of "eunuchs" close to the king. A similar issue arises with the Hebrew or Akkadian term סריס. One scholar has asked facetiously (quoted at Briant, p. 276): "is it necessary to castrate half the Assyrian administration and nearly everyone at court?"

102. Ctesias had just mentioned "the aged Mardonius" as an influential advisor to Xerxes. But Mordechai cannot be Mardonius. Herotodus had told us that Mardonius was Darius' nephew and son-in-law, and was a

later, there is a reference to a eunuch of Xerxes named Matacas. Probably, there was textual corruption and the reference is to the same individual.[103] But we do not know whether the correct name is Matacas or Natacas. Thus, what we have in Ctesias is a report that a Matacas (Ματακας) or Natacas (Νατακας) was the most influential of Xerxes' eunuchs. "Matacas" suggests a Persian name with the consonants *mtc*,[104] which would be very close to the consonants of the name Mordechai, *mrdc*.[105] Even the name "Natacas" is not significantly different, since *n* and *m* are related consonants, both being nasal stops; it is not uncommon for one to transform into the other. With either form of the name, the information provided by Ctesias bears a significant resemblance to the last verse in the Megillah, which records that by the end of the story, Mordechai was *mishneh* (=second) to the king.[106]

However, there is a potential problem with identifying Matacas/Natacas with Mordechai. The context of the reference to Matacas is that, as Xerxes was retreating from his invasion, he sent Matacas (presumably with a division) to plunder the temple at Delphi. If Mordechai did not achieve a high position with the king until the twelfth year of Xerxes,[107]

---

general in the invasion of Greece by Darius. Mardonius encouraged Xerxes to undertake his own invasion.

I have seen the following translation in at least one edition of Photius/Ctesias: "His other confidential advisors were the aged Mardonius and Matacas the eunuch." In this translation, Matacas/Natacas is more than a confidential/influential eunuch; he is a confidential/influential advisor. But this is not an exact translation of the Greek.

103. Textual corruption could have arisen in the manuscripts of Photius, or could already have been present in the text of Ctesias that Photius used. Or Photius himself may have erred, writing or dictating in haste. Matacas/Natacas is not referred to in any other sources. See Joan M. Bigwood, "Ctesias as Historian of the Persian Wars," *Phoenix* 32 (1978), pp. 19-41 (38-39). There are many manuscripts of Photius, but all derive from two, one of which is from the early tenth century (Stronk, p. 147). Both of these read "Natacas" in the first passage and "Matacas" in the second passage.

104. The *-as* at the end is almost certainly a Greek addition.

105. A contemporary parallel is that the name Mordechai is often shortened to "Moti."

106. See also Est. 9:4. Perhaps we do not have to take *mishneh* literally; the import may merely be "very high official." If "Matacas" is Mordechai, this confirms one of the main elements of the plot of the Purim story.

107. See Est. 3:7 and 8:2.

Matacas/Natacas could not be Mordechai. But given the unreliability of Ctesias on details regarding Xerxes' invasion of Greece,[108] it would be a very reasonable approach to accept his summary statement that Matacas/Natacas was the most influential of the eunuchs, without accepting the detail he provides that Matacas/Natacas had an important role in plundering a temple at the time of Xerxes' retreat.[109] In fact, there does not seem to have been a plundering of the temple at Delphi, or the plundering of any temple, at the time stated by Ctesias.[110]

Conclusions

Achashverosh is to be identified with the king the Greeks had called "Xerxes." This was determined when it was discovered that the name of the king that the Greeks had been calling "Xerxes" was in fact "Khshayarsha" in Old Persian. Achashverosh/Xerxes is mentioned in

108. See, e.g., Bigwood, "Ctesias As Historian of the Persian Wars," pp. 19-41. Bigwood concludes (p. 36):

> [T]here is exceedingly little in this whole account of the Wars which could be right and nothing which suggests concern for the truth or careful investigation. Instead we have all the ingredients which one associates with Ctesias—reckless army statistics, misidentified characters, simplifications, astounding confusions, chronology which is muddled, some degree of anachronism, and a certain amount of bias. Finally there is... sensationalism....

109. We are told as early as Est. 2:19 and 2:21 that Mordechai sat at the king's gate, and many interpret this to mean that he was employed by the king. See, e.g., *Chamesh Megillot* (*Daat Mikra*), commentary to Est. 2:19. See also Dan. 2:49 (and the comments in the Soncino edition), and Xenophon, *Cyropaedia*, VIII, 1, 6. Berlin, p. 31, suggests that Mordechai's job was a government informer. But this is a far cry from a leader of a military expedition.

110. Herodotus does not mention any plundering of the temple at Delphi at this time. Some view Ctesias as referring instead to a plundering of the temple at Didyma, and believe him (see, e.g., Briant, p. 535). But according to Herodotus, the plundering of the temple at Didyma occurred years earlier, in the reign of Darius. Most historians believe Herodotus on this issue. See Bigwood, "Ctesias as Historian of the Persian Wars," p. 38. See also Kuhrt, pp. 294-95.

his correct historical position at Ezra 4:5-7, between Daryavesh (Darius I) and Artachshasta (Artaxerxes I).[111]

Almost certainly, Esther is to be identified with Amestris. Given the identity of Achashverosh and Xerxes, there should be a presumption that the one queen-like wife of Xerxes described in the Greek sources and the *malkah* described in the Megillah are one and the same. Looked at closely, the names essentially match. Three consonants are the same and in the same order. The issue is not whether there is enough evidence to equate Esther with Amestris, but whether there is sufficient evidence to rebut the presumption that they are identical. The contradiction on the detail of the name of the father is woefully insufficient to rebut such a presumption.

Artaxerxes turns out to be at most around ten years old at the beginning of his reign. But our only source for the details that Darius and Hystaspes were sons of Amestris and that all three sons were close in age is the unreliable work of Ctesias (in a hastily prepared summary by Photius). The possibilities that Darius and Hystaspes were both sons of the forgotten Vashti and that the three sons were not close in age should be seriously considered. The age of Artaxerxes at his accession could then be increased.[112]

111. As mentioned at the outset, the *SO*/Talmudic chronology differs and places Achashverosh before Daryavesh.

In this context, it should be mentioned that there is no statement in *SO* or either Talmud that Daryavesh was the son of Achashverosh. The view that Daryavesh was the son of Achashverosh and Esther is first recorded in *Leviticus Rabbah* (13:5) and *Esther Rabbah* (8:3), and is recorded in the name of R. Judah b. R. Simon. It seems to be only a minority view. Moreover, if this view of R. Judah b. R. Simon is superimposed upon the *SO*/Talmudic chronology, it makes Daryavesh very young when he began to reign. Esther was first brought to Achashverosh in his seventh year, and Achashverosh reigned only fourteen years in the *SO*/Talmudic chronology.

112. Writers have written novels about Xerxes and Esther, and it is interesting to see how they integrate the material in the Greek sources about Amestris with the material in the Megillah about Vashti and Esther. One such novel is Rebecca Kohn's *The Gilded Chamber* (New York: 2004). Kohn does not include any character named Amestris, but in one of her descriptions of Vashti (pp. 112-13) she incorporates the story about the cruelty of Amestris found in Herodotus. Also, Xerxes' sons Darius and Artaxerxes are portrayed as sons of Vashti. (There is no mention of the other son, Hystaspes). Depicting Artaxerxes as a son of Vashti enables an

Identifying Esther with Amestris does not mean that one has to accept the tales told about her by Herotodus and Ctesias. Even outside the Orthodox world, these tales are frequently disregarded.

At verse 10:2, the Megillah invites us to search outside the Bible for additional information about Achashverosh. I hope that this search has proven an interesting one!

---

interesting plot twist. After Xerxes is assassinated, Artaxerxes brings his mother Vashti back to the palace as queen, and Esther and Mordechai have to flee! Esther is then able to reunite with Mordechai!

Earlier, I had mentioned that Herodotus tells of an agreement between Darius I and his six co-conspirators that the Persian king would not marry outside their families. I added that even if we believe that there was such an agreement, this is the kind of agreement that would surely be violated when a king was attracted to a woman who was not from one of these families. Kohn takes such an approach as well. When an official in Xerxes' court objects to his choice of Esther on the grounds that she is not of royal lineage, the king summarily dismisses the objection: "You dare speak in clever contradiction to me? I who by the favor of Ahura Mazda smote the men of Egypt and Babylonia? She shall be my queen and none other: I hereby proclaim it!"

Appendix: List of the Persian Kings

The following is a list of the major Persian kings who reigned during the period from Cyrus (Koresh) to Alexander the Great: [113]

Cyrus	539-530 B.C E.
Cambyses[114]	530-522
Darius I	522-486
Xerxes	486-465
Artaxerxes I	465-424
Darius II	423-404
Artaxerxes II	404-358
Artaxerxes III	358-338
Arses	338-336
Darius III	336-332[115]

113. The above list only includes kings whose reigns spanned one year or more. The conventional chronology also views the Persian period as spanning the reigns of additional kings: Gaumata, Xerxes II, and Sogdianus. Gaumata (also referred to as Smerdis and Bardiya) pretended to be the brother of Cambyses and reigned for several months in 522 B.C.E. He was assassinated in a conspiracy by Darius I and six others. Xerxes II was a son of Artaxerxes I. He reigned for a very brief period immediately after his father's death. (Ctesias gives him 45 days. Diodorus gives him one year. Other sources give him two months. See Kuhrt, p. 332.) He was killed by his brother Sogdianus who reigned for a few months before his brother Ochus killed him. Ochus then took the name Darius and is the Darius II mentioned above. (Babylonian texts now show that his name was Umakush. See Kuhrt, p. 331.)

114. The name of Cambyses was discovered to be "Kabujiya" in Old Persian. His name is recorded as כנבוזי in Aramaic documents from Egypt from the fifth century B.C.E. He did not reign long enough to be Achashverosh. Nor did he reign over Hodu. See my *Jewish History in Conflict*, p. 167.

115. With regard to the question of why the *SO*/Talmudic chronology leaves out the many Persian kings who reigned after Daryavesh/Darius I, and views the period from the second year of Daryavesh/Darius I until the end of the Persian period as spanning only 34 years, see my *Jewish History in Conflict*, particularly pp. 128-137. As I explain there, the author of this chronology (probably R. Yose b. Chalafta, second century C.E.) was trying to create a chronology which corresponded with the 490-year period predicted at Dan. 9:24-27. The author certainly had a firm tradition

that the exilic period spanned 70 years and probably had a firm tradition that the destruction of the Second Temple occurred in the 381st year of *minyan shetarot* (= the Seleucid Era). Given these firm traditions, a strong desire to make the chronology fit with the 490 year period predicted at Dan. 9:24-27, and his choice of the beginning of the exilic period and the end of the Second Temple period as the terminii of this 490 year period, would have forced him to reduce the length of the period from the building of the Second Temple to the beginning of *minyan shetarot* to approximately 40 years. He probably also had a tradition or made a calculation that the length of time from the beginning of the Greek period until the commencement of *minyan shetarot* was six years. This would have forced him to assign only 34 years to the length of Daryavesh's rule after the rebuilding, and to equate the Artachshasta of the time of Ezra and Nehemiah with Daryavesh. It also would have forced him to place Achashverosh between Koresh and Daryavesh. For a further detailed discussion of all of this, see Milikowsky, vol. 2, pp. 462-75, particularly pp. 470-71.

9

Mah Nishtannah: The Three Questions[1]

I. How Many Questions Were There in the *Mah Nishtannah* of the Mishnah?

It is well-known that the Mishnah in the tenth chapter of *Pesaḥim* includes a set of *mah nishtannah*. If one opens a standard printed Babylonian Talmud (*Pesaḥim* 116a), one sees four questions in the text of the Mishnah (matzah, *maror*, roast, and dipping). But if one opens a standard printed Jerusalem Talmud, one sees only three questions

---

1. I would like to acknowledge Dr. Jay Rovner, Rabbi Mordy Friedman, and Sam Borodach for their thoughts and assistance. An earlier version of this article was published at seforim.blogspot.com (Mar. 26, 2010): "Some Observations Regarding the *Mah Nishtannah*."

Several sources will be cited throughout:

- Daniel Goldschmidt, *Haggadah shel Pesaḥ* (Jerusalem: 1960), cited as "Goldschmidt."
- Menaḥem Kasher, *Haggadah Shelemah* (Jerusalem: 1967, third ed.), cited as "Kasher."
- Yosef Tabory, *Pesaḥ Dorot* (Tel Aviv: 1996), cited as "Tabory."
- Shmuel and Ze'ev Safrai, *Haggadat Ḥazal* (Jerusalem: 1998), cited as "Safrai."
- Shamma Friedman, *Tosefta Atikta: Massekhet Pesaḥ Rishon* (Ramat Gan: 2002), cited as "Friedman."
- Richard Steiner, "On the Original Structure and Meaning of Mah Nishtannah and the History of Its Reinterpretation," *Jewish Studies, an Internet Journal* 7 (2008), pp. 163-204, cited as "Steiner."

(dipping, matzah, and roast).[2] Is this one of those rare instances of a disagreement between the text of the Mishnah preserved in Babylonia and the text of the Mishnah preserved in Palestine?[3]

It turns out that it is practically certain that the original text of the Mishnah recorded only three questions: dipping, matzah, and roast. This

---

2. I will call them questions, even though some have argued that they are best understood, in the context of *Mishnah* 10:4, as explanations or exclamations. See, e.g., Safrai, pp. 31 and 206, and the sources cited by Steiner, pp. 183-84.

Steiner strongly defends the traditional understanding of the *mah nishtannah* as questions (actually, as one long question). He points out that the Talmud (*Pesaḥim* 116a) includes the following passage:

> ת"ר חכם בנו שואלו ואם אינו חכם אשתו שואלתו ואם לאו הוא שואל לעצמו ואפילו שני תלמידי חכמים שיודעין בהלכות הפסח שואלין זה לזה מה נשתנה הלילה הזה מכל הלילות שבכל הלילות אנו מטבילין פעם אחת הלילה הזה שתי פעמים.

(Although the printed editions have punctuation between שואלין זה לזה and מה נשתנה, this punctuation is only a later addition. See Steiner, p. 188, n. 95, and Kasher, p. 35. But see Goldschmidt, p. 11, and Safrai, p. 112, for a different approach to the above text.)

Steiner argues that the Mishnah is most properly understood as intending only one long question, i.e., "what special characteristic of this night is causing us to depart from our normal routine in so many ways?" He shows that R. Saadiah Gaon and every early medieval source understood the *mah nishtannah* as only one long question. It was not until the thirteenth century that a medieval source first referred to them as שאלות (plural).

A study of the *mah nishtannah* inevitably raises other issues. Is the *mah nishtannah* to be recited by the child only if he cannot formulate his own questions? Is it perhaps something recited by the father? On these issues, see, e.g., Goldschmidt, pp. 10-11, Kasher, pp. רב-רד, Safrai, p. 31, *ArtScroll Mishnah Series*, commentary to *Pesaḥim* 10:4 (Brooklyn: 1994, second ed.), p. 210, and Joshua Kulp, David Golinkin, and David Harel, *The Schechter Haggadah: Art, History, and Commentary* (Jerusalem: 2009), p. 196. Most likely, the correct understanding of Mishnah *Pesaḥim* 10:4 is that the child who lacks understanding is taught to ask the *mah nishtannah*. See Steiner, pp. 188, and 195-98. It was not a mandated piece of liturgy.

3. There are such instances. A well-known example is the first Mishnah in the fourth chapter of *Bava Metzia*. On this topic generally, see Melech Schachter, "Babylonian-Palestinian Variations in the Mishnah," *JQR* 42 (1951-52), pp. 1-35.

is what the earliest and most reliable Mishnah manuscripts record.[4] As we should have expected, there is no distinction between a Babylonian Mishnah and a Palestinian Mishnah here.[5]

Moreover, if one opens up a standard *Massekhet Pesaḥim* of the Babylonian Talmud and looks at the text of the Mishnah recorded in the Rif (R. Isaac Alfasi, 11th century) and the Rosh (R. Asher b. Yeḥiel, 13th century), one sees that they too record a Mishnah which included only the above three questions. Also, Rambam (12th century) utilized a text of the Mishnah which included only the above three questions.[6]

4. See Safrai, p. 26 and Tabory, pp. 260, 262, and 361.

Many scholars claim that the three explanations of R. Gamliel at Mishnah 10:5 (*pesaḥ*, matzah, *maror*) are the answers to the three *mah nishtannah* questions. But this approach must be rejected. As Steiner explains (pp. 194-95), although the topics of the *mah nishtannah* match the topics of the three explanations (the dipping question was the *maror* question of the time), the "explanations" given do not specifically answer the questions posed. Moreover, the *mah nishtannah* is most properly understood as only one long question, i.e., "what special characteristic of this night is causing us to depart from our normal routine in so many ways?" If so, we should look for one fundamental answer and not three piecemeal ones. According to Steiner, מתחיל בגנות... כל הפרשה is the answer expressed in the Mishnah to the *mah nishtannah*. (The prevalent view among the Rishonim was that *avadim hayinu* was the answer to the *mah nishtannah*. But *avadim hayinu* is not found in the Mishnah, and was not even included in the Palestinian *seder* ritual. See Steiner, p. 194 and below, n. 23.)

5. It is unfortunate that the new *Encyclopaedia Judaica* (Detroit and Jerusalem: 2006), in its entry "*Mah Nishtannah*," includes the statement that "[t]he Mishnah enumerates four questions." The new edition merely reprinted the original entry from the 1972 (Jerusalem) edition. The fact that the original entry took this position was surprising as well. In its bibliography, the original entry cited only Goldschmidt's work from 1960 and one other less scholarly work, and Goldschmidt clearly took the position that the original text of the Mishnah included only three questions. See Goldschmidt, pp. 11-12.

The "*Mah Nishtannah*" entry also includes the statement that the roast question did not survive after the *ḥurban*. This view has long been refuted as well, as I will explain in Part II.

6. See the edition of Rambam's commentary on the Mishnah published by R. Yosef Kafaḥ (1963-67). Rambam copied a text of the Mishnah (presumably one that he felt was authoritative) and wrote his commentary on that text. For most of the *sedarim* of the Mishnah (including *Pesaḥim)*, we have this text of the Mishnah and Rambam's commentary, all written in

Almost certainly, the familiarity of later copyists and printers with the *maror* question from the texts of their *Haggadah* led some of them to erroneously insert the *maror* question into their texts of the Mishnah, generating a new four-question Mishnah.[7]

II. Variety in the Number of Questions After the Period of the Mishnah and the Survival of the Roast Question Throughout the Centuries[8]

A widely quoted explanation of the Vilna Gaon takes the positions that there were always four questions, and that the roast question did not survive after the *ḥurban* (the reclining question substituting for it).[9] In Part I, I showed that there were originally only 3 questions. Now I will show that the roast question survived in some areas for 1000 years after the *ḥurban*.[10]

Rambam's hand. This text of the Mishnah with the Rambam's commentary was published by Kafaḥ. The edition of Rambam's commentary on the Mishnah included in a traditional volume of the Talmud does not include a text of the Mishnah.

7. Heinrich Guggenheimer, *The Scholar's Haggadah* (Northvale, N.J.: 1995), p. 250. See further, n. 35 below.

8. My discussion in this section is based on the Haggadah fragments from the Cairo Genizah included in Shmuel and Ze'ev Safrai, *Haggadat Ḥazal* (Jerusalem: 1998), and in the English adaptation of this work, *Haggadah of the Sages* (Jerusalem: 2009). As stated in the latter (p. xiii), not all of the Genizah fragments have been examined and more Haggadah fragments will certainly come to light. Nevertheless, due to the extensive number of fragments already examined, the present scholarly conclusions will likely remain largely unchanged.

9. The Gaon's explanation is printed in Kasher (p. 115). According to this explanation, reclining at the *seder* would not have been an unusual behavior prior to the *ḥurban*, because it was the practice to eat while reclining all year round. Only after the Temple was destroyed did reclining at the *seder* become unusual. At the same time, the *pesaḥ* sacrifice ceased.

Another widely quoted view is that of Rambam, who writes that there were originally five questions before the question about roast meat was dropped. See his *Hilkhot Ḥametz u-Matzah* 8:3.

10. The survival of the roast question for 1000 years, after the *ḥurban*, has been implicitly acknowledged in the *Haggadah Shel Pesaḥ: Torat Ḥayyim* (Jerusalem: 1998). See p. 29, n. 59 (notes to *Shibbolei ha-Leket*).

Documents from the Cairo Genizah in Egypt generally date from the tenth to thirteenth centuries.[11] It is reasonable to assume that this is roughly the period of the Haggadah fragments as well. Of course, not all of the Haggadah fragments from the Genizah span the *mah nishtannah* section. But of those that do, many include the roast question.[12]

---

11. Robert Brody, *The Geonim of Babylonia and the Shaping of Medieval Jewish Culture* (New Haven: 1998), p. 32.

12. For some published examples, see: 1) Israel Abrahams, "Some Egyptian Fragments of the Passover Haggadah," *JQR* (O.S.) 10 (1898), pp. 41-51, fragments # 2, 7, 8 and 10; 2) the Haggadah manuscript first described briefly in an article by Julius H. Greenstone in 1911, and later published in full by Goldschmidt; 3) the Haggadah manuscript (JTS MS 9560) published by Jay Rovner, "An Early Passover Haggadah According to the Palestinian Rite," *JQR* 90 (2000), pp. 337-396, and 4) MS Cambridge T-S H2.152 (photograph at Kasher, p. צג). There are other such fragments as well. For example, see Safrai, p. 53, n. 21, p. 114, nn. 9 and 11, and Haggadah of the Sages, p. 102, n. 5. (The manuscript published by Rovner is probably, but not certainly, from the Genizah.). In only one of these texts (T-S H2.152) was the text of the question amended to היינו אוכלים בבית המקדש כולו צלי.

Most Genizah fragments can now be viewed at genizah.org.

To date, with one exception (see below), the roast question is found only among sets of *mah nishtannah* that are based on the three questions included in the Mishnah. These sets either follow the set of three included in the Mishnah, or have a modified version of the set which leaves out the matzah question (perhaps erroneously, see the discussion in the text). (But not all of the fragments which include the roast question include a complete set of questions, so the above conclusions are not absolute.)

The exception is T-S H2.152 which includes the roast question along with four other questions. This set is so aberrant that it may not reflect an actual rite. See below, n. 21.

At least one text from the Genizah (Abrahams, fragment #5) includes the following blessing immediately after *ha-motzi*:

> ב' א' ה' ... מלך העולם אשר צוה את אבותינו לאכול מצות מרורים בשר צלי אש
> להזכיר את גבורותיו ב' א' ה' זוכר הברית.

Whatever community was using this text was almost certainly eating roast meat at their meal, although Tabory (p. 103) raises the possibility that they may have only been partaking a small, symbolic amount. A similar blessing is found in a different Genizah fragment printed at Safrai, p. 289. There,

Furthermore, although most of the *mah nishtannah* Haggadah fragments found in the Genizah record four questions the way they are asked today,[13] we also find the following:[14]

- Several record three questions: matzah, dipping, and roast,[15] just like the original text of the Mishnah.

  (It has been suggested that the fragments with these three questions reflect the original Palestinian tradition of the Haggadah,[16] and that the fragments with four questions reflect the later Babylonian tradition,[17] which gradually penetrated into Palestine and its surrounding areas.[18])

---

however, the blessing is included before the blessing for washing and *ha-motzi*, so it is less clear that the blessing was meant to precede the actual eating of roast meat. See also the fragments referred to at Safrai, p. 30.

Regarding the concluding blessing זוכר הברית, there are other fragments from the Genizah that include such a blessing in this section of the Haggadah (without reference to בשר צלי אש). See, e.g., the Greenstone-Goldschmidt manuscript (Goldschmidt, p. 83), and Abrahams, fragment #7. For further discussion of this concluding blessing, see Goldschmidt, p. 60, n. 10.

13. Safrai, p. 113. (I am not concerned with variation in the order of these four questions.)

14. In this section, I am only including fragments whose total number of questions in their *mah nishtannah* set can be determined. Therefore, I am not including fragments such as Abrahams #7 and Abrahams #8, which include *mah nishtannah* questions but which are cut off mid-set. For example, Abrahams fragment #7 starts with the roast question, but is cut off before it. Abrahams fragment #8 starts in the middle of the matzah question.

15. See, e.g., Abrahams, fragments #2 and #10. See also our discussion below of the Greenstone-Goldschmidt fragment. According to the Safrais (p. 65), "מספר ניכר" of the Haggadah fragments from the Genizah are of this type.

16. Safrai, pp. 26, 64 and 113.

But a few fragments which include the roast question follow the Babylonian rite in other essential respects. See Safrai, p. 30, n. 55, and p. 114, n. 9.

17. Safrai, pp. 113 and 206.

18. It is known from many other contexts that Babylonian customs gradually penetrated into Palestine and its surrounding areas and became the majority custom. See, e.g., Brody, *The Geonim of Babylonia*, pp. 111, 115, and 117. (An example is the practice of reciting *Kedushah* in the daily

- One records the following three questions: dipping, matzah and reclining.[19]
- One records five questions: dipping, matzah, roast, *maror*, and reclining.[20] (In this fragment, the roast question is phrased: והלילה הזה היינו אוכלים בבית המקדש כולו צלי. This is the only fragment in which the roast question is phrased with such a qualification.[21])
- Two record only the questions of dipping and roast.[22] (There does

---

Amidah. The letter of Pirkoi ben Baboi, early ninth century, describes how Babylonian Jews moved to Palestine and forced Palestinian Jews to adopt the Babylonian practice of reciting *Kedushah* daily.) See also Israel M. Ta-Shema, *Ha-Tefillah ha-Ashkenazit ha-Kedumah* (Jerusalem: 2004), p. 7.

19. See Kasher, p. 113, n. 11. Kasher calls this manuscript "21ק." It is MS Cambridge T-S H2.145. It is possible that this is not a legitimate variant and that the *maror* question was omitted in error by the scribe who copied this fragment. As explained in the text, the reclining question was almost certainly the last question added, and there was little reason for a community to have dropped the *maror* question.

There is also evidence of a *mah nishtannah* set of dipping, matzah, and *maror*. This does not come from the Genizah, but from additions made to a text of the *siddur* of R. Solomon b. Nathan (twelfth century). These additions, added at the end of the *siddur* by its owner, describe various local rites, and include a *mah nishtannah* set of dipping, matzah, and *maror*. See Shmuel Ḥagai, *Siddur Rabbeinu Shelomoh be-Rabbi Natan* (Jerusalem: 1995), p. 249. For more on this *siddur*, see Uri Ehrlich, "The Contribution of Genizah Texts to the Study of Siddur Rabbi Solomon Ben Nathan," pp. 127-137, in *"From a Sacred Source": Genizah Studies in Honor of Stefan C. Reif*, eds. Ben Outhwaite and Siam Bhayro (Leiden and Boston: 2010).

20. T-S H2.152. See the photograph at Kasher, p. צג.

21. Safrai, p. 53. This set is so aberrant that it may not reflect an actual rite. Possibly, the set was created by a lone scribe who combined the various questions that he knew of into one set. Since this set records the language of the roast question in a manner found nowhere else, this is evidence that the scribe who copied this fragment may have been a creative one.

22. The Haggadah manuscript published by Rovner clearly records only these two questions. The Greenstone-Goldschmidt manuscript initially recorded only these two questions, but a later scribe inserted the matzah question. See the last line of fragment ד/א and the first line of fragment ד/ב, in the photos at Goldschmidt, p. ii. These photos show that these lines are in a different handwriting. (At Safrai, pp. 286-289, a text of the Goldstone-Goldschmidt manuscript is printed. But it is printed as if it included all three questions initially.)

not appear to be any reason why the matzah question would have been intentionally discontinued. Perhaps the matzah question was accidentally dropped by a scribe in one source, and further copies were later made from that source. It would have been easy for a scribe to accidentally turn his eye to the wrong *mah nishtannah* line in the source he was copying from, and thereby omit a question.)

- One records only the questions of dipping and matzah.

◆ ◆ ◆

I would like to focus on this last source, which is not actually a Haggadah fragment, but is a section of an anonymous Geonic responsum that includes an outline of the procedures at the *seder*. It can be deduced that the responsum was composed in Babylonia because it includes *avadim hayinu*, which was not a part of the Palestinian *seder* ritual in this period.[23] This responsum was first published by Louis Ginzberg, in his *Ginzei Schechter*.[24]

Theoretically, it is possible to argue that the author of this responsum provided only an abbreviated version of the *mah nishtannah*, and listed only the first two questions, even though his practice was four. This seems to be the understanding of Ginzberg, who writes: נוסח מה נשתנה נתקצר ולא נאמרו כאן אלא ב' השאלות הראשונות.[25] B. M. Lewin included this responsum in his *Otzar ha-Geonim, Pesaḥim*, and he seems to agree with Ginzberg.[26] But this interpretation seems very unlikely. The whole purpose of the responsum was to spell out the procedures and text of the *seder*. Abbreviation here would have defeated its purpose.

---

23. Safrai, p. 50. See also the responsum of R. Natronai Gaon quoted, for example, at Kasher, pp. 27-28, Goldschmidt, p. 73, and Safrai, pp. 56-57. (In this responsum, R. Natronai criticizes an alternative Haggadah ritual for many reasons, one of which was the ritual's omission of *avadim hayinu*. R. Natronai thought it was a sectarian Haggadah ritual, but it turns out that he was criticizing the Palestinian Haggadah ritual. See Goldschmidt, p. 74, Safrai, pp. 56-59, and Brody, p. 96.)
24. Vol. 2 (1929), pp. 258-60. It is cited in Kasher, p. 113, n. 11 with the symbol ש. It is known as Cambridge T-S Misc. 36.179.
25. *Ginzei Schechter*, vol. 2, p. 259, n. 1.
26. Benjamin Menashe Lewin, *Otzar ha-Geonim* (Haifa and Jerusalem: 1928-43), *Pesaḥim*, p. 154, n. 13: נוסח מה נשתנה נתקצר.

Shmuel and Ze'ev Safrai take a different approach to this responsum in their monumental work, *Haggadat Ḥazal.* They write that the third and fourth questions are *ḥaserot be-sof he-amud*,[27] implying that these questions were originally included in this responsum but were cut off. Moreover, in their chart at the end of the work,[28] they put brackets over a supposed area of the third and fourth questions in this responsum, implying that these questions were once there. They take this approach so that the set of questions in our responsum could then parallel the set of questions found in the other known Babylonian Geonic sources of the Haggadah text: *Seder Rav Amram Gaon*, *Siddur Rav Saadiah Gaon*, and the Haggadah text published in 1984 by M. R. Lehman.[29]

27. Safrai, p. 64, n. 53. See also their later English adaptation, *Haggadah of the Sages*, p. 65, n. 30.
28. Safrai, p. 266. (The English adaptation does not include the chart.)
29. Menashe Refael Lehman, *Seder ve-Haggadah shel Pesaḥ le-Rav Natronai Gaon al Pi Ketav-Yad Kadmon*, in *Sefer Yovel li-Chevod Morenu ha-Gaon Rabbi Yosef Dov ha-Levi Soloveitchik Shelita*, eds. Shaul Yisre'eli, Naḥum Lamm, and Yitzḥak Refael (Jerusalem and New York: 1984), vol. 2, pp. 976-993 (986). The title of Lehman's article is unfortunate. The text of the article does not even claim that the Geonic Haggadah text published there served as the Haggadah of R. Natronai Gaon. Lehman composed the article initially based on a manuscript which spanned three sections, one of which was a Haggadah text. The first section of the manuscript included a caption stating that the material in that section (a long *paytanic* version of kiddush for Passover, and a long *paytanic* version of the blessing before the second cup) was enacted and arranged by R. Natronai. The Haggadah section had its own caption which stated that what followed was the text of the Haggadah accepted by the Talmud and the Geonim (with no mention of R. Natronai). Three Passover-related responsa followed, without any caption. Later, Lehman acquired another page from the same manuscript. He writes that the body of his article was already in final form by this time, but he was able to add his discussion of the new page at the end of the article. The new page included three anonymous responsa, one of which is recorded elsewhere in the name of R. Hai Gaon. This made Lehman realize (p. 991) that his pages were part of a collection of material from various Geonim, and not material that may all have had some connection to R. Natronai. Probably, the article was given its title (by Lehman or perhaps by someone else) before Lehman acquired the additional page. But even before Lehman acquired the additional page, the title was unjustified, as the Haggadah section had its own caption which did not connect it to R. Natronai. (Despite its caption, even the material in the first section of the manuscript may not have been composed by R. Natronai.)

All these sources record the standard four questions: dipping, matzah, *maror*, and reclining.[30]

But anyone can now view this responsum (Cambridge T-S Misc. 36.179) at genizah.org. It is clear that the third and fourth questions were never there. The first side ends with the last words of the matzah question, the next side continues immediately with *avadim hayinu,* and there are no missing lines in between.

Assuming we reject the unlikely interpretation of Ginzberg, this source records a two-question set in Babylonia.[31] The idea that we have now been able to "excavate" such a set, evidence of a period before four questions became the universal practice there, is truly remarkable.[32] On

It is unfortunate that the Safrais refer to Lehman's text throughout their work as the "Haggadah of R. Natronai Gaon." It is evident from their discussion of this text (p. 261) that all they were really willing to accept was that the text reflected a Haggadah from the time of the Geonim in general.

30. See Safrai, pp. 261 and 266.

31. See Kasher, p. 42, Jay Rovner, "An Early Passover Haggadah: Corrigenda," *JQR* 91 (2001), p. 429 (correcting p. 351, n. 59 in his original article), and Kulp, Golinkin, and Harel, *The Schechter Haggadah*, p. 199.

R. Isaac Alfasi quotes a text of Mishnah *Pesaḥim* 10:4 that includes only the questions of dipping, matzah, and roast, and then remarks והשתא לא לימא בשר צלי דלית לן פסחא. It can be argued based on this that the *mah nishtannah* at the *seder* in his community may have only included the questions of dipping and matzah.

32. The responsum does have at least one other unique aspect. It includes the statement: *etmol hayinu avadim ve-hayom bnei ḥorim.* The responsum follows an alternative *nusaḥ* for *kiddush*, but this *nusaḥ* is widely attested to. See, e.g., *Siddur Rav Saadiah Gaon*, eds. Israel Davidson, Simḥah Assaf, and Yissakhar Joel (Jerusalem: 1941), pp. 141-142, Kasher, pp. 183-85 and ב-ג, Safrai, p. 61, and Lehman, pp. 977-980 and 982-83. The responsum records the Sages in Bnei Brak as having been מסיחין about *yetzi'at mitzrayim* all night. But there is other evidence for this reading or its equivalent: משיחין. See Safrai, p. 208.

The language *etmol hayinu avadim hayom bnei ḥorim* is recorded in the Haggadot of Djerba (which also include the standard language that we are now slaves and will be free next year). See Kasher, p. רא, and Safrai, p. 111, n. 6. (Djerba is an island off the coast of Tunisia; the Jewish community there has ancient roots.) R. Shlomo Goren saw fit to include the language *etmol hayinu avadim ve-hayom bnei ḥorim* (along with the standard language) in the Haggadah he composed for the use of the Israeli

a paleographical basis, the responsum has been estimated to date to the tenth century.[33]

Regarding the issue of when the questions about *maror* and reclining were added, the following are some reasonable observations that some scholars have made:

- The reclining question was probably the last question to be added.[34] Unlike the *maror* question, it did not make its way into in any manuscripts of the Mishnah,[35] and in all communities, it is the last question of the set.[36]
- The *maror* question probably did not arise until after the text of the dipping question was changed in Babylonia (see *Pesaḥim* 116a[37]) and the dipping question lost its connotation as a *maror* question.

---

army. See, e.g., Kasher, p. רא, citing the 1956 edition of the *Haggadah shel Pesaḥ* published by *Ha-Rabbanut ha-Tzevait ha-Roshit*. Many editions of this Haggadah were published and this language appears in later editions as well.

The two-question *mah nishtannah* follows an earlier section of the responsum that includes a *piyyut* for the *hoshanot* of Sukkot and instructions regarding the *hoshanot*.

33. This is the opinion of Dr. Edna Engel of *The Hebrew Palaeography Project* at The National Library of Israel, in private correspondence. She also opines that the script is Oriental, i.e., from Egypt, Palestine, or Syria. Since the responsum reflects the Babylonian ritual, perhaps the last is most likely. The surviving responsum may be a copy of an earlier responsum.

In 2013, a *siddur* from the ninth century came to light. Its text is expected to be published in 2015. I anxiously await to see if it includes a set of *mah nishtannah* and which questions it records.

34. Tabory, p. 260.

35. The *maror* question made its way into at least one manuscript of the Mishnah and into many early printed editions. See Tabory, p. 261 and David Henshke, "*Al Rovdei Haggadat ha-Pesaḥ ba-Mishnah*," *Tarbiz* 81 (2013) pp. 25-45 (26, n. 8).

36. Tabori, p. 261, n. 36.

37. In Amoraic Babylonia, there was no practice of dipping throughout the year. This led the Babylonian Amoraim to rephrase the question. Based on the statements by the Babylonian Amoraim expressed at *Pesaḥim* 116a, the text of the dipping question was changed in many Mishnah manuscripts. Various forms of the question developed. See Safrai, p. 27, and Goldschmidt, p. 77.

Once the dipping question lost this connotation, it was probably viewed as necessary to add a question relating to *maror*.[38]

- The reclining question probably originated in Babylonia as well.[39] It was probably added, after the *maror* question, due to a desire to fix the number of questions at four, parallel to the themes of four cups of wine and four sons.[40]

Aside from Haggadah fragments found in the Genizah, the earliest sources that include the reclining question are: *Seder Rav Amram Gaon*,[41] *Siddur Rav Saadiah Gaon*,[42] and the Haggadah text published by Lehman in 1984. (With regard to *Seder Rav Amram Gaon*, it is accepted that many additions and changes were made to it in the centuries after R. Amram's death in the late ninth century. The three surviving manuscripts of the work are only from the fourteenth to sixteenth centuries. With regard to the *Siddur Rav Saadiah Gaon*, the main surviving manuscript dates from the twelfth or thirteenth century, but it is usually viewed as representing a largely reliable version of the original tenth-century work by R. Saadiah.[43] With regard to the Haggadah text published by Lehman, see above, n. 29.)

---

39. In suggesting that both the *maror* and reclining questions arose in Babylonia, I am following the approach of the Safrais. They believe that even though the majority of the *mah nishtannah* Haggadah fragments from the Genizah include dipping, matzah, *maror*, and reclining, these fragments do not reflect the original Palestinian custom. These fragments only show that the Babylonian custom became the majority custom in Palestine and its surrounding areas.

40. Guggenheimer, p. 250.

41. P. 113 (ed. Goldschmidt).

42. P. 137.

43. Admittedly, there are some differences between the text in the main surviving manuscript and the text in the Genizah fragments, perhaps due to the Aleppine origin of the manuscript. See Ehrlich, p. 128, n. 5.

Also, Naomi Cohen has noted several contradictions between the instructions provided by R. Saadiah and the liturgical texts, and between parallel prayer texts in different sections. Therefore, some of the liturgical texts included in the *Siddur Rav Saadiah Gaon* may have been supplied by later copyists, or at least changed by them. See Cohen, "*Le-Ofiyyo ha-Mekori shel Siddur Rav Saadiah Gaon*," *Sinai* 95 (1983/84), pp. 249-67.

III. The *Mah Nishtannah* May Have Been First Composed After the Destruction of the Temple in 70 C.E.

A main issue of debate among scholars is whether the *mah nishtannah* set included in the Mishnah reflects questions from Temple times. If we focus on the roast question (הלילה הזה כולו צלי), a reasonable initial assumption is that this question is referring to the *pesaḥ* sacrifice, since the *pesaḥ* sacrifice was something that was required to be roasted. This would suggest that this question and perhaps all the questions were composed during Temple times.

But many scholars argue that the roast question is not referring to the *pesaḥ* sacrifice and that this question was composed after the *ḥurban*. They make the following arguments:

1. A practice arose after the *ḥurban*, approved (or perhaps initiated) by Rabban Gamliel of Yavneh, of eating a *gedi mekulas* as a method of commemorating the *pesaḥ* sacrifice.[44] This practice is referred to at Mishnah *Betzah* 2:6-7 and Mishnah *Eduyyot* 3:10-11. Although these two sources do not specify that the Rabban Gamliel they are referring to is Rabban Gamliel of Yavneh, it seems fairly clear, for a variety of reasons, that this is the case.[45] The *gedi mekulas* was

44. A *gedi* (young goat) was one of the animals permitted for the *pesaḥ* sacrifice. Ex. 12:5 states that the *pesaḥ* sacrifice must come מן הכבשים ומן העזים (from a lamb or a goat).

45. One such reason is that plain references to Rabban Gamliel (i.e., without the description "*ha-Zaken*") are almost always references to Rabban Gamliel of Yavneh. See Safrai, p. 28, n. 50, Emil Schürer, *The History of the Jewish People in the Age of Jesus Christ*, revised and edited by Geza Vermes, Fergus Millar, and Matthew Black, vol. 2 (Edinburgh: 1979), p. 368, n. 48, and Tos. *Niddah* 6b, s.v., בשפחתו. A story referring to a practice of preparing a *gedi mekulas* among Roman Jewry, and the objection of the Sages of Palestine, is found in many sources. See, e.g., *Pesaḥim* 53a:

> תודוס איש רומי הנהיג את בני רומי לאכול גדיים מקולסין בלילי פסחים שלחו לו אלמלא תודוס אתה גזרנו עליך נדוי שאתה מאכיל את ישראל קדשים בחוץ...

See also *Berakhot* 19a, *Betzah* 23a, and in the Jerusalem Talmud *Pesaḥim* 7:1 (34a), *Betzah* 2:7 (61c), and *Moed Katan* 3:1 (81c). Most scholars believe that Todos lived after the ḥurban. See Tabory, p. 98. But there are some scholars who believe that Todos lived during Temple times. See

not designated as a *pesaḥ* sacrifice, but was arranged on the spit during the roasting process in the same manner as a *pesaḥ* sacrifice, and was *roasted in its entirety* (כולו צלי) just like a *pesaḥ* sacrifice.[46]

Safrai, p. 28, n. 52. Even if it can be shown that there was a practice outside of Palestine of preparing a *gedi mekulas* during Temple times, this does not mean that there was such a practice in Palestine, where going to Jerusalem and participating in an actual *pesaḥ* sacrifice was largely possible. (The version of the above story in the standard printed edition of the Talmud at *Berakhot* 19a states that the message to Todos was sent by Simeon b. Shetaḥ. But this is an erroneous reading. See Tabory, p. 98.)

Aside from being recorded in both Talmuds, the above story is also recorded in the Tosefta (*Betzah* 2:11). But the Tosefta has a slightly different reading:

תודוס איש רומי הנהיג את בני רומי ליקח טלאים בלילי פסחים ועושין אותן מקולסין...

טלא is the Aramaic term for שה, a broader term than גדי. Regarding the significance of this reading, see Saul Lieberman, *Tosefta ki-Feshutah*, 5, p. 959.

46. See Tosefta *Betzah* 2:11:

איזהו גדי מקולס? כולו צלי, ראשו וכרעיו וקרבו. בישל ממנו כל שהוא שלק ממנו כל שהוא אין זה גדי מקולס ...

See also *Pesaḥim* 74a:

איזהו גדי מקולס דאסור לאכול בלילי פסח בזמן הזה כל שצלאו כולו כאחד. נחתך ממנו אבר נשלק ממנו אבר אין זה גדי מקולס.

(Perhaps it was only the preparation of a *gedi mekulas* that the Sages forbade, or perhaps the preparation of any kind of שה מקולס was forbidden as well. See the version of the story involving Todos recorded in Tosefta *Betzah* 2:11 and Lieberman, *Tosefta ki-Feshutah*, 5, p. 959.)

There was a dispute as to the proper manner of positioning the legs and entrails of the *pesaḥ* sacrifice while it was being roasted. See Mishnah *Pesaḥim* 7:1. The view of R. Akiva was that they are hung outside it. This perhaps sheds light on the meaning of the difficult term *mekulas*. *Mekulas* in Aramaic can be interpreted as wearing a helmet (see the similar word at Targum Pseudo-Jonathan to 1 Sam. 17:5). According to Rashi (on *Pesaḥim* 74a), when R. Akiva expressed the view that the legs and entrails were roasted outside the animal, he meant that they were placed above its head. This made the goat look like it was wearing a helmet. *Mekulas* would therefore be another way of describing the method of positioning according to R. Akiva. (Rashi elsewhere gives a slightly different interpretation of

The Sages prohibited the *gedi mekulas*,[47] but it is possible that a large section of Jewry followed the leniency of Rabban Gamliel and engaged in this practice.[48] The roast question could have been composed after the *ḥurban* in an area which followed this practice.[49]

2. The Mishnah at *Pesaḥim* 4:4 records: מקום שנהגו לאכול צלי בלילי פסחים, אוכלים; מקום שנהגו שלא לאכול, אינן אוכלין. It is possible that this Mishnah was composed during Temple times and is referring to a practice of eating roast meat on the *seder* night outside the Temple. But just as likely, this Mishnah was composed after the *ḥurban* and is referring to a post-*ḥurban* practice of eating roast meat as a commemoration of the *pesaḥ* sacrifice.[50] It is possible to understand the roast question in the Mishnah as composed, after the *ḥurban*, in an area which followed this practice.[51]

---

how the term *mekulas* accords with the view of R. Akiva. See Rashi on *Pesaḥim* 53a and *Betzah* 22b.) An alternative approach is to understand *mekulas* as "beautiful" or "praised." See, e.g., Rambam, commentary to Mishnah, *Betzah* 2:6. The root קל"ס often has the meaning "to beautify" or "to praise" in rabbinic literature, derived from the Greek word καλος (beautiful). See also Joel Gereboff, *Rabbi Tarfon: The Tradition, the Man, and Early Rabbinic Judaism* (Missoula, Mont.: 1979), p. 70, where two other Greek derivations for *mekulas* are suggested: καλως, an animal led on a string, and κολος, a horneless animal. Gereboff also cites Samuel Krauss for the view that χαυλος in Greek means "helmeted." See also Tabory, p. 97, n. 248.

47. No reason is given in the Mishnah for the Sages' prohibition. But in the response to Todos, a reason is given. If the practice of preparing a *gedi mekulas* is permitted, people will think that *kodshim* can be eaten outside the *azarah*, because the practice was to refer to the *gedi mekulas* as if it were a *pesaḥ* offering. Probably, Palestinian Jewry as well as Roman Jewry referred to the *gedi mekulas* as if it were a *pesaḥ* offering. See below, n. 55.

48. There would be evidence of this if the custom referred to at Mishnah *Pesaḥim* 4:4 is the custom to prepare and eat a *gedi mekulas*.

49. The Safrais (p. 28), for example, take this approach, as does Friedman (p. 92).

50. Some scholars argue that the custom being referred to in this Mishnah is simply the custom to prepare and eat a *gedi mekulas*. See, e.g., Safrai, pp. 27-28. But this is not the plain sense of the Mishnah.

51. Scholars who take this approach include Gedaliah Allon, *The Jews in their Land in the Talmudic Age* (English translation, Jerusalem, 1989), pp. 264-65, and Goldschmidt, p. 12. In this approach, the roast question arose in connection with what was perhaps the practice of a large section

But the precise phrasing of the roast question does not support either of these interpretations. When read in light of the parallel matzah question, the roast question implies that the question is about a *required* behavior of the evening. While there were areas that had a custom on this evening, after the *ḥurban*, to eat a *gedi mekulas* or to eat roast meat, these were not required behaviors. It is hard to imagine that the roast question refers to something optional, rather than to a required commemorative rite. The language of the roast question, read in light of the parallel matzah question, best fits the *pesaḥ* sacrifice.[52]

Does it follow from this interpretation that the roast question was composed during Temple times? Not necessarily. Even if the roast question is referring to the *pesaḥ* sacrifice, it very possibly could have been composed after the *ḥurban,* as a simulation of a question that might have been asked during Temple times. Once the idea for a *mah nishtannah* question about matzah took hold, it would be have been natural and instructive to create a parallel question covering such an important commandment as the *pesaḥ* sacrifice, even if the *pesaḥ* sacrifice was no longer being offered.[53]

(It is also possible to understand the roast question as having been composed after the *ḥurban* if the *pesaḥ* sacrifice itself continued after the *ḥurban*.[54] But the evidence for this is weak.[55])

---

of Jewry. By contrast, the custom to prepare a *gedi mekulas* may not have been widespread.

52. A response to this would be that the roast question was phrased this way so it could parallel the matzah question, even though the phrasing did not perfectly fit the concept of an optional commemorative practice.

53. All the more so if practices commemorating the *pesaḥ* sacrifice were ongoing.

54. There are those who suggest that the *pesaḥ* sacrifice (and other sacrifices as well) continued after the *ḥurban* (perhaps outside the *makom ha-mikdash* and without the permission of the Sages). See, e.g., Yehoshua Brand, "*Korban Pesaḥ le-Aḥar Ḥurban Bayit Sheni,*" *Ha-Hed* 12/6 (1937) and 13/7 (1938), and the references at J. David Bleich, *Contemporary Halakhic Problems*, vol. 1 (New York: 1977), pp. 247-48. See also Yosef Tabory, *Moadei Yisrael be-Tekufat ha-Mishnah ve-ha-Talmud* (Jerusalem: 1995), p. 99, n. 65.

55. For example, Mishnah *Pesaḥim* 7:2 records a story in which Rabban Gamliel told his slave Tavi to go out and roast "the *pesaḥ*" on the roasting tray. (The Rabban Gamliel who had a slave named Tavi was Rabban Gamliel

The Mishnah that concerns us, *Pesaḥim* 10:4, is found in the last

---

of Yavneh. See Safrai, p. 28.) But this story can easily be interpreted as involving only the preparation of a *gedi mekulas*, after the *ḥurban*, with the term "*pesaḥ*" being used only loosely. For similar probable loose usages of the term "*pesaḥ*," see Tosefta *Ohalot* 3:9 and 18:18, and J. Talmud *Megillah* 1:11 (1:13, 72b). See also Tabory, pp. 100-101.

The argument that the *pesaḥ* sacrifice continued after the *ḥurban* has also been made based on a passage in *Antiquities*. Josephus writes (II, 313): "to this day we keep this sacrifice in the same customary manner, calling the feast Pascha…." Josephus writes (XX, 267) that he completed this work in the 13th year of the reign of Domitian (93-94 C.E.). (The precise year that book II was written is unknown.) But Josephus was writing in Rome, not Palestine, and almost certainly all he meant is that the *pesaḥ* sacrifice has been kept throughout the centuries through approximately his time. See also Baruch M. Bokser, *The Origins of the Seder* (Berkeley: 1984), p. 106.

The historian Procopius, describing events in Palestine in the sixth century, wrote:

> [W]henever in their calendar Passover came before the Christian Easter, [Justinian] forbade the Jews to celebrate it on their proper day, to make then any sacrifices to God or perform any of their customs. Many of them were heavily fined by the magistrates for eating lamb at such times….

In the late 4th or early 5th century, the church father Jerome wrote:

> Take any Jew you please who has been converted to Christianity, and you will see that he practices the rite of circumcision on his newborn son, keeps the Sabbath, abstains from forbidden food, and brings a lamb as an offering on the forteenth of Nissan.

See *Secret History of Procopius*, ed. Richard Atwater (Chicago: 1927), pp. 260-261 and Samuel Krauss, "The Jews in the Works of the Church Fathers," *JQR* (O.S.) 6 (1893/1894), pp. 225-61 (237). But almost certainly, these passages are only referring to the practice of slaughtering a *gedi mekulas*. See Safrai, p. 30, n. 55. (Obviously, the references to "sacrifices" and "offering" in the above passages are only translations.)

The Safrais suggest that the practice of preparing a *gedi mekulas* for the *seder* may have continued in Palestine through at least the seventh century. They point to the work *Sefer ha-Maasim* which includes the following passage:… גדי מקולס זה ניצלה שלם ראשו על כרעיו על קרבו. See Tzvi Meir Rabinovitz, "*Sefer ha-Maasim le-Vnei Eretz Yisrael: Seridim*

chapter of this *massekhet*. This suggests that this Mishnah was composed after the *ḥurban*, since it is reasonable to presume that *mishnayyot* that are presented in the early parts of a *massekhet* were composed first and that *mishnayyot* that are presented later were composed later.[56] Moreover, there is specific evidence suggesting that this particular chapter was composed after the *ḥurban*. Mishnah *Pesaḥim* 10:3 includes the statement: ובמקדש מביאין לפניו גופו של פסח. This statement suggests that the normative statements in this chapter describe only post-*ḥurban* practice.[57] Of course, the questions themselves could still

---

Ḥadashim," *Tarbiz* 41 (1972), pp. 275-305 (284). The Safrais believe that *Sefer ha-Maasim* was composed in Palestine around the seventh century and that it was a work whose purpose was to record decisions of *halakhah* applicable in its time. See Safrai, p. 30, and Rabinovitz, p. 280. The provenance, date of composition, and genre of *Sefer ha-Maasim* are still subject to debate. See Debra Reed Blank, "It's Time to Take Another Look at "Our Little Sister" Soferim: A Bibliographical Essay," *JQR* 90 (1999), pp. 1-26 (3, n. 9), and Brody, *The Geonim of Babylonia*, pp. 110-111.

56. Actually, the matter of the order of the chapters in Mishnah *Pesaḥim* is not so simple. Some manuscripts of the Talmud and commentaries by Rishonim follow an arrangement in which the tenth chapter follows the first four chapters. All these chapters together are called *Massekhet Pesaḥ Rishon* and the other chapters are called *Massekhet Pesaḥ Sheni*. R. Menachem Meiri writes that this alternative arrangement dates from the time of the Geonim or later. See Safrai, p. 19, n. 1. But some scholars, such as Shamma Friedman, believe that this alternative arrangement has a more ancient origin. See Friedman, p. 12, n. 5. If this alternative arrangement was the original arrangement, it is a mistake to view the tenth chapter as if it were the last of ten chapters.

57. Also, the names of the Sages included in the tenth chapter are: R. Tarfon, R. Akiva, R. Yose, R. Yishmael, Rabban Gamliel, and R. Eliezer b. R. Tzadok. (References to "Rabban Gamliel" in the Mishnah, without the description "*ha-zaken*," are almost always references to Rabban Gamliel of Yavneh. As to R. Eliezer b. R. Tzadok, he was active both before and after the *ḥurban*.) Mishnah *Pesaḥim* 10:6 records that R. Akiva included a prayer for the rebuilding of Jerusalem at his *seder*.

The introductory statement ערבי פסחים סמוך למנחה לא יאכל אדם עד שתחשך and the detailed instructions governing the drinking of wine also give the impression of a chapter composed after the *ḥurban*, detailing how an individual was obligated to conduct himself in his home. See Friedman, p. 409.

Two arguments between Bet Hillel and Bet Shammai are also included in this chapter. In general, these reflect arguments from Temple times. See, e.g., *Encyclopaedia Judaica* (1972) 4:738. But the author or editor of chapter 10 could simply have inserted this earlier material into a chapter

reflect questions from earlier times that were recorded in a chapter composed after the *ḥurban*.

But another argument can be made to support the idea that the questions were composed post-*ḥurban*. The *mah nishtannah* is not included in the tenth chapter of the Tosefta. Several scholars have studied the relationship between the Mishnah and Tosefta in the tenth chapter of *Pesaḥim* and elsewhere, and concluded that here, and often elsewhere as well, it is the Tosefta that reflects the earlier stage.[58] This also tends to support a post-*ḥurban* origin for the *mah nishtannah.*

So far, I have not discussed the precise role that the *mah nishtannah* serves in the Mishnah. But most likely, the *mah nishtannah* of the Mishnah was not a mandated piece of liturgy. Rather, it was what the child who lacked understanding was taught to ask (אם אין דעת בבן אביו מלמדו מה נשתנה).[59] This might also imply that the *mah nishtannah* text was a later development.

---

composed after the *ḥurban*. See Safrai, p. 19.

Many printed editions of Mishnah 10:3 read: ובמקדש היו מביאין לפניו גופו של פסח. But היו is a later addition. (See Safrai, p. 25 and Friedman, pp. 89 and 430.) Some have argued that the absence of היו provides a basis for dating this section of the Mishnah, and by implication, the rest of the chapter, to Temple times. In this interpretation, the Mishnah first states the practice in the גבולין in its time (הביאו לפניו...), and then continues with the practice in the מקדש (ובמקדש מביאין...). But as the Safrais (p. 25) and Friedman (pp. 89, 430-32 and 438) point out, such an interpretation is very unlikely, and the addition of היו does not change the meaning of the phrase, but correctly clarifies the original meaning.

The debate about whether the tenth chapter was composed before or after the *ḥurban* is summarized nicely by Friedman (see, e.g., pp. 88-92, 430-432, and 437-38). Friedman strongly advocates the position that the chapter was composed after the *ḥurban*.

58. See, e.g., the Friedman, who studied the relationship between the Mishnah and the Tosefta in the tenth and the first through fourth chapters of *Pesaḥim* in his *Tosefta Atikta*. See also the work of Judith Hauptman, e.g., "How Old is the Haggadah?," *Judaism* 51, no. 1 (2002), pp. 5-18, and *Rereading the Mishnah: A New Approach to Ancient Jewish Texts* (Tübingen: 2005). See also the entry "Tosefta" in the new *Encyclopaedia Judaica* (2006). Robert Brody agrees in principle that the Tosefta can sometimes reflect earlier material than the Mishnah, but thinks that this is not the case in the tenth chapter of *Pesaḥim*. See his *Mishnah and Tosefta Studies* (Jerusalem: 2014), pp. 141 and 151-54.

59. Steiner, pp.188, and 195-98. Steiner suggests that we should read this statement elliptically as if it includes the words לשאל after אין דעת בבן, and again after אביו מלמדו.

◆ ◆ ◆

The Talmud, at *Pesaḥim* 70a, records and accepts a statement by R. Ḥisda that the roast question was authored by Ben Tema. Ben Tema took the position that the *ḥagigah* too had to be roasted. In the view of R. Ḥisda, the language of the roast question, הלילה הזה כולו צלי, fits only the position of Ben Tema. Ben Tema is only mentioned at *Pesaḥim* 70a and *Yoma* 83a, and there is not enough information to determine if he lived during Temple times. (Some suggest that he is to be identified with R. Judah Ben Tema, who probably dates to the 2nd century C.E.,[60] but this identification is only conjecture.)

The above statement of R. Ḥisda is not recorded again at *Pesaḥim* 116a, where one would expect it.[61] Moreover, R. Ḥisda's statement is surprising, because it takes an overly literal approach to the roast question. There is also no statement in the Jerusalem Talmud expressing the view that the roast question was authored by Ben Tema.[62]

60. See *Encyclopaedia Judaica* (1972) 10:354 and Shamma Friedman, *Le-Ofiyyan Shel ha-Beraitot be-Talmud ha-Bavli: Ben Tema u-Ben Dortai, in Netiot le-David: Sefer ha-Yovel le-David Halivni*, eds. Yaakov Elman, Ephraim Betzalel Halivni, and Tzvi Aryeh Steinfeld (Jerusalem: 2004), pp. 195-274 (248-255).

61. But see Tosafot, s.v., כולו.

62. Many authorities seem to disregard the statement of R. Ḥisda. For example, R. Isaac Alfasi writes that the *ḥagigah* is to be commemorated at the *seder* by an item that is *mevushal*. Yet he implies in a different passage that the roast question was a normative question during Temple times. Similarly, Rambam does not follow the position of Ben Tema (see *Hilkhot Korban Pesaḥ* 10:13), but at the same time, he includes the roast question in his list of *mah nishtannah* from Temple times. See *Hilkhot Ḥametz u-Matzah* 8:2 (and *Leḥem Mishneh* there). Note that R. Joseph Caro, *OH* 473, takes the position that the egg that commemorates the *ḥagigah* should be מבושלת. Compare Tosafot *Pesaḥim* 114b, s.v., שני (the *halakhah* follows Ben Tema), and R. Moses Isserles, *OH* 473 (the egg that commemorates the *ḥagigah* must be roasted).

Friedman, in his *Tosefta Atikta*, pp. 91-92, accepts the essence of the interpretation of R. Ḥisda, but believes that the roast question must have been composed in accordance with a majority view. This leads him to conclude that the roast question must have been composed after the *ḥurban*. (In Temple times, a *ḥagigah* offering was brought, and according to the majority view, it was not roasted. Since the roast question includes the

◆ ◆ ◆

To summarize, it is possible that the *mah nishtannah* was composed during Temple times, but it also possible that it was composed after the *ḥurban*. In support of the latter is that the *mah nishtannah* is found in the last chapter of the *massekhet*, and in a chapter whose normative language suggests that it was composed after the *ḥurban*. The inclusion of a question about roast meat is not inconsistent with this approach. This question could have been composed after the *ḥurban* in an area which followed the post-*ḥurban* practice of preparing a *gedi mekulas* or in an area which followed the post-*ḥurban* practice of eating roast meat. But much more likely, if the question was composed after the *ḥurban*, it is referring to the *pesaḥ* sacrifice and was composed for educational purposes, as a simulation of a question that might have been asked during Temple times. The fact that the *mah nishtannah* is not included in the Tosefta also tends to support a post-*ḥurban* origin for it.

---

phrase הלילה הזה כולו צלי, it could not have been composed in accordance with the majority view in Temple times.) In his later article, *Le-Ofiyyan shel ha-Beraitot be-Talmud ha-Bavli*, Friedman discusses the Ben Tema passage extensively and takes a different approach.

10

Arami Oved Avi: Uncovering the Interpretation Hidden in the Mishnah

Introduction[1]

The book of Deuteronomy requires the following declaration to be made when the first fruits are brought: ...ארמי אבד אבי וירד מצרימה (Deut. 26:5). It is widely assumed that the Tannaim and Amoraim uniformly understood the word *arami* here as a reference to Lavan, and that the alternative understanding, "my father was a homeless/wandering/lost[2] Aramean," originated in the time of the Rishonim.

1. An earlier version of this article was published in *Ḥakirah*, vol. 13 (2012).

Several sources will be cited throughout: 1) Daniel Goldschmidt, *Haggadah shel Pesaḥ* (Jerusalem: 1960), cited as "Goldschmidt"; 2) Menaḥem M. Kasher, *Haggadah Shelemah* (Jerusalem: 1967, third ed.), cited as "Kasher"; 3) Yosef Tabory, "*Al Nusaḥ ha-Haggadah be-Zeman ha-Bayit*," *Sinai* 82 (1978), pp. 97-108, cited as "Tabory"; 4) David Henshke, "*Midrash Arami Oved Avi*," *Sidra* 4 (1988), pp. 33-51, cited as "Henshke"; 5) Richard Steiner, "The 'Aramean' of Deuteronomy 26:5: *Peshat* and *Derash*," in *Tehillah le-Moshe: Biblical and Judaic Studies in Honor of Moshe Greenberg*, eds. Mordechai Cogan, Barry Eichler, and Jeffrey Tigay (Winona Lake, Ind.: 1997), pp. 127-138, cited as "Steiner"; 6) Shmuel and Ze'ev Safrai, *Haggadat Ḥazal* (Jerusalem: 1998), cited as "Safrai"; 7) Jay Rovner, "An Early Passover Haggadah According to the Palestinian Rite," *JQR* 90 (2000), pp. 337-396, cited as "Rovner (2000)"; and 8) Rovner, "Two Early Witnesses to the Formation of the *Miqra Bikurim Midrash* and Their Implication for the Evolution of the Haggadah Text," *HUCA* 75 (2004), pp. 75-120, cited as "Rovner (2004)". All my citations to the *Encyclopaedia Judaica* are to the original edition (Jerusalem: 1972), unless otherwise noted.

2. Other widely proposed interpretations are: "perishing," "ready to perish," "persecuted," "poor," and "fugitive." See Part II.

This article will show that Mishnah *Pesaḥim* 10:4, a Tannaitic source, already understood *arami oved avi* to mean "my father was a homeless/wandering/lost Aramean."[3] The Rishonim who later offered this interpretation were not offering something new, but were resurrecting what was a mainstream Tannaitic interpretation.[4]

I. An Ancient Jewish Interpretation: The Subject of the Phrase is *Arami* and the Reference is to Lavan Seeking to Destroy Jacob

The interpretation of *arami oved avi* as a reference to Lavan seeking to destroy Jacob is an ancient one. It is recorded in early Jewish sources such as Onkelos,[5] *Sifrei Deuteronomy*,[6] *Midrash*

3. This point has already been made by Tabory and Henshke in the articles (in Hebrew) cited above. The present article expands the analysis.

More generally, readers should also be referred to Henshke's most recent article on Mishnah *Pesaḥim* 10:4-5, one which is groundbreaking but speculative. See his "*Al Rovdei Haggadat ha-Pesaḥ ba-Mishnah*," *Tarbiz* 81 (2013) pp. 25-45.

4. The widespread assumption that the Tannaim and Amoraim uniformly understood *arami* here as a reference to Lavan is also incorrect because another interpretation of *arami oved avi* is included as the first interpretation in *Sifrei Deuteronomy* (see below). See also the discussion below of a passage in *Sefer Pitron Torah*. Also, Targum Pseudo-Jonathan to Deut. 26:5 roughly parallels *Sifrei Deuteronomy*. The Septuagint had translated: "my father abandoned Syria."

5. Commentary to Deut. 26:5: לבן ארמאה בעא לאובדא ית אבא. (Another version has לאבדא, instead of לאובדא.) Onkelos lived in the second century, but a widespread view is that the translation known by his name did not reach its final form until the third century (*Encyclopaedia Judaica* 4:844). It is also possible that changes occurred in the text after that. Our earliest manuscripts of Targum Onkelos are medieval, although there are quotations and references to Onkelos in earlier sources.

The traditional reading in the Targum Pseudo-Jonathan to Deut. 26:5 will be mentioned below. But the Neofiti manuscript of this Targum follows Targum Onkelos: לבן ארמייה סבר למובדה לאבונן יעקב.

6. It is the second of what seems to be two different interpretations expressed here. See *Sifrei Deut.* 301: מלמד שלא ירד יעקב לארם אלא

Tanḥuma,[7] and the Haggadah.[8]

לאובד, ומעלה על לבן הארמי כאלו איבדו. The meaning of the first interpretation is unclear. (There are some variants in its text as well. For example, some texts read לאבד מן העולם.) For some attempts at understanding it, see, e.g., Tabory, p. 105, n. 29, and p. 106, and Yeshayahu Maori, *Targum ha-Peshiteta la-Torah ve-ha-Parshanut ha-Yehudit ha-Kedumah* (Jerusalem: 1995), p. 275. R. David Zevi Hoffmann speculated that the second interpretation was a later addition by someone attempting to reconcile the passage with the interpretation of Onkelos and the Haggadah. See his *Midrash Tannaim* (Berlin: 1909), p. 172, n. 5.

There is a parallel to the passage in the *Sifrei Deut.* at *Midrash Tannaim*, p. 172. Regarding this work, see below, n. 22. Targum Pseudo-Jonathan to Deut. 26:5 roughly parallels *Sifrei Deut.*, even though Lavan's name is not mentioned: לארם נהריא נחת אבונן יעקב... ובעא לאובדותיה.

7. *Midrash Tanḥuma*, Ekev 3: ואחרי כן בקש להרגו שנאמר ארמי אבד אבי. (See also Buber's edition, Ekev 5, p. 18.) The identification of the *arami* of Deut. 26:5 with Lavan is also found at *Mishnat R. Eliezer*, p. 163 (ed. Enelow), *Aggadat Bereshit* 53, and *Midrash Tehillim* 30:4. (In this last source, it is brought down in the name of R. Neḥemiah.) See also Targum Pseudo-Jonathan to Num. 31:8 and 1 Chron. 1:43. See also the passage at Jerusalem Talmud *Peah* 1:1 (16b) that interprets Obadiah 9-10, and Steiner, p. 136, n. 60. Finally, R. Nathan b. Jeḥiel (eleventh century) in his *Arukh*, entry: ארם, quotes a passage from an unknown *Yelammedenu* on Genesis that identifies the *arami* of Deut. 26:5 with Lavan.

8. צא ולמד מה בקש לבן הארמי לעשות ליעקב אבינו שפרעה לא גזר אלא על הזכרים ולבן בקש לעקר את הכל, שנאמר ארמי...

This section is generally found in the earliest Haggadot. See, e.g., Kasher, pp. 46-47, Safrai, pp. 271 and 287, Rovner (2000) p. 374, and Rovner (2004) pp. 83 and 91. Almost certainly, it was composed as a continuation of the *ve-hi she-amdah* section, and did not originate as part of any section of *derashot* on Deut. 26. See, e.g., Goldschmidt, pp. 38-39.

Scholars have frequently assumed that most of the *derashot* on Deuteronomy 26 now included in the *seder* ritual are Tannaitic. But Rovner, in his 2004 article, provided evidence for a late, Babylonian, origin of many. For example, the two earliest Haggadot from the Genizah (the fragment published by Rovner in 2000, and what Safrai calls "the Greenstone fragment," both of which reflect the Palestinian ritual) include the *ve-hi she-amdah* and *tzei u-lemad* sections, but do not

An additional allusion to this interpretation is perhaps found in the commentary of the church father Jerome (fourth century). Jerome translates *arami oved avi* as *Syrus persequebatur patrem meum*, "a Syrian pursued my father." It is possible that Jerome is not alluding to Lavan here, or that he is alluding to Lavan and came up with this translation on his own. But the influence of Jerome's Jewish teachers on other portions of his commentary has long been noted,[9] and it has been suggested that this is another such instance.[10]

The antiquity of the Lavan interpretation is also evidenced by the cantillation. According to most authorities, the cantillation sequence *pashta, zakef katon* on *arami oved avi* was formulated in accordance with the Lavan interpretation.[11]

In the period of the later Geonim and early Rishonim, both R. Saadiah Gaon[12] (d. 942) and Rashi (d. 1105) interpret *arami* as Lavan in their commentaries to Deut. 26:5.

---

include many of the traditional *derashot* on Deuteronomy 26. See Safrai, p. 287, and Rovner (2000), pp. 373-374. Rovner's view is followed in *The Schechter Haggadah* (Jerusalem: 2009), Joshua Kulp, David Golinkin, and David Harel, pp. 215-221.

It has long been observed that some of the language in *tzei u-lemad* (שפרעה לא גזר אלא על הזכרים) seems to be borrowed from *Sotah* 12a.

9. See, e.g., *Encyclopaedia Judaica* 9:1377, and Jay Braverman, *Jerome's Commentary on Daniel: A Study of Comparative Jewish and Christian Interpretations of the Hebrew Bible* (Washington DC : 1978), p. 6.

10. Goldschmidt, p. 35.

11. See, e.g., Goldschmidt, p. 34, Simḥa Kogut, *Ha-Mikra bein Taamim le-Parshanut* (Jerusalem: 1994), p. 65, Steiner, p. 131, n. 21, and A.M. Silbermann and M. Rosenbaum, eds., Pentateuch (Jerusalem: 1933), Deut., p. 223. The accents seem to divide the three words into the sections *arami* and *oved avi*. According to the approach described in Part II, the words should be divided into the sections *arami oved* and *avi*. (There are those who believe that the accents support the approach described in Part II. See, e.g., R. Samson Raphael Hirsch on Deut. 26:5.)

12. לבן הארמי קרוב היה לאבד את אבי (ed. Yosef Kafaḥ, Jerusalem, 1984, p. 181, translation from the Arabic).

II. Many Rishonim Take An Alternative Approach: The Subject of the Phrase is *Avi*

In the period of the Rishonim, commentaries that emphasized plain sense interpretation and grammar pointed out that the verb אב"ד is always intransitive when it is in the *kal* construct.[13] Thus *oved,* if it is being used as a *kal* verb at Deut. 26:5, cannot mean that Lavan was destroying or seeking to destroy one of our forefathers. Rather, the entire phrase should be looked at differently. The subject is *avi,* and *arami oved* is a description of *avi.* The meaning of the phrase is "my father was a homeless/wandering/lost Aramean."[14]

---

13. An intransitive verb does take a direct object. See, e.g., the use of the verb אבד in the *kal* in the *Shema* (Deut 11:17): "va-*avadetem meherah*..." This is not a statement that we will destroy someone quickly; it is a statement that we will lose our land quickly. Aside from Deut. 26:5, *oved* (with and without the *vav* as the second letter) is found ten other times in *Tanakh* (Num. 24:20 and 24:24, Deut. 32:28, Ps. 31:13 and 119:176, Job 4:11, 29:13, and 31:19, Eccl. 7:15, and Prov. 31:6). In none of these cases is it used as a transitive verb. It is only in the *piel* and *hif'il* tenses that the root אב"ד means destroy. (As examples, the *piel* third person present is *me'abbed* and third person past is *ibbed.*) Fundamentally, the root אב"ד means to lose something. But when used in the *piel* and in the *hif'il,* it refers to causing someone else to lose something.

Reading *oved* as the transitive present tense *kal,* "is destroying," had always been difficult in the context. The context seemed to require a statement about the past.

Some have suggested that Biblical Hebrew had a *poel* construct in which *oved* could be transitive. On such suggestions, see, e.g., Tabory, p. 102, n. 23, and Steiner, pp. 133-135. Neḥama Leibowitz cites approvingly Maharal's suggestion that *oved* is used as a noun here: an Aramean was the destroyer of my father. (But she still prefers the approach of Part II.) See her *Studies in Devarim* (trans. by Aryeh Newman, Jerusalem, 1980), p. 271, and see Maharal, *Gur Aryeh,* commentary to Deut. 26:5, and *Gevurot Hashem,* ch. 54.

Of course, contextually it made little sense for there to be a reference to Lavan in *mikra bikkurim.* These verses were intended to provide only a capsule summary of the origin of the Israelites.

14. It is usually thought that the first authorities to propose this explanation were R. Abraham Ibn Ezra and Rashbam. Steiner, p. 128, points out that it was proposed a generation earlier by R. Judah Ibn Balam in his

These rabbinic commentaries did not agree on whether "my father" refers to Abraham or to Jacob. For example, Rashbam[15] and R. Joseph Bekhor Shor identified "my father" with Abraham, while R. Judah Ibn Balam, R. Abraham Ibn Ezra, and R. David Kimḥi identified "my father" with Jacob.[16] (An alternative approach is to view "my father" as

---

commentaries (composed in Arabic) to Deut. 26:5 and Hoshea 12:13. (Much of the literature on this explanation is collected and summarized by Steiner, pp. 127-130.)

As I will argue in the text, this explanation is implicit in Mishnah *Pesaḥim* 10:4. It is also probably the view of R. Shimon b. Yoḥai. See below, n. 22.

Additional midrashic material on *mikra bikkurim* has come to light in recent decades in a work known as *Sefer Pitron Torah*, edited in the ninth or tenth century, and published by Ephraim Urbach (Jerusalem: 1978). This work includes midrashic material from Tannaitic, Amoraic and Geonic times. According to Menaḥem Yitzḥak Kahana, *Sifrei Zuta Devarim* (Jerusalem: 2002), pp. 33-36, the *derashot* on *mikra bikkurim* included in this work probably reflect Tannaitic material. (Rovner disagrees. See Rovner, 2004, pp. 115-20, and especially, p. 118, n. 130.) The explication on *arami oved avi* here is: לארם ירד אבי וכבר היה אביד שם. See Kahana, p. 415. As Kahana observes, this seems to reflect a form of our explanation. (The actual reading in the second to last word is אביך, but the proposed emendation by Urbach and Kahana to אביד seems reasonable.) See also Kahana's comments on the words גולה ומטורף in this same passage.

Steiner refers, p. 131, n. 24, to two interpretations reported by the tenth-century Karaite Biblical commentator Yefet ben Eli. In these, אב"ד is intransitive, but ארמי is still identified as Lavan.

15. Aside from his comments on Deut. 26:5, see also his comments on Gen. 20:13 (כאשר התעו אתי).

16. Steiner, pp. 128-29. Also, Rambam believed that the reference was to Jacob. See his *Sefer ha-Mitzvot*, positive commandment, #132.

Arami fits Abraham better than Jacob. The land of Aram is the area that Abraham identified as his native land. See, e.g., Gen. 24:10. (Eliezer is sent to Aram Naharayim to find a wife for Isaac.) See also Naḥmanides to Gen. 11:28 and 12:1. (Compare the view of Rashi. See, e.g., his comments to Gen. 12:1.) The term *arami* does not seem consistent with the Biblical description of Jacob (see, e.g., Gen. 31:20 and 47), even though Jacob served Lavan in Aram for 20 years (Gen. 31:38).

The continuation of Deut. 26:5, *va-yered mitzraimah va-yagar sham bi-metei me'at va-yehi sham le-goy gadol atzum va-rav*, fits Jacob better than Abraham.

combining the forefathers into one composite figure.[17])

(The issue of the location of Abraham's native land is a fascinating one. In addition to Rashi and Naḥmanides, see, e.g., Shubert Spero, "Was Abram born in Ur of the Chaldees?" *JQR* 24:3 (1996), pp.156-159, Patricia Berlyn, "The Journey of Terah: to Ur-Kasdim or Urkesh?" *Jewish Bible Quarterly* 33:2 (2005), pp. 73-80, Hershel Shanks, "Abraham's Ur: Is the Pope Going to the Wrong Place?" *BAR* March-April 2000, pp. 62-63 and 69, and Alan R. Millard, "Where was Abraham's Ur?" *BAR* May-June 2001, pp. 52-53 and 57. See also the commentary of Samuel David Luzzatto to Gen. 11:28, in *The Book of Genesis: A Commentary by ShaDaL*, ed. Daniel A. Klein, Northvale, N.J., 1998, pp. 118-119 and Klein's note.)

Regarding the precise meaning of the word *oved* here, widely suggested interpretations are: homeless, wandering, lost, perishing, ready to perish, persecuted, and poor. See, e.g., the commentaries of Ibn Balam, Rashbam, Ibn Ezra, Radak (*Sefer ha-Shorashim*), Seforno, Bekhor Shor, R. Samson Raphael Hirsch, and S.R. Driver, *A Critical and Exegetical Commentary on Deuteronomy* (New York: 1965, third ed.), p. 289. See Steiner, pp. 128-29. See also Jer. 50:6. In most instances in *Tanakh*, the meaning of *oved* seems to be "perishing" or "poor." At Ps. 119:176, the meaning seems to be "wandering." At Deut. 32:28, the meaning seems to be "lacking." At Num. 24:20 and 24:24, the meaning seems to be "destroyed." Akkadian parallels suggest a nuance of "fugitive" or "refugee. See Steiner, p. 128, n. 6, and Hayim ben Yosef Tawil, *An Akkadian Lexical Companion for Biblical Hebrew* (Jersey City: 2009), p. 2. In Papyrus Anastasi I, from the thirteenth century B.C.E., the verb אב"ד is found in a Canaanite sentence which some believe to be a close parallel to Ps. 119:176. Steiner, p. 128, n. 6.

17. See similarly the use of אבי at Ex. 15:2, and of אביך at Ex. 3:6. As stated by Luzzatto (commentary to Deut. 26:5):

אבי: כולל כל האבות כאחד שהיו תועים מגוי אל גוי והראשון בא מארם...

Luzzatto points out that Rashbam also alluded to this approach. Even though the Rashbam begins with a statement that *arami* refers to Abraham, Rashbam concludes with the following statement: מארץ נכריה באו אבותינו לארץ הזאת. The *Biur* of Moses Mendelssohn had taken such an approach earlier than Luzzatto. See Steiner, p. 129. Steiner suggests (p. 130) that the referent of *avi* can be expanded to include Jacob's sons as well (e.g., all but one were born in Aram of Aramean mothers). R. Judah he-Ḥasid suggests that the reference is specifically to Joseph. See Ephraim Kanarfogel, *The Intellectual History and Rabbinic Culture of Medieval Ashkenaz* (Detroit: 2013), p. 236.

III. The View of the Above Rishonim Was the View of the Mishnah

Mishnah *Pesaḥim* 10:4 includes the following statement:[18]

מתחיל בגנות ומסיים בשבח ודורש מ"ארמי אובד אבי" עד שהוא גומר את כל הפרשה.[19]

The Talmud records an Amoraic dispute about the meaning of the word גנות (disgrace, shame) here:[20]

מאי בגנות רב אמר מתחלה עובדי עבודה זרה היו אבותינו [ושמואל] אמר עבדים היינו.

Philo (1st century B.C.E.) also offered an interpretation based on a composite approach, even though he translated *oved* differently. Philo translated: "the leaders of our nation renounced Syria." See his *Special Laws* II, XXXV, 216. (Philo's translation was based on that of the Septuagint. See above, n. 4.)

18. In the mishnah, this passage is preceded by: 1) *ve-im ein daat ba-ben, aviv melamdo*, 2) the *mah nishtannah* section, and 3) *u-le-fi daato shel ben, aviv melamdo*. Most likely, *mah nishtannah* was only what the child who lacks understanding was taught to ask. See, e.g., Richard Steiner, "On the Original Structure and Meaning of *Mah Nishtannah* and the History of Its Reinterpretation," *Jewish Studies, an Internet Journal* 7 (2008), pp. 163-204 (188 and 195-98). (It was only in the post-Talmudic period that *mah nishtannah* began to be treated as a mandated piece of liturgy.) *Mathil be-genut... kol ha-parashah* seems to be the answer in the *seder* ritual. It can be argued that it too was addressed only to the child who lacks understanding, but one does not have to take this approach.

The correct text in the mishnah of what follows is not רבן גמליאל היה אומר, but רבן גמליאל אומר. Steiner, p. 196, n. 123, Safrai, pp. 35, 279, and 288, and Kasher, p. 128 (note to line 1). These words signal a disagreement with the previous statement, i.e., a different answer is now being provided.

19. Even though many texts continue with the word *kullah*, this word is almost certainly a later addition. See, e.g., Safrai, p. 33. It is not found in the similar passage at Mishnah *Bikkurim* 3:6. See below, n. 29.

20. The standard printed Talmud (*Pesaḥim* 116a) lists the disputants here as Rav and (in brackets) Samuel. Kasher (p. 22) points out that different disputants are named in some Rishonim and manuscripts. There is no Amoraic discussion of the *shevaḥ* of the mishnah.

Neither opinion seems to consider the *arami oved avi* section (Deut. 26:5 and the verses that follow) as relating to the *genut* referred to in the mishnah.[21]

But what if we would consider the mishnah on our own? The mishnah instructs one to begin with an exposition of *genut* and end with one of *shevaḥ*. It then refers immediately to Deut. 26:5-9, a section that can easily be understood (as will be explained below) as beginning with *genut*[22] and ending with *shevaḥ*. This can be mere coincidence,

21. Of course, the above Amoraic statements are very unclear. Is each referring to the beginning of a *derashah* that was known at their time, similar or identical to the ones we recite today? Is each merely stating an idea or minimum words that need to be expressed? Is each referring exclusively or primarily to a verse? In the Jerusalem Talmud (*Pesaḥim* 10:5, 37d), the second statement is not brought at all, and Rav's statement is a citation to Josh. 24:2-3. In light of this, it is possible to understand the first statement in the Babylonian Talmud (assuming it was made by Rav) as a reference to Josh. 24:2-3. No matter how the first statement is understood, it is hard to connect it to Deut. 26:5 and the verses that follow. If Samuel's statement is referring to a verse, the most likely candidate is Deut. 6:21: ואמרת לבנך עבדים היינו. Of course, it is possible that Samuel was referring to Deut. 26:6 and its surrounding verses, but the phrase עבדים היינו does not appear in these verses.

22. Two passages elsewhere in rabbinic literature, in the name of the Tanna R. Shimon b. Yoḥai, label the section that begins with Deut. 26:5 as a section of *genut*:

1) *Midrash Tannaim*, p. 172:

> ועניח ואמרת ... ר' שמעון בן יוחאי אומר שבחו של אדם אומרו בקול נמוך גניו אדם אומרו בקול גבוה.

See also, p. 175. (ועניח means "you shall say with a raised voice.") Only a small portion of *Midrash Tannaim* has been recovered. For further discussion of this work, see *Encyclopaedia Judaica* (1972) 11:1518-19, *Encyclopaedia Judaica* (Detroit and Jerusalem: 2006) 13:793-94, and Rovner (2004), p. 79. Despite its title, the work may not be Tannaitic.

2) *Sotah* 32b:

> תניא רשב"י אומר אדם אומר שבחו בקול נמוך וגנותו בקול רם שבחו בקול נמוך מן וידוי המעשר גנותו בקול רם ממקרא ביכורים.

(Admittedly, the subsequent discussion at *Sotah* 32b reinterprets or emends גנותו to צערו.)

but much more likely the adjacency suggests that Deut. 26:5-9 is the *genut-shevaḥ* section referred to.[23] Moreover, to follow the alternative interpretation is to view the mishnah as providing a *genut-shevaḥ* instruction that is very vague.

R. Shimon b. Yoḥai would probably agree that this section should be considered one of both *genut* and *shevaḥ*. He only called it a section of *genut* because he was making a point relating to the first part of the section.

23. R. David Zevi Hoffman, a rabbinic figure in modern times, took the position that the verses from Deuteronomy 26 constituted the *genut* and the *shevaḥ* of the mishnah. He took this position in his *Melammed Leho'il* (Frankfurt: 1926-32), vol. 3, sec. 65, and in various other places (see Tabory, p. 97, n. 2 for the references.) Hoffmann argued that even Rav and Samuel understood that the verses from Deuteronomy 26 constituted the *genut* and *shevaḥ* of the mishnah. He suggests that they gave new interpretations of *genut* because the *genut* and *shevaḥ* of the mishnah had to be reinterpreted when the original *shevaḥ*, verse 26:9, was no longer appropriate for recital

Long before Hoffmann, Ibn Balam took the position that the verses from Deuteronomy 26 constituted the *genut* and the *shevaḥ* of the mishnah. Isaac Abrabanel took this position as well, at least in one place; see his *Tzeli Eish* commentary on the Haggadah, quoted in Abraham Aderet, "*Arami Oved Avi*," *Alei Siaḥ* 12-14 (1982), pp. 70-93 (76). The Maharal took this position in his *Gur Aryeh* commentary to Deut. 26:5 and in his *Gevurot Hashem* 54. In the modern period, scholars who have taken this position include Goldschmidt, p. 14, Henshke, pp. 33-39, Tabory, *Pesaḥ Dorot* (Tel Aviv: 1996) pp. 356-59, Steiner, p. 195 (2008 article), Kahana, pp. 417 and 423, and Samuel Tobias Lachs, "Two Related Arameans," *Journal for the Study of Judaism* 17 (1986), pp. 65-69 (65). (But others, such as Safrai, p. 32 and Kulp, Golinkin and Harel, p. 214, disagree. David Halivni disagrees as well. See below, n. 31.)

The *Seder Rav Amram Gaon* (ed. Daniel Goldschmidt, Jerusalem, 1971), p. 113, includes a statement that the verses from Deuteronomy 26 constitute the *genut*. This statement would appear to be based on the statement of R. Shimon b. Yoḥai quoted above, and on an overly literal reading of the statement. See above, n. 22, last paragraph.

Since the Talmud nowhere discusses what the *shevaḥ* was, rabbinic authorities were free to take the position that the verses from Deuteronomy 26 constituted the *shevaḥ*. Some who do are cited by Kasher, pp. 30-32 and Henshke, p. 36, n. 11. This also seems to be the position taken by Rambam; see his *Hilkhot Ḥametz u-Matzah* 7:4, and Henshke, ibid. (As pointed out by Henshke, Kasher mischaracterizes the view of Rambam in his *Haggadah Shelemah*, p. 30. Kasher's quote of Rambam ends too soon here.)

Deut. 26:5-9 reads:

(5) ועניּת ואמרת לפני ה׳ אלהיך ארמי אבד אבי וירד מצרימה
ויגר שם במתי מעט ויהי שם לגוי גדול עצום ורב
(6) וירעו אתנו המצרים ויענונו ויתנו עלינו עבדה קשה
(7) ונצעק אל ה׳ אלקי אבתינו וישמע ה׳ את קלנו
וירא את ענינו ואת עמלנו ואת לחצנו
(8) ויוצאנו ה׳ ממצרים ביד חזקה ובזרע נטויה ובמרא גדל
ובאתות ובמפתים
(9) ויבאנו אל המקום הזה ויתן לנו את הארץ הזאת ארץ
זבת חלב ודבש.

A very reasonable approach to understanding the mishnah is that the *genut* referred to focuses on the phrase *arami oved avi* and the *shevaḥ* referred to focuses on verse 9.[24] This *shevaḥ* can be either the implicit praise of our ancestors for becoming worthy of being given the land,[25] or the praise of God for giving it to them. A *genut* of "my father was a homeless/wandering/lost Aramean" contrasts perfectly with this *shevaḥ*. Moreover, a statement that "Lavan was trying to destroy my father" does not, on the simplest level, amount to a *genut*; it is merely a statement about an attempt to make our ancestor into a victim.[26] Thus,

---

24. Scholars who take this approach include Henshke, pp. 37-39, Tabory, p. 106 and *Pesaḥ Dorot*, p. 358, and Kahana, p. 423.

25. Alternatively, being described as a people who live in their own land is probably enough to be considered a *shevaḥ*, since it contrasts with the previous *genut* (no matter how defined). One does not have to rely on the idea of implicit praise.

26. If the *shevaḥ* is not a praise of God, but of the Israelites, it implies some kind of a change in status. There is no such change if "Lavan was trying to destroy my father" is the *genut*.

Of course, it is a reproach or embarrassment on some level to have been weak enough to be a potential victim. But this is not the simplest implication of the term *genut* (Henshke, pp. 37-38).

We can now understand Rashi's unusual comment at *Sotah* 32b. Here, the Talmud refers to *mikra bikkurim* as *genut*, and Rashi explains the *genut* as the confession that our ancestor Lavan was a *rasha*. Why did Rashi not write that the *genut* was that Lavan tried to destroy Jacob? As Henshke suggests (p. 38), Rashi understood that this would not be a *genut* in the simplest meaning of the term. Rashi had to find a *genut* within his approach that the Aramean was Lavan.

the mishnah itself implicitly understands *arami oved avi* as "my father was a homeless/wandering/lost Aramean."

Of course, it is possible to view the *genut* and *shevaḥ* of the mishnah differently. One can argue that being ill-treated, afflicted and put to hard work in Egypt is the *genut*, and being taken out (and brought to Israel) is the *shevaḥ*. But in this interpretation, the *genut* does not begin until the sixteenth word וירעו.[27] Moreover, verse 6 only describes what the Egyptians did to us; it does not call us *avadim* or directly assign to us a negative status. Reading the *genut* as focusing on the first few words of the section, words that do clearly portray a *genut* in the non-Lavan understanding, seems to be the simplest understanding of the mishnah.

Our assumption that verse 9 was part of the ritual at the time of the mishnah is a compelling one.[28] The mishnah describes the section

---

Even if Lavan's attempt to destroy Jacob could be considered a *genut*, for the mishnah to have decided to commence an exposition at the *seder* with a reference to Lavan seems farfetched. The purpose of the *seder* was to commemorate the Exodus. Fundamentally, an exposition at the *seder* should commence with either the beginning of slavery, or the beginning of the story of our ancestors, and not with a side matter, such as one involving Lavan (Henshke, p. 39).

27. It is hard to consider anything in verse 5 after *arami oved avi* as a *genut*. Being small in number might be a *genut* but it is followed immediately by *va-yehi sham le-goy gadol atzum ve-rav* and it is difficult to view this as the *genut/shevaḥ* contrast contemplated by the mishnah.

28. It is made by many scholars. See, e.g., Goldschmidt, p. 14, Tabory, pp. 106-08 and *Pesaḥ Dorot*, p. 358, Lachs, p. 65, and Kahana, p. 423. (But others, such as Safrai, p. 33 and Kulp, Golinkin and Harel, p. 214, disagree.) Some rabbinic authorities who have taken the position that verse 9 was part of the Mishnah *Pesaḥim* ritual include R. Shimon b. Tzemaḥ Duran (see Tabory, Pesaḥ Dorot, p. 358), R. David Zevi Hoffmann (see above, n. 23), and R. Joseph B. Soloveitchik (see, e.g., Abraham R. Besdin, *Reflections of the Rav*, Jerusalem, 1979, pp. 210-11). It can even be argued that the *mikra bikkurim* section was chosen as the section for exposition at the *seder* precisely because it included a verse about the Jews being brought to Israel.

Sifrei Deut. 301, which includes explications on Deut. 26:5-8, also includes an explication on Deut. 26:9. If we take the position, as some do (see, e.g., Safrai, p. 33) that this section of the *Sifrei* is derived from an early Haggadah text, this would be further evidence that verse 9 was part of the *seder* ritual of the mishnah. *Midrash Tannaim* (pp. 173-74) also includes

to be expounded upon as running from *arami oved avi* through *kol ha-parshah*. To read the mishnah as implying that only up to verse 8 was expounded upon is farfetched. Verse 9 is a direct continuation of the capsule history ongoing in verses 5 through 8; the mishnah would have had to be more specific to indicate that verse 9 was not part of the ritual. Moreover, Mishnah *Bikkurim* 3:6 specifies a ritual in the *bikkurim* context beginning with *arami oved avi* and continuing through *kol ha-parashah*.[29] It is evident from Deuteronomy 26 that verse 9 was part of the ritual recitation there.[30]

---

an explication on verse 9. Also, the *mikra bikkurim* section in *Sefer Pitron Torah* includes an explication on verse 9. If we adopt Kahana's view of the dating of this section (see above, n. 14), this would be further evidence that verse 9 was part of the *seder* ritual of the mishnah. See Kahana, p. 423. (But according to Rovner, most of the *mikra bikkurim* section in *Sefer Pitron Torah* did not develop from the original Palestinian *seder*, but was created later, in a Babylonian or Persian setting. See Rovner, p. 120, 2004.)

It is likely that the tenth chapter of Mishnah *Pesaḥim* reflects the ritual after the *ḥurban*, not before. See Shamma Friedman, *Tosefta Atikta: Massekhet Pesaḥ Rishon* (Ramat Gan: 2002), pp. 88-92, 430-432, and 437-38, and Henshke (2013), p. 29. The Tannaim still lived in Israel after 70 C.E. One can easily take the position that all the *mah nishtannah* questions were composed after the *ḥurban*. See my article on the *mah nishtannah* in the present volume.

Admittedly, verse 9 is not found in any surviving Haggadah text. But our earliest Haggadah texts are only from the Geonic period (from Babylonia and from Palestine/Egypt), long after the period of the Mishnah. Our position is only that verse 9 must have been part of the *seder* ritual at the time of the Mishnah. It may have already been gone from the ritual by the time written Haggadot began to be composed. Admittedly, why it would disappear from the Palestinian ritual requires explanation. Perhaps the statements of Rav and Samuel eventually influenced the Palestinian ritual.

29. וקורא מ"ארמי אבד אבי" עד שהוא גומר כל הפרשה.

30. The *bikkurim* ritual also includes the first part of verse 10 (*ve-attah hinneh heveti et reshit pri ha-adamah asher natattah li Hashem*). If we make the reasonable assumption that these words were not part of the *seder* ritual at the time of the mishnah, we have to admit that the term *kol ha-parashah* does not mean exactly the same thing in both cases.

Alternatively, we can suggest that the term *kol ha-parashah* means exactly the same thing in both cases; it refers to the capsule history. We can view the first part of verse 10 as a mere addendum, applicable in the *bikkurim* ritual only. (But *Midrash Tannaim*, p. 172, seems to view the

◆ ◆ ◆

It has been argued that *ve-doresh* means some form of extended exposition beyond the reading of verses.[31] If it does, then perhaps the statement beginning with *ve-doresh* introduces a new requirement and is not merely a specification of the manner of fulfilling the *genut/shevaḥ* requirement. Alternatively, even if the statement beginning with *ve-doresh* is meant as such a specification, perhaps the *genut* and *shevaḥ* are found in the extended exposition and not in the verses themselves.

But although we are used to the root *doresh* as indicating an extended exposition, or a resort to *midrashim* or hermeneutical principles, this was probably not the meaning of this root at the time of the mishnah. As one scholar has written:

> The Mishnah probably did not assume knowledge of midrash, even the simple midrash in our Haggadot.... [T]he verb דרש was used to mean 'expound,' 'explain,' 'explicate'....[32]
>
> ◆ ◆ ◆
>
> [T]he addition of midrashic elements [to *miqra' bikurim*] progressed slowly, giving the impression that earlier the *miqra' bikurim* lection was simply recited by itself or else it was variously "expounded" according to each leader's tastes and abilities....
>
> The usage of *drš* to indicate recourse to hermeneutical principles develops in the amoraic period....[33]

---

first part of verse 10 as within *kol ha-parashah*. Despite its title, *Midrash Tannaim* may not be a Tannaitic work. See above, n. 22.)

Those disagreeing with the view that verse 9 was part of the *seder* ritual can argue that the author of Mishnah *Pesaḥim* 10:4 merely borrowed the term *kol ha-parashah* from Mishnah *Bikkurim* 3:6, even though nothing past verse 8 was included in the *seder* ritual. But this is farfetched. Precision was surely intended in Mishnah *Pesaḥim* 10:4; this mishnah was composed to give instruction with regard to the proper *seder* ritual. (I do not view the imprecision with regard to the first part of verse 10 as significant.)

31. Both David Halivni and Safrai take this position. See Safrai, p. 32 and his reference to Halivni there. In their view, the word *ve-doresh* would not be used if the focus was mainly on the verses themselves.

32. Rovner (2000), p. 354.

33. Rovner (2004), p. 72, n. 2.

Thus, Mishnah *Pesaḥim* 10:4 most likely did not mean that *derashot* of the Sages on *mikra bikkurim* were expounded upon at this point. All it meant was that some explanation above and beyond the mere recital of the verses was required or customary. In this interpretation of *doresh*, there is not an implication that the statement beginning with *ve-doresh* introduces a new requirement,[34] or that the *genut* and *shevaḥ* are found in the exposition and not in the verses themselves.

CONCLUSION

Reading the *genut* as focusing on the first few words of the Deut. 26:5-9 section seems to be the simplest understanding of the mishnah. If the *genut* is to be located in these words, the mishnah almost certainly understood *arami oved avi* to mean "my father was a homeless/wandering/lost Aramean."[35] If we make the compelling assumption that verse 9 (*va-yevienu el ha-makom ha-zeh va-yitten lanu et ha-aretz ha-zot…*) was part of the *seder* ritual at the time of the mishnah, a *genut* of "my father was a homeless/wandering/lost Aramean" contrasts perfectly with the *shevaḥ*.

Our approach to Mishnah *Pesaḥim* 10:4 is very satisfying, since we are no longer forced to take the position that a widespread interpretation of the Sages was ungrammatical.[36] There is other evidence that the Sages knew that *oved*, as a verb, was intransitive.[37]

Over the centuries, due to the influence of Onkelos and the Haggadah, and due to the statements made by the Amoraim about Mishnah *Pesaḥim* 10:4, the way the mishnah originally understood

---

34. Since the statement of R. Shimon b. Yoḥai cited in *Midrash Tannaim* and *Sotah* 32b refers to the *mikra bikkurim* verses as *genut*, this strongly suggests that we are reading the mishnah correctly in viewing the *mikra bikkurim* verses as the *genut* and the *shevaḥ*. This point was made by Hoffmann.

35. This was probably the view of the Tanna R. Shimon b. Yoḥai as well (see above, n. 22). See also our discussion of a passage in *Sefer Pitron Torah*, above, n. 14.

36. Also, as mentioned earlier, contextually it made little sense for there to be a reference to Lavan in either *mikra bikkurim* or the beginning of the story told at the *seder*.

37. Steiner, p. 132, citing *Sifrei Deut.*, secs. 354, 324 and 43.

arami oved avi was forgotten.[38] It did not occur to the Rishonim who argued for the homeless/wandering/lost Aramean interpretation that they were advocating the interpretation already implied in this mishnah.[39]

Of course, a fascinating question is what motivated the Lavan interpretation.[40] This question is even stronger if we make the reasonable assumption that whoever authored the interpretation knew that the verb אב"ד, in the *kal*, is intransitive. Many answers to this question have been suggested. The best answer is that the author of the Lavan interpretation wanted to avoid tying the origins of the Jewish people to the Arameans. The interpretation was probably authored at a time and locale when such a connection would have been thought of as disparaging.[41] The author's desire to avoid a Jewish-Aramean connection was probably

38. The fact that the *trop* also seems to be consistent with the Lavan interpretation perhaps contributed to this as well. Also, because of its location in the Haggadah and utilization of Deut. 26:5, it was probably often erroneously assumed that the passage in the Haggadah with the Lavan interpretation was connected to the following section of the Haggadah, which comprised *derashot* of the Sages on Deut. 26:5-8. This made the Lavan interpretation appear to be the official interpretation of the Sages on Deut. 26:5. See Lachs, pp. 68-69, and Tabory, *Pesaḥ Dorot*, p. 358, n. 38. *Sifrei Deut.* included another interpretation aside from the Lavan interpretation, but this may not have been well-known.

Ironically, because the Lavan interpretation has usually been viewed as the official interpretation of the Sages, many rabbinic authorities have gone to great lengths to attempt to justify it, and have severely criticized Rishonim who adopted the alternative "homeless/wandering/lost Aramean" interpretation. See, e.g., the Maharal's *Gur Aryeh* commentary to Deut. 26:5, and his *Gevurot Hashem* 54, and see Steiner, pp. 132-34.

39. The only exception is Ibn Balam. He cited Mishnah *Pesaḥim* 10:4 and understood it the way I am suggesting here.

40. It bears repeating that the Lavan interpretation may have originated after the time of Onkelos himself. See above, n. 5.

41. See, e.g., Kogut, p. 66 and 192, and Steiner, p. 129, n. 9. Steiner writes:

> If the meaning 'Gentile, heathen' (attested for ארמי in Jewish and Christian dialects of Late Aramaic) developed early enough, the standard Jewish interpretation [=the Lavan interpretation] may have been a response to it, as well.

Similarly, Tabory, p. 104, n. 27 (citing Abraham Geiger) writes that the term ארמי became the usual term for idolators.

strong enough to outweigh any concern about the odd grammatical construct that resulted from the new interpretation.[42]

---

42. Some other suggestions include:

1) The author of the interpretation interpreted the word *oved* as though it were Aramaic. Steiner writes (pp. 136-138):

   In Aramaic, אובד is not a *Qal* participle with the meaning 'perishing, wandering' but rather, a third masculine-singular *'Apel* perfect with the meaning 'he destroyed.'.... It is perhaps not fortuitous that the rabbis chose to read this particular verb as Aramaic; after all, it describes an activity of an ארמי 'Aramean.'

2) The author of the interpretation had a different vocalization of אבד in his text of Deut. 26:5. He had a vocalization which would be consistent with the verb being in the *piel*. See, e.g., Steiner p. 135, citing Arnold Bogumil Ehrlich.
3) The author of the interpretation was employing a pun, based on his knowledge of Greek. In Greek, ἐρημόω is a rough equivalent of "destroy." (In a widely used *Greek-English Lexicon*, it is defined as: "to strip bare, to desolate, lay waste."). See David Berger, "Three Typological Themes in Early Jewish Messianism: Messiah Son of Joseph, Rabbinic Calculations, and the Figure of Armilus," *AJS Review* 10 (1985), pp. 141-64 (161, n. 77).

It should be mentioned that the only individuals referred to as Aramean in the Torah are Lavan and Betuel. This also could have motivated or been a contributing factor to the interpretation. See, e.g., Goldschmidt, p. 34. The word order *arami oved avi* also perhaps contributed to *arami* being viewed as the subject.

Louis Finkelstein suggested that the Lavan interpretation arose in the 3rd century B.C.E., when Palestine was under Egyptian rule and the Syrians were viewed as enemies. He suggested alternatively that the interpretation arose in Maccabean times. The Syrians were viewed as enemies in this period as well. See Finkelstein, "The Oldest Midrash: Pre-Rabbinic Ideals and Teachings in the Passover Haggada," *Harvard Theological Review* 31 (1938), pp. 291-317 (300). Most scholars today reject these suggestions. It is complete speculation to pinpoint the origin of the Lavan interpretation to these particular periods.

It is noteworthy that Josephus (1st cent. C.E.) did not mention Lavan in his brief paraphrase of *mikra bikkurim* at *Antiquities* IV, 242:

Another fascinating question is what motivated the two Amoraim to deviate from the plain sense of the mishnah that the *genut* is found in the *mikra bikkurim* verses. Many answers to this question have been suggested as well.[43]

◆ ◆ ◆

I will close with a description of how the all-important *Maxwell House Haggadah* has revised its translation of our passage. The original edition, published in 1932, translated *arami* as "Syrian." Because of Syria's ongoing conflict with the State of Israel, it was decided to avoid this term in the new translation, published in 2011. The new translation is "Aramite." According to the translator, "Aramite" was chosen over "Aramean" because "Aramite" sounded nastier, and "Laban, as a nasty customer, deserves a nasty description."(!) [44]

[L]et him... render thanks to God for having delivered his race from the insolence of the Egyptians and given them a good land and spacious to enjoy the fruits thereof.

43. As mentioned earlier (above, n. 23), Hoffmann deals with this question. Attempts have also been made to interpret the two Amoraic statements in a manner consistent with *mikra bikkurim* being the *genut* and *shevaḥ* of the mishnah. On all these issues, see, e.g., Goldschmidt, p. 14, Tabory, pp. 97-99 and *Pesaḥ Dorot*, pp. 358-59, and Henshke, pp. 33-35 and 39-46.
44. Deena Yellin, "Haggada on the House," *The International Jerusalem Post*, April 15-21, 2011, p. 25.

11

The *Pe/Ayin* Order in Ancient Israel and its Implications for the Book of *Tehillim* [1]

The first four chapters of the book of *Eikhah* are alphabetical acrostics.[2]

---

1. I would like to acknowledge Sam Borodach and Rabbi Mordy Friedman for their thoughts and assistance.

An earlier version of this article was published at seforim.traditiononline.org on July 26, 2009. A short version (with photos) was published as "Can Archaeology Help Date the Psalms?" *BAR*, July-August 2012, pp. 47-50 and 68. Another version was published in *JSOT*, "Using the *Pe-Ayin* Order of the Abecedaries of Ancient Israel to Date the Book of Psalms," 38 (2014), pp. 471-485.

2. In the third chapter, there are three verses for each letter.

The fifth chapter consists of exactly twenty-two verses, just like the first, second, and fourth chapters, even though it is not an acrostic. This is probably not a coincidence. See, e.g., Elie Assis, "The Alphabetic Acrostic in the Book of Lamentations," *Catholic Biblical Quarterly* 69 (2007), pp. 710-724 (711). One scholar has suggested that the lack of an acrostic in the fifth chapter may be a subtle way of indicating that the intensity of the poet's grief has exhausted his poetic powers. See John Brug, "Biblical Acrostics and their Relationship to Other Ancient Near Eastern Acrostics," in William W. Hallo, Bruce William Jones and Gerald L. Mattingly, eds., *The Bible in the Light of Cuneiform Literature* (Lewiston, N.Y.: 1990), p. 286. Meir Bar-Ilan has suggested that the fifth chapter was a communal lament with many different authors and originally included more than twenty-two verses; it was then shortened to precisely twenty-two. See his

In the acrostics of chapters 2, 3 and 4, the verses that begin with *pe* precede the verses that begin with *ayin*. The Soncino commentary to *Eikhah* remarks: "This unusual order has never been satisfactorily explained."[3]

In light of the archaeological discoveries of recent decades, it is time to provide this explanation. Thereafter, we will discuss the implications of this explanation for the dating of the book of *Tehillim*. The book of *Tehillim* includes alphabetical acrostics in chapters 9-10,[4] 25, 34, 37, 111, 112, 119, and 145. We will also discuss the implications for the book of *Mishlei*, which includes such an acrostic at 31:10-31.

◆ ◆ ◆

Preliminarily, it will be noted that the Talmud includes a comment on the unusual order of *pe* preceding *ayin* in *Eikhah*. The suggestion is made that it alludes to the sin of the spies: *she-amru be-fihem*[5] *mah she-lo ra'u be-eineihem* (who spoke with their mouths what they had not seen with their eyes).[6] The sin of the spies is connected to the ninth of Av in a well-established rabbinic tradition.[7]

"*Ha-Kol ha-Nashi mi-Karov u-me-Raḥok*," in *Or le-Mayer*, ed. Shamir Yona (Be'er Sheva: 2010), p. 47, n. 46.

3. Commentary to *Eikhah* 2:16 (London: 1946).

4. These two chapters together constitute one long acrostic. But seven of the twenty-two letters are missing.

5. The letter *pe* seems to have its origin in either the representation of a mouth (פה) or a corner (פאה). See *Encyclopaedia Judaica* 13:194 (Jerusalem: 1972). (In this article, all my citations to this work are to the 1972 edition.) Since the names of many of the other letters are based on parts of the body, the former seems more likely. See further Aaron Demsky, *Yediyat Sefer be-Yisrael be-Et ha-Atikah* (Jerusalem: 2012), p. 176.

6. This explanation is recorded in the Talmud at *Sanhedrin* 104b (as a comment on 2:16), and twice in *Eikhah Rabbah* (as a comment on *Eikhah* 2:16 and as a comment on *Eikhah* 3:46). No explanation is given in these sources for why the first chapter is in the regular order. Maharsha (commentary to *Sanhedrin* 104b) suggests that the first chapter was kept in the regular order to prevent someone from claiming (as I will shortly!) that *pe* preceding *ayin* was the standard order at the time of *Eikhah*. Compare the explanation of the *Siftei Ḥakhamim* to *Eikhah* 2:16.

7. See, e.g., M. *Taanit* 4:6. See further Shmuel Hakohen, "*Al ha-Yaḥas she-Bein Tzurah le-Tokhen be-Megillat Eikhah*," *Sinai* 89 (1981), pp. 119-133 (128).

But on a simple level, the book of *Eikhah* is not related to the story of the spies. More importantly, even prior to the archaeological discoveries of recent decades, evidence of *pe* preceding *ayin* was found *outside* the book of *Eikhah*. In the two earliest texts of the Septuagint of *Mishlei* 31:10-31 (=*Eshet Ḥayil*), the translation of the *pe* verse precedes the translation of the *ayin* verse.[8] These texts, Codex Vaticanus and Codex Sinaiticus, date from the fourth century C.E., hundreds of years earlier than the earliest Hebrew texts of *Mishlei*.[9]

The relevant archaeological discoveries of recent decades from the land of Israel are as follows:

- In the one Dead Sea text of *Eikhah* that has been found that spans the *ayin* and *pe* verses of the first chapter, the *pe* verse precedes the ayin verse.[10]
- In 1976, a potsherd was discovered at Izbet Sartah, in Western Samaria. The potsherd has five lines of Hebrew[11] writing on it, one of which is an abecedary.[12] In this abecedary, the *pe* precedes the

8. See, e.g., *Septuaginta*, ed. Alfred Rahlfs (Germany: 1935), vol. 2, p. 237.
9. In the other main witness to the text of the Septuagint, Codex Alexandrinus (fifth century), the *ayin* verse precedes the *pe* verse. Most likely, this reflects a later conformity of the Greek text to the Masoretic text.
10. See *DJD* XVI (Oxford: 2001), p. 234. The script of this text dates to c. 30 B.C.E.-1 C.E. Ibid., p. 229. According to this *DJD* volume (p. 230), this text (4QLam) "preserves a considerable number of readings that appear to be superior" to those of the Masoretic text.

With regard to the second and third chapters of the book of *Eikhah*, the Dead Sea scrolls only include verses 2:5 and 3:53-62, so there is not enough of a text to confirm the Masoretic *pe-ayin* order. The *pe-ayin* order is confirmed in the Dead Sea texts from the fourth chapter (although the texts of the relevant verses, 4:16-17, are very fragmentary). See *DJD* III (Oxford: 1962), pp. 176-78.
11. I am calling this writing "Hebrew" because it was likely composed by an Israelite. But paleography scholars would not use the term "Hebrew" here, since it was probably not until the ninth century B.C.E. that a "Hebrew" script evolved that was distinct from the Phoenician script. The same issue of terminology arises with respect to the find at Tel Zayit.
12. An abecedary is a text meant to record all or some of the letters of the alphabet in order. On the Izbet Sartah abecedary, see Moshe Kochavi, "An

ayin. Based on the shape of the letters, the writing can be dated to about 1200 B.C.E.[13] There is a scholarly consensus that Izbet Sartah was an Israelite settlement in this period.[14]

Ostracon of the Period of the Judges from 'Izbet Ṣarṭah ," *Tel Aviv* 4 (1977), pp. 1-13; Aaron Demsky, "A Proto-Canaanite Abecedary Dating from the Period of the Judges and its Implications for the History of the Alphabet," *Tel Aviv* 4 (1977), pp. 14-27; Demsky and Kochavi, "An Alphabet from the Days of the Judges," *BAR* Sept.-Oct. 1978, pp. 23-30; and Kochavi and Demsky, "*Alphabeit bi-Khetav Proto-Canaani me-Izbet-Tzartah*," *Kadmoniot* 11 (1978), pp. 61-67.

The Izbet Sartah abecedary reads from left to right; the writing direction was not yet fixed in this early period. See Joseph Naveh, *Early History of the Alphabet* (Jerusalem: 1987, second ed.), p. 42. For another inscription from around this time that reads from left to right, see Naveh, p. 36, describing an inscription from the northwestern Negev. See also Naveh, p. 24, figure 16, inscription on the top right. The Khirbet Qeiyafa ostracon, discovered in 2008 and dating from the eleventh or tenth century B.C.E., also may read from left to right. According to most scholars, the first four lines on the Izbet Sartah potsherd seem to be just random letters (and seem to have been inscribed by someone else). The whole potsherd may simply reflect an exercise by two students. Also noteworthy in the abecedary is that the *ḥet* precedes the *zayin*. There are grounds to suspect that this was a scribal slip. See Demsky, pp. 17-18. But interestingly, this same order is found in the Tel Zayit abecedary.

13. Kochavi, p. 12, and Demsky and Kochavi, p. 24. Three occupational strata were found at Izbet Sartah, but the potsherd was found in a silo that was unattached to any house, so we do not know in which stratum this silo was used. The earliest stratum probably dates to the late thirteenth century B.C.E. The latest probably dates to the tenth cent. B.C.E. For more on Izbet Sartah, see Israel Finkelstein, *'Izbet Sartah: An Early Iron Age Site near Rosh Ha'ayin, Israel* (Oxford: 1986).

14. For example, the site contains the typical Israelite storage silos and pillar-courtyard style houses. See William G. Dever, *Who Were the Early Israelites and Where Did They Come From?* (Grand Rapids and Cambridge: 2003), p. 83. Kochavi, p. 3, writes that the identification of Izbet Sartah as an Israelite site "is not open to question." See also Israel Finkelstein, *The Archaeology of the Israelite Settlement* (Jerusalem: 1988), pp. 31-33. The quantity of pig bones found at Izbet Sartah was nil. See Finkelstein, p. 31, n. 2.

The Philistine site of Aphek is to the west of Izbet Sartah. It is widely believed that Izbet Sartah is the Biblical Even Ha-Ezer. According to 1 Samuel, chapter 4, the Philistines, camped at Aphek, defeated the Israelites at Even Ha-Ezer and seized the Ark.

- During excavations in 1975-76 at Kuntillet ‘Ajrud, a site in the northeast Sinai, a jar fragment was discovered that included three Hebrew abecedaries in which the *pe* precedes the *ayin*.[15] The site dates to approximately 800 B.C.E. The opinion of the archaeologist who led the excavations is that the site was established at the order of King Jehoash of the northern kingdom of Israel, after he defeated King Amaziah of Judah.[16]
- In 2005, a Hebrew abecedary inscribed on a stone was discovered at Tel Zayit, a site north of Lachish. The stone had been used in the construction of a wall belonging to a tenth-century B.C.E. structure. This abecedary seems to follow the order of *pe* preceding *ayin*.[17]

In the unlikely event that the Izbet Sartah, Kuntillet ‘Ajrud, and Tel Zayit abecedaries were inscribed by non-Israelites, these abecedaries would still be relevant. The Israelites utilized the same alphabet as their neighbors in Canaan, and the order of the letters within the alphabet would presumably have been the same.

15. See Ze’ev Meshel, *Kuntillet ‘Ajrud (Ḥorvat Teman): An Iron Age II Religious Site on the Judah-Sinai Border* (Jerusalem: 2012), pp. 102-03, for the most accurate photo, sketch and transcriptions. Above these three abecedaries is another, largely incomplete, that does not include *pe* or *ayin*.

16. Meshel, pp. 66-69. The nature and function of the site (two buildings) has been much debated. The literature on this topic is cited by Meshel. Almost all of the fifty inscriptions discovered at the site are in the Hebrew language and script, like the abecedaries. Four inscriptions are in the Phoenician script, but in the Hebrew language. While the approximate date of the site is clear, that it was established by King Jehoash of the northern kingdom of Israel is merely Meshel’s educated conjecture based in part on the strong northern influence found at the site; no inscriptions mention King Jehoash.

King Jehoash’s defeat of King Amaziah is described at 2 Kings 14 and 2 Chronicles 25.

17. See Ron E. Tappy, P. Kyle McCarter, Marilyn J. Lundberg, and Bruce Zuckerman, “An Abecedary of the Mid-Tenth B.C.E. from the Judaean Shephelah,” *Bulletin of the American Schools of Oriental Research* 344 (2006), pp. 5-46 (26). In this article, the authors admit that some of the letters on this abecedary are less visible than others, and that the *pe* and *ayin* are among the less visible ones. Interestingly, a disc comes with the book *Literate Culture and Tenth-Century Canaan: The Tel Zayit Abecedary in Context*, edited by Tappy and McCarter in 2008 (Winona Lake, Ind.), and the sketch of the abecedary on the disc cover does not include the *pe* and *ayin* letters.

Most probably, Tel Zayit was part of the area of the tribe of Judah in the tenth century B.C.E.[18]

- In recent years, another ostracon with three Hebrew abecedaries with *pe* preceding *ayin* has come to light.[19] The provenance of the ostracon is unknown, but the writing can be dated to the late seventh or early sixth century B.C.E.

The abecedaries mentioned above are the only abecedaries in the traditional *aleph-bet* scheme[20] that have been discovered in ancient

---

The Tel Zayit abecedary departs from the traditional order in three other instances: 1) *vav* precedes *he*, 2) *ḥet* precedes *zayin*, and 3) *lamed* precedes *kaf*. (As to the last, there is evidence that the author of the abecedary realized that this was a mistake.)

18. Tappy, et al, pp. 6-7, 22, and 42. The authors write (p. 22) that in the tenth century, "the stratigraphic and cultural history of the site seems to be parallel closely that of nearby Lachish… with both sites maintaining their principal cultural affinities with the highlands to the east and serving as borderland settlements that marked the westernmost Judahite frontier." As to the script, the authors write (p. 5): "The Tel Zayit abecedary represents the linear alphabetic script of central and southern Canaan at the beginning of the first millennium B.C.E., a transitional script that developed from the Phoenician tradition of the early Iron Age and anticipated the distinctive features of the mature Hebrew national script."

19. See Martin Heide, "Impressions from a New Alphabetic Ostracon in the Context of (Un)Provenanced Inscriptions: Idiosyncracy of a Genius Forger or a Master Scribe?" pp. 148-182, in Meir Lubetski, ed., *New Seals and Inscriptions, Hebrew, Idumean and Cuneiform* (Sheffield: 2007). Although the ostracon is unprovenanced, the prevailing view is that it is genuine. Supposedly, it came from the debris of the Temple Mount.

20. An abecedary in cuneiform from the thirteenth century B.C.E. was found in 1933 at Beit Shemesh. But this abecedary follows an entirely different scheme, one that corresponds to the scheme found in South Arabian inscriptions from the first few centuries C.E. In this alternative scheme (one that includes more than 22 letters), the order begins: *h, l, ḥ, m*. See Wayne Horowitz, Takayoshi Oshima, and Seth L. Sanders, *Cuneiform in Canaan and the Land of Israel: Cuneiform Sources from the Land of Israel in Ancient Times* (Jerusalem: 2006), pp. 157-60. It was not until 1987 that it was realized that the Beit Shemesh find was an abecedary. An abecedary in this same scheme was found in 1988 at Ras Shamra (RS 88.2215.) These discoveries are forcing scholars to rethink many of their assumptions about the history of the alphabet. See, e.g., Horowitz, et al, pp. 159-60. As stated there:

Israel that date from the period of the Judges and the First Temple which also span the letters *ayin* and *pe*.[21] *Pe* precedes *ayin* in every one.[22] As we have seen, these abecedaries come from different regions in ancient Israel and not merely from one area.

On the other hand, the ancient abecedaries in Western Semitic[23] languages from this same period from regions outside Israel reflect the *ayin-pe* order:

- Ugaritic texts from Ras Shamra, on the Mediterranean coast of North Syria, include abecedaries that date from the thirteenth century B.C.E. In the several abecedaries in the *aleph-bet* scheme

---

> The Beth Shemesh tablet… indicates that there was a language variety being taught in the southern Levant at the end of the Late Bronze Age which contained as wide a phoneme inventory as standard Ugaritic. It renders implausible the idea that the south possessed a single, reduced "southern" or "Canaanite" alphabet…

The scheme later reflected in the South Arabian inscriptions may have originated in Canaan or its surroundings, and not Arabia. See Demsky, *Yediyat*, p. 106

21. Other Hebrew First Temple period abecedaries have been found, but they are much shorter. For example, אבגדה was found incised on one of the steps of the palace at Lachish. Other finds in ancient Israel include: אבגד, הוזחט (see the note below), וזח, and זחט. Most of these are collected in André Lemaire, *Les écoles et la formation de la Bible dans l'ancien Israël* (Fribourg, Switz.: 1981). For additional references, see Menahem Haran, "On the Diffusion of Literacy and Schools in Ancient Israel," *Supplements to Vetus Testamentum*, vol. 40 (Leiden and New York: 1988), pp. 81-95 (86).

22. There is an eighth-century B.C.E. inscription from Lachish that Emil Puech believes follows the ayin/pe order, but André Lemaire rejects Puech's readings as unsubstantiated. See David Ussishkin, *The Renewed Archaeological Excavations at Lachish (1973-1994)* (Tel Aviv: 2004), vol. IV, pp. 2116-2117. (This section of the work was written by Lemaire.) According to Lemaire, the letters הוזחט are readable on the middle of the first line, and the second line includes צקר, followed immediately by אב. But the letters preceding צקר on the second line are unclear.

23. Ancient Semitic languages are traditionally divided into three branches: Eastern, Western, and Southern. The Eastern Semitic languages (i.e., Babylonian and Assyrian) were written in Sumerian cuneiform, which was not an alphabetic cuneiform script. Southern Semitic languages (i.e., South Arabian, Ethiopian, and Arabic) have a different alphabet order altogether.

that are long enough to span *ayin* and *pe*, the cuneiform sign for the *ayin* precedes the cuneiform sign for the *pe*.[24]

- Among the other Western Semitic languages, i.e., Aramaic, Ammonite, Moabite, and Phoenician, only one abecedary has been discovered from this period that is long enough to span *ayin* and *pe*. This is an eighth-century B.C.E. inscription in Aramaic from Tell Halaf, a site in northeastern Syria. Here, too, *ayin* precedes *pe*.[25]

◆ ◆ ◆

It was mentioned earlier that in the earliest texts of the Septuagint of *Mishlei* 31:10-31, the translation of the *pe* verse (פיה) precedes the translation of the *ayin* verse (עז). Based on the widespread evidence for *pe* preceding *ayin* in ancient Israel, it seems evident that what lay behind the Septuagint version of *Mishlei* 31:10-31 was a Hebrew text in which the *pe* verse preceded the *ayin* verse.[26]

24. See Manfried Dietrich, Oswald Loretz, and Joaquín Sanmartín, eds., *The Cuneiform Alphabetic Texts from Ugarit, Ras Ibn Hani and Other Places,* (Münster: 1995, second ed.), pp. 490-495. For an illustration of one of these abecedaries in which *ayin* precedes *pe*, see Naveh, p. 30. (One Ugaritic abecedary was discovered that follows the alternative alphabetical scheme that begins h, l, ḥ, m. See RS 88.2215.)

In the Latin alphabet that we use today, "o" precedes "p." This also reflects the *ayin-pe* order. (As should be obvious, the Latin alphabet ultimately derives from the same source as the Hebrew one.) The letter "o" is the parallel to the letter *ayin* (originally drawn to look like an eye).

25. See Rainer Degen, "Ein aramäisches Alphabet von Tell Halaf," in Rainer Degen, Walter W. Müller & Wolfgang Röllig, *Neue Ephemeris für semitische Epigraphik*, vol. III (Wiesbaden: 1978), pp. 1-9. The article "Alphabets," by G. Wilhelm Nebe, in *Encyclopedia of the Dead Sea Scrolls*, vol. 1, pp. 18-20 (New York: 2000), states that this inscription follows the *pe-ayin* order, but this is a mistake.

For references to other abecedaries that have been discovered in Aramaic and the other Western Semitic languages from the early first millennium B.C.E., see André Lemaire, "Abécédaires et exercises d'écolier en epigraphie nord-ouest-sémitique," *Journal Asiatique* (1978), pp. 221-35 (225-28). See also *Semitica* 28 (1978), pp. 7-10, and *Semitica* 32 (1982), p. 33, no. 16.

26. Unfortunately, we have no Dead Sea text of *Mishlei* chap. 31.

Let us take a closer look at this section. In the traditional order, verses 24-26 read as follows:

כד) סדין עשתה ותמכר וחגור נתנה לכנעני.
כה) עז והדר לבושה ותשחק ליום אחרון.
כו) פיה פתחה בחכמה ותורת חסד על לשונה.

In this order, the women of valor laughs to the last day because she makes cloaks and sells them, delivers belts to the merchant, and is clothed with might and splendor. But if the original order here was *pe-ayin*, the qualities that enable her to laugh to the last day would also include her *ḥakhmah* and *ḥesed*! A much more profound description!

◆ ◆ ◆

Now it is time to focus on the balance of the alphabetical acrostics in the Bible, the ones found in the book of *Tehillim*.[27] Alphabetical acrostics are found in the book of *Tehillim* at chapters 9-10, 25, 34, 37, 111, 112, 119 (every letter 8 times), and 145.

In chapter 34 (*le-David be-shannoto*), verses 17 and 18 have troubled Biblical commentators throughout the ages. In verse 17, we are told:

> The face (פני) of the Lord is against those who do evil, to cut off the remembrance of them from the earth.

Yet immediately following this, at verse 18, we are told without explanation:

The Greek translation of *Mishlei* differs in many other ways from the Masoretic text. It has been argued that the Greek translation was based on a different recension altogether. See Emanuel Tov, "Recensional Differences Between the Masoretic Text and the Septuagint of Proverbs," in Harold W. Attridge, John J. Collins, and Thomas H. Tobin, eds., *Of Scribes and Scrolls: Studies on the Hebrew Bible, Intertestamental Judaism, and Christian Origins* (Lanham: 1990), pp. 43-56.

27. It has also been suggested that a partial acrostic, up to *kaf*, was once found at the beginning of Nahum chapter 1 and that there has been some textual corruption here. See, e.g., *Encyclopaedia Judaica* 2:229. There are no alphabetical acrostics in the Torah.

They cried (צעקו) and the Lord heard, and delivered them from all their troubles.

Why should God listen to and save the evildoers, when we have just been told that He wants to cut off the remembrance of them from the earth?[28]

However, if we make the assumption that *pe* preceded *ayin* here, then God listens to and saves the righteous, not the evildoers:

34:17. The face (פני) of the Lord is against those who do evil, to cut off the remembrance of them from the earth.
34:16. The eyes (עיני) of the Lord are toward the righteous, and his ears to their cry.
34:18. They cried (צעקו) and the Lord heard, and delivered them from all their troubles.

The theological problem disappears and the sequence of verses makes perfect sense![29]

28. R. Abraham Ibn Ezra believes that an explanation is provided in the following verse, verse 19:

קרוב ה' לנשברי לב ואת דכאי רוח יושיע.

He suggests that the evildoers were depressed by their actions and changed their ways (see his commentary to 34:18-19). But if this is the explanation, it is stated very indirectly by the text. Also, we would have expected it to be stated earlier, before the acceptance of the outcry was described in verse 18.

29. There is no Dead Sea text of 34:16-17.

The suggestion that these verses need to be re-ordered is found at *Encyclopaedia Judaica* 2:229, and is repeated by many modern scholars. The *Daat Mikra* commentary on *Tehillim*, authored by Amos Ḥakham, is even willing to consider the possibility of re-ordering these verses. See *Sefer Tehillim* (*Daat Mikra*, Jerusalem: 1979), vol. 1, pp. 189-90, n. 9. The suggestion that these verses need to be re-ordered was made long ago. See, e.g., S. R. Driver, *An Introduction to the Literature of the Old Testament*, p. 346 (Edinburgh: 1892, fourth ed.), Julius Wellhausen, *The Book of Psalms, Critical Edition of the Hebrew Text*, p. 81 (Leipzig: 1895) (citing the German Bible scholar Hermann Hupfeld, d. 1866), and Solomon Judah Rapoport (d. 1867), *Erekh Millin*, vol. 2 (Warsaw, 1914), pp. 42-43. (I would like to thank Chaim Sunitsky for the last reference.)

Now it is time to address the acrostics in the rest of the book of *Tehillim*. If we can agree that *pe* must have preceded *ayin* in the original version of chapter 34, does that mean that *pe* originally preceded *ayin* in all the other acrostics in *Tehillim*? This is very unlikely. Chapter 119 is an eightfold acrostic. Eight complete verses would have had to have been rearranged if this chapter once reflected an older *pe-ayin* order that was later changed to *ayin-pe*.[30]

Our approach to the acrostics of *Tehillim* will focus instead on the likely distinction between early (pre-monarchic and First Temple period) and late (early Second Temple period) books of *Tehillim*.

Jewish tradition divides the 150 chapters into five books.[31] This

---

There is a rabbinic tradition that interprets verse 18 as relating back to the prayers of the *tzaddikim*. See the Baraita of 32 Rules in *Midrash ha-Gadol*, Genesis (ed. Mordecai Margaliot, Jerusalem, 1997), p. 38. See also R. Saadiah Gaon, *Emunot ve-Deot* (end of the fourth treatise), and one view cited and rejected by R. Abraham Ibn Ezra. None of these suggest that the verses themselves need to be re-ordered. Similarly, Targum Yonatan adds the word צדיקיא (righteous ones) into its translation of verse 18. ArtScroll has inserted the phrase "the righteous" (in brackets) in several of its English translations of verse 18.

Verse 7 supports the idea that the subject of verse 18 is the righteous ones if we take the reasonable approach that its subject, the עני, is sometimes a synonym for the צדיק in the book of *Tehillim*. Verse 7 reads: זה עני קרא וה' שמע ומכל צרותיו הושיעו.

Interestingly, the contemporary writer Leon Wieseltier happened to choose verse 34:18 as the verse to be inscribed on his father's tombstone. He writes: "[t]he words are plain, vernacular, direct. They are unusually artless for this great poet..." *Kaddish* (New York and Toronto: 1998), p. 167. Little did he know that he chose a controversial verse whose subject needed to be redefined, the verse that is the key to our whole analysis.

30. That there was a re-ordering of chapter 145 also seems unlikely because the *ayin* and *pe* lines in chapter 145 seem to be parallel to the following lines in chapter 104 (27-28):

כלם אליך ישברון לתת אכלם בעתו.
תתן להם ילקטון תפתח ידך ישבעון טוב.

31. See, e.g., *Kiddushin* 33a (and Tosafot, s.v., שני חומשין). See also Roger Beckwith, *The Old Testament Canon of the New Testament Church* (Grand Rapids: 1986), pp. 112-13. A text from Qumran Cave 1 refers to ספרים חומשים.

division is already reflected in the Bible, as certain verses seem to serve as the divisions between the books.[32] Almost certainly, the books originated as independent collections.[33] This is seen, for example, by the fact that chapter 53 is an almost identical repetition of chapter 14, and chapter 70 (a superscription plus five verses) is an almost identical repetition of chapter 40:14-18.[34]

But it is hard to date most of the chapters because of the lack of reference to historical events. The prefix "ל," attached to the name of an individual, is found in the superscription to most of the chapters. But the precise connotation of this prefix is ambiguous.[35]

There is a widespread view that the first three books are the earlier collections. Among these, the first book is often viewed as the earliest.[36]

See *DJD* I (Oxford: 1955), p. 132. This may be an early allusion to the division of *Tehillim* into five books. But it may merely be a reference to the Pentateuch.

32. Verses 41:14, 72:18–20, 89:53, and 106:47–48.

33. See *Encyclopaedia Judaica* 13:1308.

34. Also, verse 72:20, at the conclusion of the second book, reads: *kallu tefillot David ben Yishai*, "the prayers of David son of Yishai are finished." It seems very unlikely that an individual who was aware of the eighteen psalms connected to David in the subsequent chapters would have written such a line.

35. I.e., does it express authorship by the individual named? Or that the chapter is connected to some event in the life of the person named? Or that the chapter is dedicated to the person named? Many other possibilities have been suggested. See, e.g., *Encyclopaedia Judaica* 13:1313, Ḥakham, *Sefer Tehillim* (*Daat Mikra*), intro., p. 9, John Goldingay, *Psalms*, Vol. 1 (Grand Rapids: 2006), pp. 26-27, and Hayyim Angel, *Vision from the Prophet and Counsel from the Elders* (New York: 2013), p. 217. Moreover, the meaning of the prefix "ל" probably varies throughout the various superscriptions. It is also possible that some of the superscriptions were added long after the original composition. Seventy-three of the one hundred fifty chapters are designated *le-David.*

36. For example, the following statement is found at *Encyclopaedia Judaica* 13:1309: "the earliest collection is undoubtedly Book I, or rather Psalms 3-41 within it."

One of arguments made there is that, with the exception of chapters 1, 2, 10, and 33, all of the chapters in the first book have superscriptions connecting them to David. (Almost certainly, the reason such a superscription is lacking in chapter 10 is that it was once united with

The acrostics in the book of *Tehillim* are found only in the first book, which comprises chapters 1-41, and in the fifth book, which comprises chapters 107-150.

One factor that points to the antiquity of the first book is that most of the acrostics in this book are missing letters.[37] The acrostic that runs

---

chapter 9; it is a continuation of one long acrostic. As to chapter 33, it has a Davidic superscription in the Septuagint.) In contrast, in books two through five, only eighteen have superscriptions connecting them to David. Of course, this argument is not compelling.

It is instructive to quote two other sources regarding the dating of the book of *Tehillim*:

1. The modern scholar Robert Alter, *The Book of Psalms* (New York: 2007), p. xv, writes:

   The dating of individual psalms has long been a region of treacherous scholarly quicksand.... [A] few of the psalms might be as early as the Solomonic court, or even the pre-monarchic period. Many of these poems appear to have been written at some indeterminate point during the four centuries of the First Commonwealth (approximately 996 to 586 BCE). Many others offer evidence in their themes and language of composition in the period of the Return to Zion....

2. Dr. A. Cohen, *The Psalms* (London: 1945, Soncino edition), intro., p. 12, writes:

   It is consequently well within the bounds of probability that [David] inaugurated a new style of Hebrew lyrical poetry, the Psalm, which became a model for poets in later generations.... As he drew upon his personal experiences for the themes of his songs, so did his successors. The urge to compose would be stimulated by stirring national events. In particular, the aggression of Assyria, the crisis of the Babylonian Exile and the Restoration were occasions of increased literary activity which produced numbers of Psalms.

37. See similarly Paul W. Gaebelein, Jr., "Psalm 34 and Other Biblical Acrostics: Evidence from the Aleppo Codex," *Maarav* 5-6 (1990), pp. 127-43 (139).

To my knowledge, there are no comments in the Talmud or other classical rabbinic sources about the missing verses in these acrostics. (I

through chapters 9 and 10 is missing seven of the twenty-two letters; the acrostic of chapter 25 is missing a *kof*, and has a *resh* twice;[38] and the acrostic of chapter 37 is missing an *ayin*. All of this suggests that we are dealing with acrostics composed at such an early stage that their texts have no longer been accurately preserved. Also, the absence of a verse for *vav* in chapters 25 and 34 perhaps suggests that we are dealing with acrostics composed at an early stage, a stage when the letter *vav* was not consistently viewed as deserving a place in a Hebrew acrostic.[39]

In contrast, the acrostics in the fifth book are perfectly, or almost perfectly, preserved. The acrostics of chapters 111 and 112 are complete, and the acrostic of chapter 119 is complete, with every letter repeated eight times. The lone possible imperfection is chapter 145 which lacks a *nun* verse. However, the fact that all the other acrostics in the fifth book are complete suggests that the *nun* verse is not missing here, but was omitted intentionally.[40]

---

do not mean to imply that these acrostics were complete in the time of the Tannaim and Amoraim. One could make such an argument from the lack of such comments, but it would be very weak.)

38. Some characterize chapter 25 as missing a *bet*, but probably the second word of 25:2 (בך) counts as the *bet*, with the first word, אלקי, being considered only an introduction.

39. Interestingly, an eighth- or seventh-century B.C.E. Aramaic text from Deir 'Alla (the Biblical Succoth, on the east bank of the Jordan River) records the following sequence of letters: *aleph*, *bet*, *gimmel*, *dalet*, *zayin*, and *ḥet*. Both *he* and *vav* were left out. See J. Hoftijzer and G. van der Kooij, *Aramaic Texts from Deir 'Alla* (Leiden: 1976), pp. 267 and 285.

Very few Hebrew words began with *vav* in the Biblical period. The concordance of Solomon Mandelkern (Lipsiae: 1896) lists only a handful: וו (hook), וזר (only at *Mishlei* 21:8), and ולד. (But *vav* is a root letter in proto-Semitic.)

40. The *nun* verse found in the Dead Sea, Septuagint, Vulgate, and Peshitta texts of chapter 145 should therefore be considered a later addition. The *nun* verse found in these sources is suspicious for other reasons as well. See, e.g., Reuven Kimelman, "Psalm 145: Theme, Structure, and Impact," *JBL* 113 (1994), pp. 37-58 (50). As Kimelman also points out, content-wise there is no indication that any verse is missing here.

For the text of the Dead Sea version of chapter 145 (which begins "*Tefillah le-David*"!), see J.A. Sanders, *The Dead Sea Psalms Scroll* (Ithaca: 1967), pp. 64-67.

In the fifth book, we find phrases such as *be-shuv Hashem et shivat Tziyyon* (126:1), and *al naharot Bavel sham yashavnu gam bakhinu be-zakhreinu et Tziyyon* (137:1).[41] Moreover, a leading scholar whose expertise is distinguishing between the Hebrew of the early Biblical period and the Hebrew of the late Biblical period (c. 600-400 B.C.E.) has pointed to chapter 103 in the fourth book, and chapters 117, 119, 124, 125, 133, 144, and 145 in the fifth book, as the chapters that have the largest concentration of late Biblical Hebrew elements.[42] Hence, he

41. Also worth noting is 147:2: *boneh Yerushalayim Hashem, nidḥei Yisrael yikannes*. Ḥakham, *Sefer Tehillim* (*Daat Mikra*), intro., p. 47, suggests that this verse may be from the *shivat Tziyyon* period, as does the Soncino commentary to this verse (p. 472).

Chapters from the third book that sound like they were composed either after the destruction of 586 B.C.E. or after the Return, include chapters 74, 79, 80, 85, and 89.

42. See Avi Hurvitz, *Bein Lashon le-Lashon* (Jerusalem: 1972). See also his *The Identification of Post-Exilic Psalms by Means of Linguistic Criteria* (1966). For example, he argues in *Bein Lashon le-Lashon* that there are nine ways in which chapter 145 exhibits the Hebrew of the early Second Temple period. One is the use of the word *malkhut* for kingdom. This word appears four times (in various forms) in chapter 145. He suggests that this word was the prevailing word for "kingdom" in the early Second Temple period, while *mamlakhah* was the prevailing word in earlier Biblical Hebrew. He points out that the book of Chronicles, a book that is usually accepted as having been composed in the Second Temple period, sometimes utilizes the word *malkhut* when a parallel passage in an earlier source had used the word *mamlakhah*. Compare, for example, 2 Sam. 5:12 with 1 Chron. 14:2, and 2 Sam. 7:12 with 1 Chron. 17:11. Moreover, outside of the book of *Tehillim*, *malkhut* (in its various forms) appears approximately eighty times in the later Biblical books: Chronicles, Ezra, Nehemiah, Daniel, Esther, and Kohelet. It appears three times in the book of Jeremiah. But it only appears three times in texts that are considered earlier than this (at Num 24:7, 1 Sam. 20:31, and 1 Kings 2:12). In the book of *Tehillim*, it appears elsewhere at 45:7 and 103:19.

Hurvitz does raise the possibility that chapters that show multiple signs of late Biblical Hebrew may only have been edited in the later period. But he takes the position (p. 182) that once he has shown that a chapter exhibits multiple signs of late Biblical Hebrew, the burden shifts to those who wish to claim that the chapter was composed earlier and edited later to provide evidence for their view.

believes that at least these chapters were likely composed in the late Biblical period.[43]

It is very easy to extrapolate from this to almost the entire fifth book, and by implication, to the entire fifth book.[44] For example, chapters 124 and 125 are part of a section of fifteen *shir ha-maalot* chapters (120-134) that were all probably composed around the same time. Chapter 117 is part of a section that runs from chapter 111 through chapter 117; each of these chapters (except for chapter 114) begins or ends with the word *halleluyah*. In addition, chapters 135, and 146 through 150, all start and end with the word *halleluyah*, evidencing their relation to chapters 111 through 117.[45]

Dating sections of *Tehillim* to a period as late as the fifth century B.C.E. should not be viewed as inconsistent with the entirety of rabbinic tradition. Although an anonymous *baraita* in the Talmud attributes the book of *Tehillim* to David *al yedei asarah zekenim* (all of whom seem to have lived either in his time or earlier),[46] this is not the only view of the authorship of *Tehillim* recorded in classical rabbinic literature. *Shir ha-Shirim Rabbah* 4:4 preserves the views of both Rav and R. Yoḥanan that Ezra (mid-fifth century B.C.E.) was one of the ten figures involved in the composition of *Tehillim*. A similar passage is found at *Kohelet Rabbah* 7:19.[47]

Ḥakham, *Sefer Tehillim* (*Daat Mikra*), intro., p. 47, takes the position that the proposed distinctions between early and late Biblical Hebrew in *Tehillim* are *mesupakim meod*.

43. The division between the fourth and fifth books of *Tehillim* is considered by many scholars to be artificial. This position is taken by the *Encyclopaedia Judaica* "Psalms" entry. This source also takes the position that the fourth and fifth books are the latest books. See *Encyclopaedia Judaica* 13:1308-1310.

44. Hurvitz engages in some limited extrapolation at *Bein Lashon le-Lashon*, p. 172.

45. The word *halleluyah* is only found in the fifth book and in the fourth book (chapters 104-06). It is found nowhere else in the Bible. This also points to the lateness of the fourth and fifth books.

46. See *Bava Batra* 14b. The ten are: Adam, Malkitzedek, Avraham, Moshe, Heman, Yedutun, Asaph and three sons of Korach. On this passage, see Angel, pp. 212-213.

A statement by R. Meir is found at *Pesaḥim* 117a that perhaps implies a different view, that the entire book of *Tehillim* was composed by David alone.

47. See also *Yalkut Makhiri* (14th century?) to *Tehillim*. Admittedly, the

Moreover, in the modern period, Malbim was willing to allow for authorship of some of the chapters of *Tehillim* as late as the time of Ezra.[48] Amos Ḥakham's commentary to *Tehillim* also takes this approach.[49]

I suggest that the difference in the era of composition of the first and fifth books is reflected in the alphabetical order originally employed in each. I propose that the acrostics of the first book, composed in the pre-monarchic or First Temple periods, were all written with the *pe-ayin* order. The acrostics in the fifth book (chapters 111, 112, 119, and 145), composed in the sixth century B.C.E. or later, were written with the subsequently arising *ayin-pe* order.

Can I prove this?

1. Regarding the acrostic that spans chapters 9 and 10, it is fairly clear that our text is corrupt. The acrostic only includes fifteen of the twenty-two letters, and is missing all the letters from *mem* through *tzade*.[50] But many scholars believe that the words פיהו (verse 10:7,

---

mention of Ezra seems out of context in the passages, and some have argued that it is an erroneous reading. (For example, the *Yafeh Kol* to *Shir ha-Shirim Rabbah* suggests the interesting emendation to עירא, based on 2 Sam. 20:26.) But since Ezra is mentioned twice in the *Shir ha-Shirim Rabbah* passage (once by Rav, and once by R. Yoḥanan), and again in the *Kohelet Rabbah* passage (which is a shorter form of the *Shir ha-Shirim Rabbah* passage), it is hardly likely that we are dealing with an erroneous reading. Also, *Yalkut Makhiri* is considered to be a work that preserves accurate readings. See *Encyclopaedia Judaica* 16:706.

48. See the introduction to his commentary to *Tehillim*. He defends this approach by pointing out that prophecy was still in existence at the time of Ezra (who is identified in one rabbinic tradition with the prophet Malachi). Malbim suggests alternatively that all of *Tehillim* may have been composed in Davidic times but some sections were kept hidden until they needed to be revealed.

An eleventh-century authority who takes the position that parts of *Tehillim* were authored in the post-exilic period is Moses Gikatilla. See Uriel Simon, *Four Approaches to the Book of Psalms* (Albany: 1991), pp. viii and 136. R. Abraham Ibn Ezra mentions such a view but rejects it. See Simon, p. 152. See also Simon, pp. 182-84.

49. *Sefer Tehillim* (*Daat Mikra*), intro., pp. 13 and 47. See also Angel's discussion of the authorship of *Tehillim* at pp. 210- 218.

50. The acrostic that spans chapters 9 and 10 is much less even with respect to the average unit length for each section than are the other acrostic psalms. This also suggests that the acrostic is textually corrupt. See Peter

second word) and עיניו (verse 10:8, third to last word) were once the first words of *pe* and *ayin* verses in the *pe-ayin* order in the original text.[51]

2. Regarding the acrostic of chapter 25, the verses present no difficulty in their present order. The relevant verses read:

> 14: The counsel (סוד) of the Lord is with those that fear Him, and His covenant, to make them know it.
> 15: My eyes (עיני) are always toward the Lord, for He will bring my feet out of the net.
> 16: Turn (פנה) to me and be gracious to me, for I am solitary and afflicted.
> 17: The troubles (צרות) of my heart have spread; bring me out of my distress.

But let us see what happens if we switch the order:

> 14: The counsel (סוד) of the Lord is with those that fear Him, and His covenant, to make them know it.
> 16: Turn (פנה) to me and be gracious to me, for I am solitary and afflicted.
> 15: My eyes (עיני) are always toward the Lord, for He will bring my feet out of the net.
> 17: The troubles (צרות) of my heart have spread; bring me out of my distress.

C. Craigie, *Psalms 1-50* (Word Bible Commentary, vol. 19) (Waco, Tx.: 1983), p. 129.

There are Dead Sea and Nachal Chever texts of limited portions of chapters 9 and 10. But these closely parallel the Masoretic text. See *DJD* XXIII (Oxford: 1998), pp. 54 and 66, and XXXVIII (Oxford: 2000), pp. 148-151. Nor does the Septuagint help in restoring the original acrostic.

51. The suggestion that פיהו was the first word of the *pe* verse, and עיניו the first word of a subsequent *ayin* verse was made long ago. See Charles Augustus Briggs and Emilie Grace Briggs, *A Critical and Exegetical Commentary on the Book of Psalms* (International Critical Comm.) (Edinburgh: 1906), vol. 1, p. 70. It is still widely accepted today. See, e.g., Demsky, p. 18, Hanan Eshel and John Strugnell, "Alphabetical Acrostics in Pre-Tannaitic Hebrew," *Catholic Biblical Quarterly* 62 (2000), pp. 441-58 (443), and Tappy, et al, p. 26.

In the new order, verse 15 flows easily after verse 16. More important, we now see a parallel between the second halves of the newly adjacent verses 15 and 17; "for he will bring my feet out of the net" parallels "bring me out of my distress."

Critically, chapter 25 parallels chapter 34 in two significant ways: both lack a *vav* verse and both add a *pe* verse at their conclusion.[52] This makes it very likely that chapter 25 originally paralleled chapter 34 in its *pe-ayin* order as well.[53]

3. Regarding chapter 37, this is an acrostic where the *ayin* section is missing. However, close examination of the verses reveals that the section for the *samekh* is unusually long.[54] Moreover, the Septuagint on the *samekh* section even has an additional phrase not found in the Hebrew text.[55] Almost certainly, there was an *ayin* verse here once and some of the original text in this section has been lost.[56] Of all the 22

---

52. Also, the added *pe* verse is from the same root (פדה) in both. Also, each letter of the alphabet is assigned only one verse in chapters 25 and 34. This is unlike the acrostics of chapters 9-10 and 37, in which there is (usually) an acrostic verse followed by a verse that begins with any letter.

The reason for the added *pe* verse has engendered much speculation. One interesting suggestion is that the addition of this verse enables the acrostic to begin with *aleph*, have a *lamed* in the middle, and end with *pe*, alluding to the word *aleph*, a word that symbolizes the alphabet. See, e.g., David Noel Freedman, "Acrostic Poems in the Hebrew Bible: Alphabetic and Otherwise," *Catholic Bible Quarterly* 48 (1986), pp. 408-31(416, n. 8).

53. The Dead Sea texts include a text of the first two words of 25:15, but there is no text of the surrounding verses.

54. It spans three verses, 37:27-29, while the sections for all the other letters span only one or two verses.

55. It is chapter 36 in the Septuagint. Codex Vaticanus and Codex Sinaiticus have the added phrase: αμωμοι εκδικηθησ; Codex Alexandrinus has the added phrase: ανομοι δέ εκδιωχθήσονται. Perhaps the Hebrew phrase being translated here began with *ayin*, and perhaps there were additional words in the Hebrew that were lost as well.

56. The observation that the *samekh* verse in chap. 37 is unusually long and that there was once an *ayin* verse here was made long ago. See, e.g., Driver, p. 346, and Wellhausen, p. 82.

Ḥakham (*Sefer Tehillim, Daat Mikra*, vol. 1, p. 215) and others have suggested that the ayin of לעולם, in the middle of verse 28, is the *ayin* of the acrostic. But the letter of the acrostic is practically always the letter that starts the verse or something very close to that. (In *Tehillim* 25:2, the

letters in the Hebrew alphabet, why is it that the main textual problem arises in the context of the *ayin* verse?[57] Probability suggests that it has something to do with the issue of the *pe-ayin* order.[58] I strongly suspect that if the correct text of this chapter is ever established, it will end up being one in which the *pe* preceded the *ayin*.[59]

---

first letter of the second word of the verse is the letter of the acrostic, and in *Tehillim* 37:39, the *tav* of ותשועת, the first word of the verse, is the letter of the acrostic.) The letter of the acrostic is never from the middle of the verse. To postulate that an acrostic letter is found mid-verse is to postulate that our verse division is off, and this too implicitly questions our received text. Moreover, nowhere else in the Biblical acrostics is a letter after an initial *lamed* used as the acrostic letter. (The utilization of the tav of ותשועת, after an initial *vav*, is much easier to accept.) That the Septuagint has an added phrase here suggests that there was some loss of text.

57. There are other abnormalities in this acrostic, but they are minor. See Ḥakham, ibid., and Eshel and Strugnell, p. 443. For example, the *dalet*, *kaf*, and *kof* letters span only one verse, while the other letters span two verses.

Here is a good place to point out that there is an egregious error in the *Encyclopaedia Judaica* "Acrostics" entry (2:229). There is a long sentence that begins: "The *ayin* is missing in Psalm 37, and the *nun* in Psalms 9-10 (originally a unity) and Nahum 1 are unmistakable torsos of originally alphabetic compositions…." The entry should read: "The *ayin* is missing in Psalm 37, and the *nun* in Psalm 145. Psalms 9-10 (originally a unity) and Nahum 1 are…." This mistake (like most others) was not corrected in the second edition.

58. Perhaps something went wrong in the course of the re-ordering of the original *pe-ayin* order to *ayin-pe*. Alternatively, perhaps at some point in the Second Temple period, a scribe used to the *ayin-pe* order was copying from a text which had the older *pe-ayin* order, and jumped to the wrong line.

59. There are no Dead Sea texts of the relevant verses in chapter 37. Neither are the relevant verses extant in the *pesher* on chapter 37, at 4Q171.

Admittedly, chapter 37 is unlike chapters 25 and 34 in that it includes a verse that begins with *vav* and does not add an end verse beginning with *pe*. Also, each letter of the acrostic (for the most part) spans two verses. But these structural forms are not inconsistent with the chapter following the *pe-ayin* order. As discussed in the text, the acrostic of chapter 9-10, in which each letter seems (for the most part) to span two verses, and which includes a *vav* in its acrostic and does not end with *pe*, may have followed the *pe-ayin* order.

A striking parallel between chapters 34 and 37 is that the *samekh* verse in both begins with *sur me-ra va-aseh tov*. Also, chapter 34 ends with

Conclusion

As discussed above, every known Hebrew abecedary from the period of the Judges and the period of the First Temple records the pe before the ayin (if the abecedary is long enough to include these letters). I believe that the *pe-ayin* order was not just a variant order,[60] but that it was *the only order* in use in Israel in these early periods. This order is reflected, if we accept the Dead Sea text of *Eikhah* 1:16-17, in all the acrostics in the book of *Eikhah*.[61] If we accept the text of the Septuagint of *Mishlei*

כל החסים בו, while chapter 37 ends with כי חסו בו. Also, the superscription לדוד (without more) is found at chapters 25 through 28, and at chapters 34, 35, and 37, perhaps indicating some relationship between these chapters. (In the other books, it is found at chapters 103, 138, and 144.)

60. Over time, scholarly awareness of the prevalence of the order is increasing, but I have not seen any scholar take the position that *pe-ayin* was the exclusive order of the period of the Judges and the First Temple. After the Izbet Sartah and Kuntillet 'Ajrud abecedaries were found, scholars typically viewed the *pe-ayin* order as a variant order. Later, after the Tel Zayit abecedary was found in 2005, the scholarly article publishing the find called the *pe-ayin* order "a well-attested alternative to the traditional order." See Tappy, et al, p. 26. In 2007, in suggesting that the scribes of the eighth through sixth centuries B.C.E. were trained in this order, Ryan Byrne called *pe-ayin* the "prevalent (if not dominant)" order of the time. See Byrne, "The Refuge of Scribalism in Iron I Palestine," *Bulletin of the American Schools of Oriental Research* 345 (2007), pp. 1-31 (5). Later, Seth L. Sanders, based on Byrne's observation, wrote that *pe-ayin* "may well have been the most popular" order of the time. See his "Writing and Early Iron Age Israel: Before National Scripts, Beyond Nations and States," in Tappy and McCarter., eds., *Literate Culture and Tenth-Century Canaan*, p. 102.

Similarly, although many who write about the *pe-ayin* order point to the suggested *pe-ayin* order in *Tehillim* 9-10 and 34 (see, e.g., Demsky, "A Proto-Canaanite Abecedary," p. 18, and Tappy, "An Abecedary," p. 26), no one that I have seen has taken the next step and argued, as I am, that *Tehillim* 25 and 37 originally followed the *pe-ayin* order as well.

61. The comments of the author of the *Encyclopaedia Judaica* entry "Book of Lamentations," in his attempt to date the various chapters of the book, are worth noting (10:1374): "Certainly none of the chapters can postdate Cyrus' proclamation of 538… since none of the hope which it engendered is reflected in the book." See also Elie Assis, "The Unity of the Book of Lamentations," *Catholic Biblical Quarterly* 71 (2009), pp. 306-329 (307):

31:25-26 as preserving the order of the original Hebrew, the *pe-ayin* order is reflected here as well.[62] I believe that all the acrostics in the first book of *Tehillim*, almost certainly its oldest section, originally reflected this order.

Recently, a scholar of paleography has analyzed the surviving Hebrew inscriptions from the eighth through sixth centuries B.C.E. and observed that when *samekh* is immediately followed by *pe*, the two letters are consistently written the same way in relation to one another.[63] Based on this, a subsequent scholar has theorized that the Israelite scribes of this period may have been trained in an order in which *samekh* was followed by *pe*.[64] This would be further evidence for the *pe-ayin* order.

Admittedly, as mentioned earlier, the earliest Western Semitic

---

"[M]ost commentators today agree that the five poems of Lamentations were all composed shortly after 586 B.C.E., or at the very least, during the exilic period."

62. Many scholars have argued that chapters 30-31 of *Mishlei* are post-exilic. They are the latest chapters in the book and are not even attributed to Solomon. Compare the first verse of the book, which tells us that what follows are the proverbs of Solomon, and verse 25:1 (introducing chapters 25-29): "These also are proverbs of Solomon, which were copied by the men of Hezekiah king of Judah." Chapter 30 is attributed to Agur son of Yakeh, and chapter 31 is attributed to king Lemuel. If 31:10-31 follows the *pe-ayin* order, this suggests that at least this acrostic dates to the First Temple period. But it is possible that the *pe-ayin* order remained in some use in the post-exilic period.

63. See Christopher Rollston, "Non-Provenanced Epigraphs I: Pillaged Antiquities, Northwest Semitic Forgeries, and Protocols for Laboratory Tests," *Maarav* 10 (2003), pp. 135-93 (160-62). Byrne (p. 4) summarizes the pattern observed by Rollston as follows: "The *samek* always ascends to a height above the register's ceiling line, while the *pe* nestles snuggly below the left edge of the *samek*'s lowest crossbar."

64. See Byrne, pp. 4-6. See also Sanders, p. 102.

Subsequent to Rollston's analysis, the unprovenanced ostracon published by Heide came to light. The way the *samekh* and its adjacent *pe* are inscribed in this ostracon do not fit the pattern observed by Rollston. This might suggest that the ostracon is a forgery. But more likely, the ostracon is not a forgery, but just an exception to the pattern observed by Rollston. The fact that not every inscription fits the pattern does not refute Byrne's suggestion.

abecedaries reflect the *ayin-pe* order.[65] These abecedaries are in Ugaritic (from Ras Shamra, Syria) and date to the thirteenth century B.C.E. But it is evident from our study that a different order existed in early Israel and that the order of letters was not as fixed in earliest times as we imagine it to have been.[66] Note also that there are now two ancient abecedaries in early Israel in which the *ḥet* precedes the *zayin*.[67]

Finally, we must explain what led the *ayin-pe* order to begin to be used in Israel in the post-exilic period. A good guess is that *ayin* preceded *pe* in the Aramaic alphabet in use in Babylonia, and that this led the exiled Judeans to use this order in Israel upon their return.[68]

This study began with a technical observation about the acrostics in the book of *Eikhah*, but led to insights into the books of *Tehillim* and *Mishlei* and into the history of the alphabet. I will leave it to someone else to consider its implications for the field of *gematria*!

---

65. But as noted earlier, abecedaries have been discovered at Ras Shamra and Beit Shemesh that follow the alternative alphabetical scheme that begins *h, l, ḥ, m*.

66. Admittedly, we see things before we eat them, suggesting perhaps that *ayin* should precede *pe*. But on this basis, perhaps *resh* (head) should precede both, and all of *resh*, *ayin*, and *pe* should precede *yod* (hand) and *kaf* (palm). Obviously, there is no natural order being followed in the order of the letters. For an interesting recent attempt to explain the meaning and order of all the letters, see Demsky, *Yediyat*, pp. 174-77.

67. Izbet Sartah and Tel Zayit.

68. As is well-known, the names of the Jewish months were adopted from Babylonia around this time as well.

There seems to be an acrostic in the last chapter of Ben Sira. See the Hebrew text of this work known as manuscript B, discovered in the Genizah. Some view this acrostic as following the *pe-ayin* order. But looked at more closely, it seems to follow the *ayin-pe* order. See the text in Abraham Kahana, *Ha-Sefarim ha-Ḥitzonim* (Jerusalem: 1978), vol. 2, p. 530. The third word of 51:23, סכלים, reflects the *samekh* letter, followed by the *ayin* and *pe* of verses 24 and 25. (Some claim that manuscript B is only a translation from the Syriac version of Ben Sira. But even if manuscript B derives directly from the original Hebrew version, it is clear that its text is corrupt.)

Suggestions for Further Reading

Aaron Demsky, "A Proto-Canaanite Abecedary Dating from the Period of the Judges and its Implications for the History of the Alphabet," *Tel Aviv* 4 (1977), pp. 14-27.

Aaron Demsky and Moshe Kochavi, "An Alphabet from the Days of the Judges," *BAR* Sept.-Oct. 1978, pp. 23-30.

Mitchell First, "Can Archaeology Help Date the Psalms?" *BAR* July-August 2012, pp. 47-50 and 68.

Mitchell First, "Using the *Pe-Ayin* Order of the Abecedaries of Ancient Israel to Date the Book of Psalms," *JSOT* 38 (2014), pp. 471-485.

Paul W. Gaebelein, Jr., "Psalm 34 and Other Biblical Acrostics: Evidence from the Aleppo Codex," *Maarav* 5-6 (1990), pp. 127-43.

Martin Heide, "Impressions from a New Alphabetic Ostracon in the Context of (Un)Provenanced Inscriptions: Idiosyncracy of a Genius Forger or a Master Scribe?" pp. 148-182, in Meir Lubetski, ed., *New Seals and Inscriptions, Hebrew, Idumean and Cuneiform* (2007).

Moshe Kochavi, "An Ostracon of the Period of the Judges from 'Izbet Ṣarṭah," *Tel Aviv* 4 (1977), pp. 1-13.

Ze'ev Meshel, *Kuntillet 'Ajrud (Ḥorvat Teman): An Iron Age II Religious Site on the Judah-Sinai Border* (2012).

G. Wilhelm Nebe, "Alphabets" in *Encyclopedia of the Dead Sea Scrolls*, vol. 1, pp. 18-20 (2000).

Ron E. Tappy, P. Kyle McCarter, Marilyn J. Lundberg, and Bruce Zuckerman, "An Abecedary of the Mid-Tenth B.C.E. from the Judaean Shephelah," *Bulletin of the American Schools of Oriental Research* 344 (2006), pp. 5-46.

Ron E. Tappy and P. Kyle McCarter Jr., eds., *Literate Culture and Tenth-Century Canaan: The Tel Zayit Abecedary in Context* (2008).

Abbreviations Used in this Book

BAR: Biblical Archaeology Review

DJD: Discoveries in the Judaean Desert

HUCA: Hebrew Union College Annual

JBL: Journal of Biblical Literature

JQR: Jewish Quarterly Review

JSOT: Journal for the Study of the Old Testament

REJ: Revue des Études Juives

INDEX

(NOTE: Citations with parenthetical numbers indicate that the source is referenced both in the body and the footnote on that page.)

Herodotus,
III, 68-69, 152 n. 72
III, 84, 149 n. 64
III, 133-135, 152 n. 72
VII, 61, 142 (n. 42), 145 n. 51
VII, 89, 137 n. 23
VII, 114, 143
VII, 152, 151
VIII, 103, 145 n. 51
IX, 10, 137 n. 25
IX, 108-113, 143
IX, 108, 137 n. 25
IX, 109, 143 n. 45
IX, 110, 143 n. 46

Josephus,
Life,
2, 79 n. 10
3, 65 n. 24
4, 79 n. 10

Antiquities,
II, 313, 184 n. 55
IV, 242, 205 n. 42
IX, 291, 113 n. 46
XII, 133-153, 94 n. 2
XII, 211-212, 75 n. 66
XII, 253, 102 n. 24, 106 n. 31
XII, 255, 99 n. 16
XII, 257, 113 n. 46
XII, 258-263, 112
XII, 263, 114 n. 47
XII, 265, 67 n. 32, 78 (n. 10), 99 n. 17
XII, 275-83, 82 n. 19
XII, 384-385, 104
XII, 402-412, 77 n. 4
XII, 412, 118 n. 2
XIII, 228, 66 n. 28
XIII, 320, 66 nn. 30-31
XV, 403, 91 n. 55

(Josephus, cont'd)
XX, 190, 78 n. 10
XX, 238, 78 n. 10
XX, 249, 78 n. 10
XX, 240, 66 n. 29
XX, 267, 184 n. 55

Jewish War,
I, 19, 78 n. 9
I, 34, 106 n. 31
I, 36, 78 n, 9, 99 n. 17
I, 64-66, 82 n. 19
II, 344, 91 n. 55
V, 139, 91 n. 55
VII, 43-44, 112

Apion,
I, 3, 151 n. 69
I, 172-175, 137 n. 23

Justin,
III, 1, 140 n. 36, 158 n. 95

Lucian,
A True Story,
I, 3, 151 n. 67
II, 29-31, 151 n. 67

Philo,
Special Laws
II, XXXV, 216, 196 n. 17

Plato,
Alcibiades,
I, 123C, 144 n. 48

Plutarch,
Life of Artaxerxes,
I, 154 n. 76
VI, 154 n. 76

Tacitus,
Histories,
V, 8, 103 n. 24

Thucydides,
I, 110, 155 n. 84
I, 128-129, 140 n. 38

Xenophon,
Cyropaedia,
VII, 1, 6, 163 n. 109

Made in the USA
Middletown, DE
27 August 2021

46963244R00144